BLOOD ALLIANCE

DEFENDER PUBLISHING
BOOKS BY MESSIANIC RABBI ZEV PORAT

- *Blood Alliance*—2023

- *Unmasking the Chaldean Spirit*—2022

- *The Rabbi, the Secret Message, and the Identity of Messiah*—2019
  (co-authored with Carl Gallups)

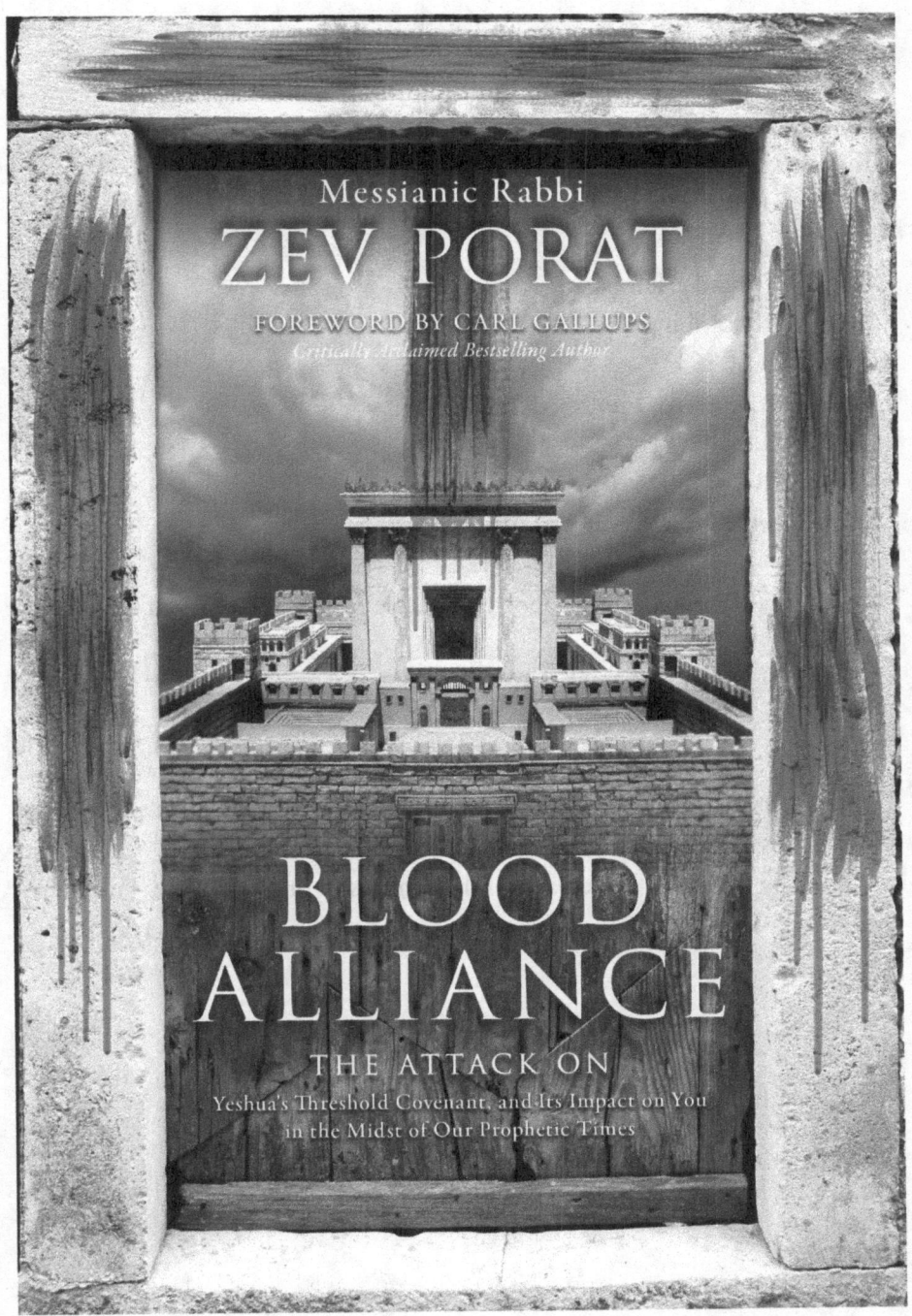

Defender

Crane, MO

Blood Alliance: The Attack on Yeshua's Threshold Covenant and Its Impact Upon You in the Midst of Our Prophetic Times
by Zev Porat

© 2023 Defender Publishing
Defender Publishing
Crane, MO 65633
All Rights Reserved. Published 2023

ISBN: 978-1-948014-73-1
Printed in the United States of America.

A CIP catalog record of this book is available from the Library of Congress.

Cover design: Jeffrey Mardis
Interior design: Pamela McGrew

Unless otherwise noted, Scripture quotations are taken from The Holy Bible, English Standard Version. ESV® Text Edition: 2016. Copyright © 2001 by Crossway Bibles, a publishing ministry of Good News Publishers

Dedicated to the glory of *Yeshua Ha Mashiach*,
the revealer of all genuine truth and wisdom.

For my precious wife, Lian.
You have always been there for me.
You are a true gift from Yahweh.

Acknowledgments

Thanks again to my dear brother and ministry partner Pastor Carl Gallups and his wife, Pam. Both of you continue to be so helpful to Messiah of Israel Ministries and my family. We love you!

My deepest gratitude to Tom and Nita Horn, SkyWatch TV, and Joe Horn, as well as the entire SkyWatch team. I especially extend my appreciation for Donna Howell and everyone at Defender Publishing. I'm honored to be affiliated with you through my books. And, of course, a special word of thanks to Angie Peters of Defender Publishing—you are an amazing editor.

Thank you Diane Roblin Lee, along with Moshe and Dina Rapaport. You have provided a ton of wonderful support from the very beginning of this work.

I also want to offer my appreciation to Jane Anne Shortly. You were an invaluable help to me in getting this book ready for its final form.

A huge thanks to all those who so faithfully and selflessly serve on the Messiah of Israel Ministries team.

And a very special thanks to my brother Haim and his wife, Sarah Levy.

When I See the Blood

The blood shall be a sign for you, on the houses where you are. And when I see the blood, I will pass over you, and no plague will befall you to destroy you, when I strike the land of Egypt.

Take a bunch of hyssop and dip it in the blood that is in the [threshold][1] and touch the lintel and the two doorposts with the blood that is in the [threshold]. None of you shall go out of the door of his house until the morning.

—Exodus 12:13, 22

CONTENTS

Foreword xiii

PART I
THE FIRST STEP

1: The Passage 3
2: Beginnings 7
3: The Night of Reckoning 13
4: The Supernatural Week 17

PART II
THE CROSSING POINT

5: Cutting a Covenant 23
6: The Sea, the Song, and the Servants 29

PART III
THE SEDITIOUS ATTACK

7: Trampled Underfoot 39
8: The Dark Marauders 45
9: Threshold Demolition Agents 49
10: Demonic Redefining of Thresholds 55

Part IV
VITAL PERSPECTIVES

11: The Threshold Portal 61
12: The Inward Parts 67
13: The Missing Nuance 73
14: The One Who Knocks 77

15: The New "Renewed" Covenant 83
16: It Has Always Been about Faith 87
17: Threshold Consequences 91
18: Often Overlooked 97
19: On or Over? 103
20: Yahweh's Message to Zephaniah 107
21: The Fall of Dagon 113

Part V
Seizing the Kingdom

22: A Carnal Kingdom 119
23: Polluting the "One New Man" Threshold 123
24 The Chaldean Holy Day 129
25: The Easter Spirit 133
26: The Astarte/Ishtar Connection 137
27: Digging Deeper 141
28: Anti-Semitic Constantine 149
29: Sins of the Fathers 155
30: Calendar Chaos 163
31: Eliminating the Easter Confusion 167

Part VI
Temple Frenzy

32: The Third-Temple Diversion 175
33: Words Have Meaning 181
34: The Thessalonian Declaration 187
35: Measuring the Revelation Temple 191
36: Daniel and the Temple 195
37: The Wing 201
38: The Temple and the Lawless One 205
39: Offerings and Sacrifices 211

Part VII
Ezekiel's Temple Vision

40: Ezekiel's Heykal 217
41: The Revelation-Ezekiel Link 225
42: The Hebrews Connection 231

Part VIII
Remember the Sabbath

43: The Sabbath Threshold 239
44: The Codification of the Sabbath 243
45: The Holy Convocation 247
46: The Purpose 251
47: Traditions, Laws, and Servitude 255
48: All About Yeshua 261
49: Making the Biblical Case 265
50: The Fulfilled Word Speaks 271
51: The Old Law or the New Covenant? 279
52: Sabbath Keeping Today 285
53: Practical Application of the Sabbath 289

Part IX
Final Thresholds

54: The New Jerusalem 297
55: Everything Is Connected 303
56: The True Aliyah 309
57: Blessing Israel 313
58: The Journey 319

About the Author 322
Notes 325

Foreword

A number of scholarly works have been written on the topic of biblical Threshold Covenants. For example, those penned by the globally renowned H. Clay Trumbull date all the way back to the late 1800s. Of course, several more recent writings delve into this rather complex topic as well. But this book is not just another work based on the often-repeated material that has come before it. It is vastly different, and it will more than likely prove to be utterly life-changing.

Messianic Rabbi Zev Porat will take you on a biblical expedition that is, to say the least, fascinating. You will soon discover not only the historical concepts of Threshold Covenant-making, but you'll also come to understand just how profoundly this truth is embedded within the Word of God, from beginning to end. More importantly, it will help you understand why this revelation is significantly applicable to the lives of born-again believers everywhere.

In the pages that follow, Zev will also uncover the details about the very real spiritual battle taking place within today's Orthodox Jewish community, as well as within the various congregations of believers in *Yeshua*,[2] and in your own daily faith life. Additionally, you'll find out why this all-out demonic warfare is intricately connected to the threshold choice our Creator holds out to all who will, in faith, "step over" from one spiritual dimension and into another. The battle is real, unbelievably vile, and unthinkably deadly. And it's right in front of our faces, but many are entirely missing the magnitude of its stark reality.

Rest assured, the one leading you on this quest is uniquely qualified. Zev's pedigree is unlike any Messianic rabbi I've ever known. He was born and raised in the heart of Israel, in one of the most traditional Orthodox Jewish communities on the planet.

His family line on his father's side is decidedly rabbinic in many important levels of the Jewish culture. On his mother's side are family members who have served at some of the highest tiers of Israeli government. In the next few pages, you'll read more about this in Zev's riveting testimony about his personal pursuit to find the truth concerning Yeshua.

There's something else to consider as you read this book: Hebrew is Zev's mother tongue. Because of this, he understands the intricacies of the original languages of the Tanakh (Old Testament) and important nuances of the Hebrew language—both ancient and modern—that many non-Hebrew speaking researchers, teachers, and writers don't recognize. This makes his insight into the Threshold Covenant refreshingly pertinent.

As you move from chapter to chapter, you'll most likely find yourself thinking many times, "Wow! I didn't know this! I had no idea!" You'll be astonished, on occasion, as you begin to realize how demonically duped most of us have become regarding several important matters of historical and biblical understanding—and for such a very long time.

You will not regret the time you'll spend exploring the following revelations. It is my prayer that this book will majestically influence your walk with the Lord…to the glory of His name and to the divine blood alliance that's tethered to that name.

Enjoy the journey!
Carl Gallups

The Mountain of Decision

Moses came and told the people all the words of the Lord and all the rules. And all the people answered with one voice and said, "All the words that the Lord has spoken we will do."

And Moses wrote down all the words of the Lord. He rose early in the morning and built an altar at the foot [threshold³] of the mountain, and twelve pillars, according to the twelve tribes of Israel.

And he sent young men of the people of Israel, who offered burnt offerings and sacrificed peace offerings of oxen to the Lord.

And Moses took half of the blood and put it in basins, and half of the blood he threw against the altar. Then he took the Book of the Covenant [a blood-alliance agreement] and read it in the hearing of the people.

And they said, "All that the Lord has spoken we will do, and we will be obedient."

And Moses took the [other half of the] blood and threw it on the people and said, "Behold the blood of the covenant that the Lord has made with you in accordance with all these words."

Exodus 24:3–8

PART I

The First Step

Jesus said, "For judgment I came into this world, that those who do not see may see, and those who see may become blind." Some of the Pharisees near him heard these things, and said to him, "Are we also blind?" Jesus said to them, "If you were blind, you would have no guilt; but now that you say, 'We see,' your guilt remains."

JOHN 9: 39–41

chapter one

THE PASSAGE

**Those diabolical grips still have their anti-Yeshua claws
tightly wrapped around many of God's own people.**

Have you ever reflected upon the fact that when you walk across the threshold of a doorway for the first time and into another person's home, you have passed from one reality into another?

That might be an odd way of considering the simple act of entering someone's residence. But think of it for just a moment: You start in the outside world—a world with which you are probably comfortably familiar—but then you enter the inside world of someone's sanctuary, their house, their *home*—and into the exclusive domain of their intimate life.

That home was previously a realm from which you were excluded. It was a domain belonging only to the homeowners, their family, and their guests. However, in that moment of entry, you are now included as a special occupant of that personal sphere of existence. You are allowed to enter the house through the open door before you, and with the permission of the homeowner.

Upon entering the home, however, you discover there are still other thresholds within. For example, the living room might be the only one immediately available to you. You are probably allowed to use a guest bathroom as well. But the study, the master bedroom, children's bedrooms, storage rooms, food pantries, the library, the children's playroom, the family den, the laundry room, and other such areas remain off-limits unless you're invited into them.

Yeshua actually spoke of these same spiritual truths, admittedly in veiled language…unless, that is, we have the spiritual *eyes to see*:

> In my Father's house are many rooms.[4] If it were not so, would I have told you that I go to prepare a place for you? And if I go and prepare a place for you, I will come again and will take you to myself, that where I am you may be also. (John 14:2–3)

But those passageways and rooms spoken of by Yeshua, marked out by biblical thresholds, can also have a much greater and transcendent meaning. They usually signify the movement of a person from a lower earthly plane of physical existence into a higher and divinely appointed, interdimensional one.

Yeshua even used the concept of a household and its special internal relationships in several of His teachings. He employed that imagery to teach us about the Kingdom responsibilities we have once we have crossed those thresholds and are living and working inside the *Kingdom house*:

> Who then is the faithful and wise servant, whom his master has set over his household, to give them their food at the proper time? Blessed is that servant whom his master will find so doing when he comes. Truly, I say to you, he will set him over all his possessions. (Matthew 24:45–47)

Even the Apostle Paul uses the household metaphor to describe a genuine reality that speaks of who we are, who we are becoming, and what our Creator has in store for us.

So then you are no longer strangers and aliens but you are fellow citizens with the saints and members of the **household of God**, built on the foundation of the apostles and prophets, **Christ Jesus himself being the cornerstone,** in whom the whole structure, being joined together, grows into a holy temple in the Lord. In him **you also are being built** together **into a dwelling place** for God by the Spirit. (Ephesians 2:19–22, emphasis added)

That first step over the ultimate *threshold* represents one's passage into a new world, and it is the boundary where the natural meets the supernatural. Once we have stepped across that divine doorway, our lives are forever changed. That is what this book is about.

The Lord of all dimensions of space and time has put it upon my heart to walk with you on a spiritual excursion of uncovering a number of profound principles that are revealed throughout the pages of God's Word. It is an exploration that should help you make much more sense of this relatively short earthly voyage each of us has embarked upon, and of the eternally important choices before us all. But mostly I pray it will help you live a victorious life, to the praise and glory of *Yeshua Ha Mashiach*—Jesus Christ our Lord.

THE BIG PICTURE

Get ready! We will soon be exposing some hugely controversial and ancient demonic strongholds. As you will discover, those diabolical influences still have their anti-Yeshua grip around many of God's own people, as well as within the halls of denominational and doctrinal thought. Sadly, most are unaware of the cavernous darkness actually staring them in the face.

The information presented in this book is well-documented, based on reliable external sources, as well as on the knowledge afforded me within the corridors of my own deep-seated Jewish heritage. I often draw upon that legacy as a guide for understanding ancient biblical customs, Hebrew word meanings, and the important nuances of those meanings.

I have worked to lay out the material in a way that is easy to read and, at times, even fun and engrossing. So, please be patient and diligent as we sort through the crusty layers of the mile-high mound of primitive deception.

From the beginning of this book to the end, I'll be building a case that will finally expose several monumental truths. Truths that should absolutely delight you, once you discover them! Our process will be similar to working an ancient archeological site that is being carefully uncovered until the layers of earth are dusted away and the great treasures we are searching for are fully visible. I assure you, this adventure will be worth your while!

Thank you for joining me. I am grateful you have already begun.

chapter two

BEGINNINGS

I felt my road had come to an end.
Obviously, the "all-knowing" rabbis were just as confused as I.

I heard the voice. It rang out in the most cavernous moments of the night.

I heard it in the same way I hear every other audible communication. In the stillness of that nocturnal moment, He spoke affectionately, as a loving father might instruct a wayward son who is on the brink of finally coming home.

"Zev! Zev! Isaiah 53, which you have been studying so diligently, this is the Messiah of Israel. Isaiah 53 is Yeshua. *It is true!*"

On that very night—in that instant—I surrendered to the One who was now speaking to the heart of my innermost being. I knew the voice that awakened me had been that of Yahweh Himself. To say my life has never been the same since is a huge understatement. That night, I instinctively knew I was crossing over a supernatural border into something unspeakably holy.

Getting to that point had not been a lightning-bolt experience. Rather, this pinpoint moment in the vastness of all eternity was the culmination of a long, tedious, and patient process, with the patience being much more on Yeshua's part than on mine. (There was mostly hardheadedness on my part.) Now I was standing at an open doorway to decision—an eternal one, one I knew I must make. My very life depended on it.

So, I stepped across the threshold.

My Own Wilderness Wandering

Let me go back a bit and briefly describe what had brought me to that night.

I was born in Israel. Hebrew is my native tongue. Our family lived in Bnei Brak, the most ultra-Orthodox and fiercely anti-Yeshua city in Israel. There, to this day, famous black-robed rabbis spend their entire lives studying in the *yeshivot*, Jewish rabbinical schools. In those schools in Bnei Brak, saying the name *Yeshua*—Hebrew for "Jesus"—or being seen with a Bible, especially a New Testament, can be a stoning offense.

I was raised in Bnei Brak and was steeped in its unmovable traditions. However, my father's brief stint as the rabbi of a synagogue in southern California equipped me to grow up speaking both Hebrew and English fluently. This was my world when I was a child. Anyone who strayed from our straight-laced norm was to be pitied for his or her "ignorance."

My father hated Jesus. Just the mention of His name, he claimed, was blasphemy against Judaism. I truly wanted to share the extent of my father's beliefs, but I was still wandering. I couldn't quite grasp why I never seemed to be able to find my own way. I just didn't know yet how deeply lost I really was.

I have shared some of the more extensive and dramatic circumstances of my life in *The Rabbi, the Secret Message, and the Identity of Messiah*, which I co-authored with Pastor Carl Gallups. I related stories about my life again, in even more detail, in my second book, *Unmasking the Chaldean Spirit*. Even so, a quick review of several important pieces of my background in this book might prove helpful for newer readers. (While the information in both of those books is extremely helpful to understanding the teachings in this one, they are not essential for you to be able to thoroughly enjoy and understand our current journey.)

BLOODLINES

Ancestral lines are like valuable currency to religious Jews, and mine was pure gold. My father, grandfather, great-grandfather, and other forerunners were rabbis. Some were even *dayans*, meaning "judges of rabbis."

My grandfather, Rabbi Pinhas Porat, was a Holocaust survivor from Poland. He lost his entire family in the gas chambers of Nazi Germany when he was a teenager, but eventually became a distinguished leader of Israel's Orthodox Rabbinate, the ruling elite. My great-grandfather was Zev Goldman, a member of the Knesset (the country's legislative body) in the Likud political party. Therefore, with my mother's side being well represented in the secular Israeli Benjamin Netanyahu government and my father's side producing a line of important Sanhedrin rabbis, that meant we had everything covered.

Little did I understand that, with my access to many Holocaust survivors and enviable family connections, all of those links would one day be important to the work to which God called me with the Jewish people. Still today, the Lord is using my ancestry to increase His Kingdom by opening doors to people who would otherwise want nothing to do with Him.

Despite the remarkable religious trappings of our family, I never felt any sense of the presence of the God of Abraham, Isaac, and Jacob. Where was He? Tradition cloaked our air with such intensity that I could barely breathe, let alone find God in the midst of my religious suffocation. I was a kid. I found no life in mere religion. In my heart, I wanted more. I wanted to "feel" the love of my Creator. I wanted not just to know the Laws and traditions of our forefathers, but I wanted to know Him personally.

Nevertheless, I, too, over time, grew into a black-robed *religious one* and began to peck through the seeds of Orthodox study, looking for sustenance like a crow picking through an almost-empty grain bin. Finding no satisfaction, then daring to constantly question my elders, I was stonewalled with assurances that if I would just study the Sabbath Laws more diligently, I would eventually be rewarded with the proper understanding. According to them, the apparent wasteland of spirituality I was experiencing was my own fault.

But then I was introduced to Matthew 12:1–8, Mark 2:23–28, and Luke 6:1–5: "They glorify the Sabbath more than the Sabbath maker." That's when I realized it was *they* who lacked understanding! Nevertheless, it took many years of the Holy Spirit working in my life before I was adequately seasoned to step into His ultimate purposes for me.

A Personal Travesty

When my father suddenly died, my beloved grandfather took on the role of a father figure. His great dream was that I would join him as an authorized Sanhedrin rabbi. But ultra-Orthodoxy didn't fit me. Despite my love and respect for my grandfather, I threw away my big black hat, cut my side curls, shaved my beard, and joined the Israel Defense Forces. However, I eventually returned to my Orthodox roots and became a Sanhedrin-qualified rabbi.

Years of disappointment and scrambling to stuff my empty soul with material things ensued. Despite financial success, anger and frustration became the doorposts of my life. Nothing was enough.

An Unlikely Alliance

Then I met Lian, a top chef from Shanghai, China, who was participating in a food expo with a tour group. We were married ten months later. Her Buddhas and my pictures of long-bearded and revered Orthodox rabbis were displayed together in the decor of our early home. Nothing made sense; our life was the joining-together of a hodgepodge of largely opposing belief systems.

The idea that Lian would one day become my ministry partner in the Kingdom of Yeshua was the farthest thing from our realm of consciousness. I was running away from God at the same time I was trying to find Him. Dissatisfaction with the status quo was eating me alive. One day, while searching for answers online, I bumped into an American Christian named Todd in a chat room. That was the beginning of my journey toward Holy-Spirit enlightenment.

For the next four years, Todd explained the Gospel of Jesus to me. The fact that I was a rabbi didn't stop him. It was obvious that he knew the Old Testament. The hairs of my Jewish heritage stood on end at the truths he revealed. How dare he explain Old Testament Scriptures as though they pointed to the New Testament account of Yeshua as Messiah! I could easily have pushed the "stop" button, but I listened to Todd's words. For four years, he taught me about the Messiah from the Old Testament. Slowly, passages such as Isaiah 53, Isaiah 9, Micah 5, Psalm 2, Psalm 110, Psalm 122, and Isaiah 7:14 began to make sense. As Todd screwed down the nuts and bolts of the Old Testament, he fastened my mind to truth.

Soon, I started having trouble sleeping. I could no longer ignore the reality that I had to face my question head-on and do my own investigation: *Who is the real Jewish Messiah?*

Like a dog with a new bone, I chewed my way through libraries, devouring the history of Christianity and Judaism, but I became thoroughly confused. I had nowhere to hide from the weighty conviction that drove me, nowhere to hide from God's presence.

The Holy Spirit began to give me visions at night that brought to life several Bible verses I had been studying. But then a voice—one I now know to be Satan's—would say, "Yeshua is the Messiah of the Gentiles. He is not the Jewish Messiah. Stay away from Him. Go the other way. Pay no attention to this teaching. You are Jewish. That is all you need." I thought I was going crazy.

I decided to approach my grandfather about some of the Scriptures Todd had shared with me. I asked him for his thoughts on Isaiah 53, Isaiah 7:14, Micah 5:2 (Micah 5:3 in Hebrew), and Jeremiah 31:31. "Who is this baby in Micah 5:2?" I asked. "Who is this child who existed before the foundation of the world and would one day be the ruler of Israel?" My usually calm grandfather became very nervous, but could give me no answer.

I questioned thirty-two other rabbis over the next two years and received twenty-six different answers. I finally met with Rabbi Israel Lau, who was then the chief rabbi of Israel, and asked him a simple question: "Rabbi Lau, I interviewed thirty-two rabbis and have received twenty-six different answers to the same question. Isn't there just one Tanakh?"

He smiled. "Zev," he said, "it's okay, because there are seventy different faces to the Torah—seventy different answers to the Tanakh."

I felt my road had come to an end. Obviously, the "all-knowing" rabbis were just as confused as I. Nevertheless, the truth had been confirmed: My years of exploration and study had proven that Yeshua was the Messiah of Israel. But I was a Jew! If I believed that, I would lose my family, my friends, my job, and maybe even my life.

I dared not believe.

chapter three

THE NIGHT OF RECKONING

*I had committed the unpardonable Jewish sin.
I had become a follower of Yeshua,
the most detested name on the planet.*

The next night, a very cold one, I woke up shaking, but in a heavy sweat. I looked at the clock. It was almost three in the morning. I could sense something supernatural happening.

Over my head shone a bright light shrouded in a shiny cloud. The experience was so real that, to this day, I firmly believe I was witnessing God's *Shekinah* glory—the same cloud through which God revealed Himself to the children of Israel as they were departing Egypt to travel to the Promised Land. That's when I heard the voice. That's when I knew something holy was taking place.

My shaking became violent, to the point of becoming uncontrollable. I dropped to my knees beside my bed, weeping, calling out for Yeshua to receive me as His own. In that moment I was transformed—reborn.

I awakened Lian. "Lian! Lian! It is true! The Messiah of Israel is Yeshua!" Still a Buddhist, she rolled over and tried to go back to sleep, but when she realized the whole bed was wet from my sweating, despite the cool temperature of the night, she knew something serious was going on.

She sat up, riveted by my experience as I told her about the entire ordeal. The next week, we diligently explored the Scriptures together. She renounced her Buddhist beliefs and called upon Yeshua to save her as well.

At that moment, our home changed. We became the "one new man" spoken of in Ephesians 2:14–18. We were a Jew and a Gentile united not only as husband and wife, but now as brother and sister in the Lord.

Changes

I was on fire with excitement! God had spoken to me one-on-one in a voice I could hear. He had told me Yeshua was the true Messiah of Israel! No more wandering. No more holding back because I was a Jew. *Yeshua* was a Jew! He was now *my* Messiah! It was my Damascus Road of revelation.

I was so full of the Spirit of God that I had to tell people, anyone who would listen. But wherever I tried to share the Good News, I was rejected. I was cursed, spat upon, and reviled by the entire Orthodox community whenever I dared to say the name of Yeshua.

My family was no different. Where I had hoped to find understanding, I met with anguish and fury. My mother tried to have me "deprogrammed" by Rabbi Stieglitz in Netanya, a man who helps parents explain to children the blasphemy of believing in Yeshua. After his best efforts, the rabbi finally gave up. He told my mother, "He's brainwashed. He's finished. I can't help him."

My grandfather, whom I loved more deeply than words can express, was no different. He was an old man, but when I began to share with him my precious knowledge that Yeshua is the Messiah of Israel, he shot out of his chair, opened the glass cabinet behind him, and started to shout, "*Goy* ("Gentile")! Traitor! Get out of here!" He started throwing plates at me, and one hit me in the head. My shirt torn and head bloody, I ran out of his home and had to go straight to the hospital for stitches. A scar on my forehead reminds me, to this day, of the overwhelming pain I felt from my grandfather's rejection. It was the last time I ever saw him. I tried to call him once after that, but he said, "Deny Yeshua or don't call."

My sister and her husband, a rabbi, filed an injunction against me that required me to stay one hundred meters away from their seven children—my beloved nieces and nephews. To them, I was dead. My aunt tried to give me money to pay for a psychiatrist, saying, "Your family shouldn't reject you because you are sick." When I declined her offer, she left. My boss, for whom I had worked more than fourteen years, called me into his office one day and said, "Zev, sit down. I've been hearing things about you. You've been talking about Yeshu [the horrendously derogatory pronunciation nonbelievers use for Yeshua[5]]. You'd better stop this! You're going to turn this place into a cult! You are brain-washing the people, and I won't allow it!"

I told him I would never deny my Lord Yeshua.

"Then you're out of here." He terminated all my years of working for him in two minutes. "Go to your office, clear your desk, return your car keys," he said. "You're leaving: no compensation, no salary, and no pension. That's it."

I knew I had grounds to file a lawsuit, but after praying for two days, I was led to the Scripture, "Vengeance is mine" (Deuteronomy 32:35). I knew I was to lay down my rights and simply pray for the salvation of my former boss.

With no one left who would recommend me for a job, eventually I found a position where no one cared what I believed: I became a dishwasher. The manager was an Arab who hated Jews, and now, he finally had a Jew under his thumb. He shouted to me every day: "Faster, faster...wash!"

I had committed the unpardonable Jewish sin. I had become a follower of Yeshua, the most detested name among Jews. I was considered an utter family disgrace. Without rent money, Lian and I resorted to living in a tent on the Mediterranean beach for three and a half months. While our surroundings were enchanting at first, the initial romance of our situation quickly dwindled as the reality of our homelessness sank in. Our ensuing despair was palpable at times.

However, on the flip side of our dejection was our increasing belief that God had a blessing for us. Somewhere, sometime soon—we hoped. We were convinced that while He hadn't been the one who put us on the beach, He *had* allowed it to happen for His purposes.

So I kept washing dishes, knowing that, somehow, God was in control. He had promised He would be!

chapter four

THE SUPERNATURAL WEEK

We knew Yeshua was not only directing our lives,
but also actively providing for our every need.

One day, I felt the Lord saying, "Zev, I didn't call you to preach the Gospel only when you live in a hotel or a penthouse. I instructed you to preach the Gospel 'in season and out of season,' wherever I lead you."

So I soon started to go out on the beach after my dishwashing hours and share the Good News with people there. I seldom received a positive response. Reactions varied from scorn and rejection to an outright physical assault that left me with a black eye. There I was—a Messianic Jew with a black eye, living on the beach with my wife, working as a dishwasher for an abusive Arab man, still looking for a job—but Lian and I had found the Pearl of Great Price, the Messiah, and we would never turn back. We were full of His joy and overall peace.

The day after I was slugged in the eye, I went to see our family's lawyer. I had received a phone call requesting my presence and supposed my whole family would be there. I knew they would be shocked at my appearance. However, as it turned out, I was the only one present. My grandfather, who had recently passed away, had named me as heir to his $43 million inheritance of cash and property. But there was one caveat: To receive what he had left me, I would have to renounce Yeshua as Messiah—something I could never do after I realized what He had done for me. I walked over to the door, turned and looked around the room, and then closed it on my earthly fortune, and on my past.

The day after seeing the lawyer, I took a bus to Jerusalem and went to the Garden Tomb. As I sat there praying and crying, a man who said he was from Australia walked up to me. "Are you a Messianic Jew?" he asked. When I said, "Yes," he said, "The Holy Spirit just told me to come and talk and pray with you." I appreciated his sensitivity and told him about my situation—how I'd gotten the black eye. We wept together. He said, "The Lord Yeshua is going to bless you!" We exchanged contact information, shook hands, and parted.

Three days later, the blessings began flowing; I experienced five days of supernatural blessings from Heaven.

On day one, I received a phone call from an insurance company. The agent said he had been looking for me for some time. "We have a check for 48,000 shekels [about $13,000 US] that has been sitting here for ten years and belongs to you." I knew that phone call was from Heaven! That same day, Lian and I got the money and found an apartment to rent.

On day two, we got a call from the family Lian had been working for, preparing food for banquets. The father of the family had left for the United States and had given Lian a bonus of $14,000. Our heads were spinning, but our hearts were full: Yeshua was honoring our faithfulness!

On day three, we both had the same dream from the Lord. We understood we needed to sow a tithe, so we went into the Garden Tomb ministry in Jerusalem to sow the tithe by faith.

On day four, we received yet another phone call. The person on the other end of the line said, "Mr. Porat, you were here looking for a job eleven months ago. Are you still looking?" The caller was from the Israeli Ministry of Defense. It was a very good management position in the army. I finally was able to put down my dish rag. I took the job!

And on day five, we got a call from a Messianic believer who had met the man from Australia I had talked and prayed with on the beach. The Messianic believer invited us to worship the Lord with him.

So, within just one week, God provided us with finances, a place to live, a lesson in God's economy, a great job, and a new brother in the Lord. Blessing after blessing had flowed our way! We knew Yeshua wasn't only directing our lives, but was also actively providing for our every need. We were in awe.[6]

THE BIRTH OF A MINISTRY

Seven months later, the Lord told me to leave my job with the Ministry of Defense and called me into full-time ministry to the Jewish people of Israel. I took a step of faith and began to serve the Lord. Thus began Messiah of Israel Ministries.

Our calling is to share Yeshua everywhere: on the streets, in synagogues, in mosques, in houses, on rooftops, through Internet video casting, on websites, in discipleship programs, through television interviews, through radio interviews, in print-media articles, in conference preaching, on tours, and in joint ministry efforts with other like-minded believers—wherever the Lord leads. We visit and minister to Holocaust survivors and those doing *aliyah*[7] in Israel, blessing them with basic necessities and the full Gospel of Yeshua the Messiah. We now preach all over the world, primarily in Israel, Europe, China, and the United States.

In those early days of intense persecution and loss of precious relationships, we had no idea our lives would soon be intricately entwined with the message of the world's most revered Orthodox rabbi, Yitzhak Kaduri. That message would send shock waves around the world and forever shatter the footings of Orthodoxy. If you have not done so already, I urge you to read *The Rabbi, the Secret Message, and the Identity of Messiah* (Defender Publishing) to learn of that astounding and intertwined relationship that was ordained by Yeshua.

Little did I know at the time, but I had stepped across a spiritual threshold. I had walked into an entirely new dimension of reality—I had "cut a holy covenant" with the Creator of the universe and the originator of my very being.

That's when everything in my life began to dramatically shift.

My entire perspective of reality and awakened perception of what was actually happening around me, as well as my understanding of Scripture itself, would never be the same.

I had stepped through a divine doorway. I now, through faith in *Yeshua Ha Mashiach*, had access to the house of Yahweh. But I have discovered that in my Father's house there are many "rooms." Each one holds additional treasures of delight and exploration. Yet, each room I enter within the boundaries of that house requires me to cross yet another threshold—a threshold of an enhanced walk of covenant, a closer walk with my Savior.

I'm still on that journey, and now want to show you what it's really all about—for you and for me—until we've successfully completed it and the Lord calls us home. I also want to explain how all of this has everything to do with the quickly changing world we live in—and our place in it.

Part II

The Crossing Point

So Jesus again said to them, "Truly, truly, I say to you, I am the door of the sheep. All who came before me are thieves and robbers, but the sheep did not listen to them. I am the door. If anyone enters by me, he will be saved and will go in and out and find pasture. The thief comes only to steal and kill and destroy. I came that they may have life and have it abundantly."

John 10:7–10

chapter five

CUTTING A COVENANT

*When God established His covenant with His people,
He incorporated elements they were already familiar with.*

In the ancient days of almost everywhere in and around the Fertile Crescent (the crescent-shaped region in Western Asia and North Africa also called the Cradle of Civilization),[8] if I were going to "cut a covenant" with you, I'd kill an appropriate sacrificial animal at my front door—at the threshold of my home. Then you would come into my house and eat a meal with me. The very act of you entering my home, crossing over the blood-soaked threshold, and then partaking of a "covenant" meal with me would indicate your partnership in the agreement I offered.[9] That form of covenant-making was still active in Syria and Egypt as recently as the early 1900s.[10]

Note the covenant was not said to have been "made," as are most of our current contract systems; rather, those solemn agreements were known as being "cut" and almost always involved the shedding of blood. The Hebrew phrase is *karat berît*, which translates to "cut a covenant."[11] This type of language is found about ninety times in the Hebrew Scriptures[12] and is generally translated into English versions of the Bible as "make" a covenant.

The animal would first be *struck down*—killed. Then it would be cut, often into pieces...and the blood that flowed would be collected to mark the threshold. That's why the practice of cutting a covenant is the root of such English phrases as "cut a deal" or "strike a bargain."[13] The implication was that whoever entered such a covenant was taking the agreement seriously. As you're probably already thinking, the idea of the literal "cutting of covenants" isn't something most people would necessarily wish to bring back into practice!

However, as a matter of fact, as we look at photos of buildings still existing from the world Yeshua walked in, we'll sometimes see an indented line—or trough—hewn into the actual thresholds. That line is called a "groover." We often also see a nearby hewn basin in which the blood of the sacrificial animal would first be collected and then poured out into the groover in the threshold.[14]

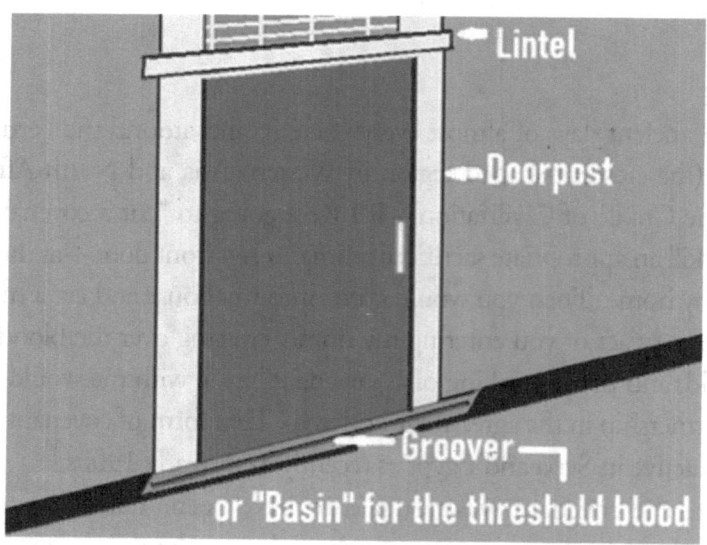

Artist Conception for Illustration Purposes (Used with permission)

The shed blood of that sacrifice wasn't to be taken lightly. It was evidence of the loss of life being surrendered for something that was ultimately designed to directly benefit the one with whom the covenant was made. The lamb killed on one's behalf would never again smell the sweet scent of a green pasture, romp with its siblings, or nuzzle close to its mother's side under the starry skies. Even those simple tidbits of contemplation were often involved in the potential covenant-maker's mind as he stepped across that threshold. Cutting a covenant was no small thing in the ancient way of doing serious business.

Those "covenant considerations" also included the fact that cutting a blood covenant with someone was understood to speak of something deadly ominous. It implied the participants' willingness to suffer a fate similar to that of the sacrificed animal if they violated the covenant's stipulations.[15]

Furthermore, in going through the "door" of that covenant, if you were to step directly *on* the blood-spattered threshold, you would be signifying your contempt for the agreement and for the person establishing it. On the other hand, properly crossing *over* the threshold would indicate your agreement regarding entering the "covenant relationship" with the host. In recent years, many ancient extrabiblical texts have been discovered that help us better understand historical context and meaning of the Threshold Covenant.[16] We'll examine that type of covenant cutting more thoroughly in the pages ahead.

THE FIRST BIBLICAL COVENANT CUTTING

The first clearly described scriptural account of *covenant cutting* was made between Abraham and God—approximately 1900 BC—when God promised to give Abraham an heir in his old age. That successor would later prove to be Abraham's firstborn son, Isaac. The covenant also included the promise that God would give Abraham's descendants a specific parcel of land and would eventually bless all the nations of the earth through his family and that land.

God's promise to Abraham was sealed with a covenant-cutting agreement. Abraham would have been familiar with this practice of the ancient lands and times in which he lived.

> And he said to him, "I am the LORD who brought you out from Ur of the Chaldeans to give you this land to possess." But he said, "O Lord GOD, how am I to know that I shall possess it?" He said to him, "Bring me a heifer three years old, a female goat three years old, a ram three years old, a turtledove, and a young pigeon." And he brought him all these, **cut them in half, and laid each half over against the other.** (Genesis 15:5–10, emphasis added)

Once Abraham complied with that direction, the Lord reiterated His promise, then His presence passed through the sacrificed portions, over the interdimensional threshold of shed blood, and into the establishment of an eternal promise—thus, the divine covenant was cut…and completed. It was sealed in sacrificial blood.

> And he said to him, "I am the LORD who brought you out from Ur of the Chaldeans to give you this land to possess." But he said, "O Lord GOD, how am I to know that I shall possess it?" He said to him, "Bring me a heifer three years old, a female goat three years old, a ram three years old, a turtledove, and a young pigeon." And he brought him all these, **cut them in half, and laid each half over against the other.** (Genesis 15:5–10, emphasis added)

Thus, when God later required every male descendant of Abraham to be circumcised as a token of the covenant that had been established, the requirement was not challenged, but accepted as legitimate. In this case, blood was shed with the cutting of the foreskin.[17]

> This is my covenant, which you shall keep, between me and you and your offspring after you: Every male among you shall be circumcised. You shall be circumcised in the flesh of your foreskins, and it **shall be a sign of the covenant between me and you.** (Genesis 17:10–11, emphasis added)

This concept of sacrifice and establishing threshold boundaries—literal and/or interdimensional—and the agreements they represented were nothing new. The pagans of those days were accustomed to sacrificing to their gods in a similar manner—a practice most likely "borrowed" from the original people of Yahweh.[18]

We have only to go back to a study of the gods of Egypt and see artifacts of entities represented on the doorposts of the Egyptians. Satan had already used his false gods as recipients of this kind of pagan tradition and religious observance. It was his counterfeit for God's genuine requirements.

The Egyptians previously might not have been putting the blood of lambs on their doorposts, but they were doing similar things in reverence to their own gods.

> They sacrificed to demons that were no gods, to gods they had never known, to new gods that had come recently, whom your fathers had never dreaded. (Deuteronomy 32:17)

The general idea of covenant cutting wasn't foreign to the Hebrew slaves in Egypt. So, apparently, when God established His covenant with His people, He incorporated several elements with which they were already familiar. But those practices would now take on an infinitely deeper and eternal significance.

The Passover Covenant would be a return to the truest form of covenant cutting…with the Creator of the heavens and earth and all that is in them—Yahweh/Elohim.

chapter six

THE SEA, THE SONG, AND THE SERVANTS

*Every step we take on our journey of sanctification—
every additional threshold we face—
rests on the foundation of our blood covenant with Yeshua,
our once-and-for-all sacrificial Lamb.*

Just before the people of Israel crossed the Red Sea, they were required to apply the blood of sacrificial lambs to the lintels (the top of the doorframes) of their homes, then they were told to place more blood on the doorposts.[19] They were not taken by surprise by this requirement. They didn't go to Moses complaining about being confused about the ritual. They understood at least its general significance. Threshold Covenants were as much a part of ancient life as marriage ceremonies.[20]

To be clear, the Israelites certainly would not have understood the foreshadowing of what that Passover ritual would ultimately mean in the context of its complete fulfillment in Yeshua's sacrifice for us. However, they did comprehend the requirement of innocent blood being shed at a threshold as part of the legal requirements. This was an element of the earliest human culture, far before the Israelites ever found themselves in bondage to Egypt.[21]

Also, there's no indication in the scriptural account of the original Passover that the *Egyptians* thought the blood requirement was strange, either. The concept of the Threshold Covenant was familiar to them as well, because of their frequent sacrifices to the idols of their gods.[22]

The Egyptians may have mistakenly thought the Israelites were paying homage to one of the Egyptian gods by smearing blood on the lintels of their homes. It could even be possible that throughout the previous nine plagues God brought on the land of Egypt via His servant Moses, the Egyptians had been smearing the blood of animals sacrificed to their gods, making appeals to them to somehow intervene and stop the plagues of Yahweh. Maybe they thought the Israelites were doing something similar. They would soon find out that Yahweh, the One they had been rejecting, was the One with whom they should have "cut a covenant" all along!

The Egyptians would discover the angel of death was unable to enter the homes of the Israelites because the blood on the lintels and doorposts demonstrated the inhabitants were identified with the properly sacrificed animal, and in the appropriate manner, proving they were in covenant with Yahweh alone. Of course, we now know the full truth. That blood was a foreshadowing of the blood of Yeshua, the Lamb of God who would ultimately bring us into the true Covenant of Salvation, the true blood alliance.

The following is from H. Clay Trumbull's "The Threshold Covenant or the Beginning of Religious Rites":

> How the significance of the Hebrew Passover rite stands out in the light of this primitive custom! It is not that this rite had its origin in the days of the Hebrew exodus from Egypt, but that Jehovah then and there emphasized the meaning and sacredness of a rite already familiar to Orientals. In dealing with his chosen people, **God did not invent a new rite or ceremonial** at every stage of his progressive revelation to them; but **he took a rite with which they**

were already familiar and gave to it a new and deeper significance** in its new use and relations.[23] (Emphasis added)

THE SEA

It wouldn't be long after leaving Egypt that the Israelites were confronted with yet another threshold—a treacherous *crossing-over* point. It was the threshold of the Red Sea. The next step required of them was to cross through that sea in an act that became the first *baptism* wherein the people of God were led through the waters. The Apostle Paul, a former Pharisee and teacher of the Law, understood this concept well:

> For I do not want you to be unaware, brothers, that our fathers were all under the cloud, and all passed through the sea, and all were baptized into Moses in the cloud and in the sea, and all ate the same spiritual food, and all drank the same spiritual drink. For they drank from the spiritual Rock that followed them, and the Rock was Christ. (1 Corinthians 10:1–4)

While there is no mention of a sacrifice being made at a literal threshold of the Red Sea, the Israelites could not have faced that very real *threshold of faith* without the foundation of having placed the blood on the lintels and the doorposts involving the sacrifice of the Passover lamb just a few days earlier. Every step we take on our journey of sanctification—every additional threshold we face—rests on the footing of our original blood covenant with Yeshua, our once-and-for-all sacrificial Lamb.

In the Hebrew mindset, it is impossible to view crossing the Red Sea without seeing it as a threshold. It was a barrier, a body of water they would have drowned in without the intervention, provision, and protection of Almighty God. It took monumental faith to take that first step off the dry beach.

The Israelites crossed the threshold and came out the other side singing the Song of Moses—a foreshadowing of believers entering the final threshold, sprinkled by the sanctifying blood of the Lamb, in the book of Revelation (15:3–4). We will eventually cross over that blood-bought Threshold Covenant into eternity, singing the Song of Moses—a song of victory—as we'll no longer be sludging through the never-ending, earthbound process of sanctification.[24]

THE SONG

Imagine Moses and the Israelites taking those first steps into the Red Sea. Looking back over their shoulders, they could see the dust of the Egyptian army and hear the thundering noise of countless thousands of troops coming after them, drawing closer with each passing second. Memories of smearing the blood of sacrificial lambs on the lintels and doorposts of the homes they had just left were still fresh. Now they faced either drowning in the sea blocking their way forward or trusting Moses to receive direction from God about their continued deliverance. They chose the latter and crossed over the threshold of faith, walking through the sea on supernaturally formed dry land and emerging alive on the opposite shore!

Imagine their shock as they watched the gigantic walls of water crashing over the advancing chariots and troops, eliminating their enemies. What a miracle! God was keeping His Threshold Covenant right before their eyes…in real time! This is why they would sing of it—forever.

> Then sang Moses and the children of Israel this song unto the Lord, and spoke, saying, "I will sing unto the Lord, for He hath triumphed gloriously; the horse and his rider hath He thrown into the sea. The Lord is my strength and song, and **He has become my salvation**; He is my God, and I will prepare Him a habitation; my father's God, and I will exalt Him. The Lord is a man of war; the Lord is His name." (Exodus 15:1–3, emphasis added)

In Exodus 15:2, where most translations read, "He has become my *salvation*," the original Hebrew says, "He has become my *Yeshua*." The word for "salvation" in Hebrew is *Yeshua*. The Israelites had just gone through the Red Sea. They had crossed over the threshold of trust and had gone through the waters of "faith-walk baptism." Of course, everything in the Old Testament is a dress rehearsal—*a shadow* of the New Covenant that was to come in Yeshua. More than 1,500 years later, the world would see that the Lord would indeed become our Yeshua—in the flesh!

Everything ties together. It's all connected. Everything in the Old Testament has significant meaning that deepens our understanding of the New Testament. And everything in the New Testament points back to, and has its foundation on, the Old Testament! That's why it's important to read and study, in context, the entire Bible, from Genesis to Revelation. If it weren't significant, God would have instructed us to ignore the First Covenant.

> Do your best to present yourself to God as one approved, a worker who has no need to be ashamed, rightly handling the word of truth. (2 Timothy 2:15)

At the time Paul wrote that instruction to Timothy, the "word of truth" was the Tanakh, what we now call the Old Testament. The earliest Church was commanded to study it thoroughly in conjunction with the then-circulating New Testament documents they were introducing into their preaching and teaching.

THE SERVANT

The events of the Exodus, Passover, and the Red Sea all foreshadowed the final threshold in the book of Revelation, where we read once again about the "sea," then the "song," and, of course, the "servant" of God.

And I saw what appeared to be a **sea of glass mingled with fire**—and also those who had conquered the beast and its image and the number of its name, standing **beside the sea** of glass with harps of God in their hands. And they sing **the song of Moses**, the **servant of God**, and the **song of the Lamb**, saying, "Great and amazing are your deeds, O Lord God the Almighty. Just and true are your ways, O King of the nations! Who will not fear, O Lord, and glorify your name? For you alone are holy. All nations will come and worship you, for your righteous acts have been revealed." (Revelation 15:2–4, emphasis added)

God was recognized as King of all the *nations*, not of Israel exclusively, because all become one in Yeshua under the blood of the ultimate covenant. All believers of every nation will become the "one new man"—a literal and physical embodiment of the deepest meaning of the Threshold Covenant. This truth is stated most beautifully in Ephesians 2, written by the Apostle Paul to the congregation of believers at Ephesus:

But now in Christ Jesus you who once were far off have been brought near by the blood of Christ. For he himself is our peace, who has made us both one and has broken down in his flesh the dividing wall of hostility by abolishing the law of commandments expressed in ordinances, that he might create in himself **one new man in place of the two, so making peace**, and might reconcile us both to God in one body through the cross, thereby killing the hostility.

And he came and preached peace to you who were far off and peace to those who were near. **For through him we both have access in one Spirit** [by stepping over one threshold!] **to the Father.** So then you are no longer strangers and aliens, but you are fellow citizens with the saints and members of the household of God, built on the foundation of the apostles and prophets, Christ Jesus himself being the cornerstone, in whom the whole structure, being joined together, grows into a holy temple in the Lord. In him **you also are being built together into a dwelling place** for God by the Spirit. (Ephesians 2:13–22, emphasis added)

There it is! Every element of the Threshold Covenant is laid out in Ephesians 2. We are brought near God's throne only by a blood sacrifice…Yeshua's blood. Through that sacrifice, we are able to move from one plane of existence to another, one realm to another, one dimension to another, as well as from the relationship of death in Satan's domain to the relationship of life in Yahweh's domain!

Since therefore the children share in flesh and blood, he himself likewise partook of the same things, that through death he might destroy the one who has the power of death, that is, the devil, and deliver all those who through fear of death were subject to lifelong slavery. (Hebrews 2:14–15)

All this happened because we were willing to accept the Covenant of Salvation offered by the Owner of the house and the spilled blood of the Lamb that was lovingly placed at the threshold—at the door. We stepped across the threshold, moving *from* the domain of Satan's destruction and eternal separation *into* the house of salvation. This eternal world wasn't previously open to us, as long as we chose to remain outside…in the earthly world, squarely in Satan's domain.

Now the door is open to us! We are members of the household of our Creator…but only through the Threshold Covenant.

We have crossed over.

PART III

THE SEDITIOUS ATTACK

Be sober minded; be watchful. Your adversary the devil prowls around like a roaring lion, seeking someone to devour.

    1 PETER 5:8

In their case the god of this world has blinded the minds of the unbelievers, to keep them from seeing the light of the gospel of the glory of Christ, who is the image of God.

    2 CORINTHIANS 4:4

chapter seven

TRAMPLED UNDERFOOT

The smooth talker had beguiled them both.
And they stepped right into Satan's house.

In the heart of the New Testament, we find a passage that speaks of the Threshold Covenant, and it does so in a shockingly pointed manner. The Hebrew minds that would have first pondered this Scripture—the earliest believers in Yeshua—would have known fully well what was being declared. And, by this point in our journey together, so will you. Have a look at Hebrews 10:29 in the fresh light of the Threshold Covenant God has offered us through the blood of Yeshua:

> How much worse punishment, do you think, will be deserved by the one who has trampled underfoot the Son of God, and has profaned the blood of the covenant by which he was sanctified, and has outraged the Spirit of Grace? (Hebrews 10:29)

After reading that passage, perhaps you'll recall some of the things documented earlier about the widely accepted ancient understanding of Threshold Covenants. One of those customs involved the belief that if a person were to step directly *on* the blood-spattered threshold, thereby trampling it "underfoot," it was a sign of contempt for the living sacrifice, a clear rejection of the covenant.[25]

How much clearer could that point have been worded than in this passage from Hebrews? It's the ultimate embodiment of the concept of "trampling" the Threshold Covenant "underfoot," dishonoring the sacrificial blood that was shed, and deeply insulting the owner of the house who was offering the covenant agreement. The very idea of taking the blood of Yeshua for granted or insulting the Spirit of grace who has sanctified us is utterly abhorrent to God. Here, in Hebrews 10, it is plainly stated as such…in Threshold Covenant language.

COUNTERATTACK

As we journey farther into the subject of the threshold and reveal additional disclosures of this theme throughout the Scripture, let's first explore how this concept ties into Satan's retaliation.

The enemy always puts forward a counterfeit effort to combat God's plan. The primary elements of his operating procedures are deception, manipulation, and coercion. He wants to keep everyone—especially the Jewish people in these last days—under his spell of beguilement. This is similar to how it all began in the Garden of Eden:

> Now the serpent was more crafty than any other beast of the field that the LORD God had made. He said to the woman, "Did God actually say, 'You shall not eat of any tree in the garden'?" And the woman said to the serpent, "We may eat of the fruit of the trees in the garden, but God said, 'You shall not eat of the fruit of the tree that is in the midst of the garden, neither shall you touch it, lest you die.'" But the serpent said to the woman, "You will not surely die. For God knows that when you eat of it your eyes will be opened, and you will be like God, knowing good and evil." (Genesis 3:1–5)

> Then the LORD God said to the woman, "What is this that you have done?" The woman said, "The serpent deceived [KJV, "beguiled"] me, and I ate." (Genesis 3:13)

Think of it! In the Garden, Satan attempted to convince Adam and Eve, humanity's first parents, to come "out" of God's house and to step across Satan's own threshold...the doorway to the path of the knowledge of good and evil. As we now know, it was nothing less than a doorway to death and destruction. However, Satan had disguised it with his smooth flattery, fanciful twisting of God's own words, outright lies, and boastful promises.

But on that fateful day, the smooth-talking cherub of God[26] had charmed both Adam and Eve and they stepped right into Satan's house. They crossed over *his* threshold. They covenanted with the fallen one. Unbeknownst to them, the blood that would be used against them would be their own! They would be the sacrificial lambs of that unholy blood alliance, the one that ultimately brought death and a fallen nature to humanity and to creation itself.

For Adam and Eve to ever have a chance to return to their Creator, they would have to begin their journey of contrition with more shedding of blood. And that's just what the Bible says happened.

> And the LORD God made for Adam and for his wife garments of skins [requiring killing an animal and shedding its blood] and clothed them. (Genesis 3:21)

Even at the most holy place of God's threshold, we face the demonic realm's efforts to block our entrance. This is because the devil wants to stop all from stepping over the final and eternal threshold into glorious union with their Lord and Creator. Once they do, and are truly born again, Satan cannot have their souls. He has lost them to God's divine eternity.

Satan understands the Threshold Covenant all too well. He knows the divinely eternal blood alliance was reversed, back upon his own head, at

Golgotha. Now it's not just the blood of an animal that seals the deal in the groover, it's the blood of Yeshua, the Lamb of God, the Good Shepherd, the One who laid down His own life and sprinkled His own blood on the threshold of Heaven's entrance.

> I am the good shepherd. The good shepherd **lays down his life for the sheep**....
>
> I am the good shepherd. I know my own and my own know me, just as the Father knows me and I know the Father; and I **lay down my life for the sheep**. And I have other sheep that are not of this fold. I must bring them also, and they will listen to my voice.
>
> So there will be one flock, one shepherd. For this reason the Father loves me, **because I lay down my life** that I may take it up again. No one takes it from me, but **I lay it down of my own accord. I have authority to lay it down, and I have authority to take it up again.** This charge I have received from my Father. (John 10:11, 14–18, emphasis added)

THE CHALDEAN SPIRIT

In the meantime, until Satan meets his ultimate and eternal demise, he continually calls out his big guns for the task of obfuscating and counterfeiting God's Threshold Covenant doorways—those divine portals that lead to righteousness and life.

What you will discover next is that these elite forces of Satan's darkest kingdom corridors have an ancient biblical name. This spirit is mentioned throughout God's Word, *from first to last*. Their main objective is to take what is not theirs—what belongs to God and His people—and try to corrupt it, steal it, hide it, belittle it, and even destroy it. They are thieves, murderers, and wicked masters of the darkest deceptions.

The thief comes only to steal and kill and destroy. I came that they may have life and have it abundantly. (John 10:10)

In my previous book, *Unmasking the Chaldean Spirit*, I engaged in a thorough uncovering of this spiritual truth of almost unfathomable depths. In that book, I also take the reader on a journey of vast discoveries of exactly how and where these demonic spirits have trod. I expose the misunderstanding of God's Word they have caused, the spiritual devastation they've left in their wake, and their continued exploitation of biblical truth.

In the next couple of chapters, I will briefly review the basics concerning this elite demonic force. This quick overview will ensure that from here on out you'll understand what I'm talking about as I refer to that highly specialized spiritual stronghold. As you'll soon see, this same class of demonic entities has focused like a laser on God's most precious of all gifts to fallen humanity: His offer of salvation through a very specific blood alliance.

It is this agreement Satan despises the most.

chapter eight

THE DARK MARAUDERS

Never doubt: The battle is always over the firstborn,
which is spiritual Israel, the "one new man."

The Chaldean spirit, spoken of in Scripture from the Tanakh (the Old Testament) through the New Testament,[27] is directly connected with the demonic outpouring of the end times.[28]

AGENTS OF SEPARATION

In Habakkuk's day, the Lord chose the Chaldeans to separate the faithful from the unfaithful, or "the wheat from the chaff" (Matthew 13). There is a reason He chose the Chaldeans in particular. It is in this sense that I and numerous renowned biblical scholars often refer to their Heaven-prompted but demonically manipulated exploits as being accomplished through the "spirit of the Chaldeans."

Here is what God instructed Habakkuk to tell the Hebrew people of his time:

> Look among the nations and see; wonder and be astounded. For I am doing a work in your days that you would not believe if told. For behold, **I am raising up the Chaldeans**, that bitter and hasty nation, who **march through the breadth of the earth, to seize dwellings not their own**. (Habakkuk 1:5–6, emphasis added)

Notice something else about this truth. This "raising up" of the literal Chaldean people of the days of Habakkuk also has an ominous spiritual aspect. It is a depth of darkness much of the world doesn't even begin to understand. The Chaldeans were steeped in practices of the most perverse occultic arts and the chasms of abominable evil attached to them. This lifestyle was foundational to their civilization. Jewish people around the world are familiar with this fact.

From the *Jewish Encyclopedia*:

> It was from Chaldea that the name "shedim" (evil demons) came to the Israelites, and so the sacred writers intentionally applied the word in a dyslogistic [noncomplimentary] sense to the Canaanite deities.[29] (Parentheses in original)

Being a native Hebrew speaker, I can attest that in the Modern Hebrew language, the word "Chaldean" (Hebrew: *Kasdim*) is frequently used to mean "ghosts, demons, or spirits" because of the grammatical, biblical, and historical connections. The historic links come from the fact that the Chaldeans were widely known for practicing astrology, the magic arts, and divination.[30]

Satan is the grand prince of those Chaldean spirits, and through his authority over that corrupt demonic host, he continues to storm throughout the earth stealing what does not belong to him, arrogantly believing he can somehow thwart the work of God.

Ephesians 6 makes clear that even the demonic realm has "rulers and authorities" associated with it. These are divisions, ranks, and regions of influence of Satan's demonic grip on the planet.

> Put on the whole armor of God, that you may be able to stand against the schemes of the devil. For we do not wrestle against flesh and blood, but against the **rulers**, against the **authorities**, against the **cosmic powers** over this present darkness, against the **spiritual forces of evil in the heavenly places**. (Ephesians 6:11–12, emphasis added)

I believe the Chaldean spirit makes up the bulk of Satan's army—especially in the last days, and specifically against the Jewish people, as well as against the assembly of the called-out ones, made up of both Jews and Gentiles—the *ecclesia*.[31]

Nevertheless, God will turn everything around for His own purposes. He always does. Yet, He still allows that same demonic spirit to act as a sort of divine "Weed Eater." In this way, the tares are continually pulled from among the wheat, right until the time of the last-days harvest. Yeshua has never hidden this great truth from us.

> He answered, "The one who sowed the good seed is the Son of Man. The field is the world, and the good seed stands for the people of the kingdom. The weeds are the people of the evil one, and the enemy who sows them is the devil. The harvest is the end of the age, and the harvesters are angels. As the weeds are pulled up and burned in the fire, so it will be at the end of the age. The Son of Man will send out his angels, **and they will weed out of his kingdom everything that causes sin and all who do evil**." (Matthew 13:37–41, emphasis added)

> **For it is time for judgment to begin with God's household**; and if it begins with us, what will the outcome be for those who do not obey the gospel of God? (1 Peter 4:17, emphasis added)

The Chaldean spirits are ominously dark in origin and faithful in continuing to serve Satan throughout the ages. This is true whether they are posing as humans—as in the "appearance" of a dead relative in a séance—or as some other ghostly apparition that is "summoned" forth at the command of someone immersed in the occult.[32]

These spirits can also work through teachers of false doctrine, as well as by simply exerting their spiritual influence in the ongoing war waged in the arenas of the human mind and soul (Romans 12:1–3; 2 Corinthians 10:5; 1 Timothy 4:1). Through all those means and countless others, their main goal is to muddy the biblical waters so people, especially God's people, know very little, if anything, about the importance of God's Threshold Covenants.

We know the centermost battle of the universe, according to God's own Word, is spiritual warfare against Israel. It started in Israel, where the Garden of Eden was first established, and it will end in Israel, where the garden is ultimately reclaimed and divinely revealed (Revelation 21–22).[33]

Satan knows these truths, and he knows his days are numbered:

> But woe to the earth and the sea, because the devil has gone down to you. He is filled with fury, because he knows that his time is short. (Revelation 12:12)

Never doubt: The battle is always over spiritual Israel, the "one new man" (Ephesians 2; Romans 11; John 10:11, 14–18; and Revelation 12). These are the ones who have *cut a covenant* with God…at the threshold to His house! They were the very first to do so on that Passover night in Egypt.

Satan will attack anyone who has anything meaningful to do with Israel, and most certainly if it involves the salvation of the Jewish people. The evil one will try to steal what does not belong to him. That stealing-killing-destroying agenda is brought about through the Chaldean spirit—the vilest of all the demonic orders, divisions, and hordes. Satan and his diabolic multitude will not give up until they are ultimately defeated at the Second Coming of our Lord *Yeshua Ha Mashiach*.

chapter nine

THRESHOLD DEMOLITION AGENTS

Without a doubt, this evil, Satanic empire of the Chaldean "special forces" spirit will be the main focus of the outpouring of God's wrath in the very last days.

No place on earth is safe from being hijacked by the marauding spirit of the Chaldeans. Unbeknownst to many, the Chaldeans are also known in the Bible as the Babylonians. In fact, the geographical designation "Chaldea" is simply another name for Babylon (and for the biblical Shinar).[34]

But here is how this becomes especially relevant for our own prophetic days: Accounts of the depraved *spirit of Babylon/Chaldea* are recorded throughout the Old Testament, and they continue to be reported in the last chapters of the book of Revelation.

Also, ancient Babylon was located in the area of what was known in the antediluvian days as the greater region of early Eden.[35] Spiritually speaking, this demonic Chaldean/Babylonian spirit was first evident in the Garden God had established in the land of Eden, the place where

Heaven's throne met with the earthly creation. That spirit of "theft" was there from the beginning, when the enemy first plotted to steal God's family along with His entire newborn creation.[36]

Babylon-Chaldea was also the geographical setting for the ancient disaster of the Tower of Babel after the days of Noah's Flood. The Bible calls that area the "plain of Shinar." It turns out, then, that Babel was the earthly command center for the great battle in Heaven when Satan and his demons once again—after the Garden of Eden and the Flood of Noah—thought they would somehow dethrone Elohim, the Creator of the universe.[37]

So, when we speak of the Chaldean spirit, always remember it's actually another name for the Babylonian spirit. The two phrases can be used interchangeably.[38] This is the demonic spirit that permeated Ur of the Chaldeans, the land we know today as Iraq—the epicenter of the ancient Babylonian empire.[39]

While Ur was a specific geographical area, the demonic powers at the controls of the earthly thrones of that region were doing all they could to rob God of His own people and of His authority over them. Because there is no place of rest for demonic spirits, they continue throughout the generations, controlling geographical areas as well as the people who open the doors of their lives to areas of demonic control, thus making the way for unsuspecting people to walk right through satanic thresholds ultimately meant to keep them from God's true threshold.

It's also interesting to note that the Chaldean word "Ur"—as in "Ur of the Chaldeans"—means "light." Of course, now we know that this Ur of Chaldea was a false light, a demonic light…a deceptive and beguiling light. That's why God removed Abraham from that area and took him into the land where, eventually, the *true light* of Yeshua would enter humanity's story. Basically, Yahweh was moving Abraham from an area where the masquerading angel of light had a colossal stronghold.

And no wonder, for even Satan disguises himself as an angel of light. (2 Corinthians 11:14)

The Time of the End

The Chaldean spirit is as active as ever, as evidenced by the increasing depravity that continues to pour out upon the earth. As previously emphasized, the Word of God warns that this same evil spirit is continually at work, right up to the end, and its purposes have not changed.

Even as we come to the final chapters of the Word of God, we run right into the Babylonian/Chaldean spirit of unmitigated evil in the book of Revelation. It is a malevolence that eventually sweeps the entire planet in the last days. This spirit, unarguably the target of God's coming wrath, is connected directly to the days of the Antichrist kingdom; it is Satan's ultimate deception and masquerade.

> The rest of mankind who were not killed by these plagues still did not repent of the work of their hands; they did not stop worshiping demons, and idols of gold, silver, bronze, stone and wood—idols that cannot see or hear or walk. Nor did they repent of their murders, their magic arts, their sexual immorality or their thefts. (Revelation 9:20–21)

Even in the Modern Hebrew, the word "Chaldean" is also used for "astrologer," "witch," "sorcerer," "or magician," speaking to the depravity just referenced in that passage from Revelation. This symbolic use of the word "Chaldean" was also true in the ancient Hebrew language. Obviously, that term speaks to the overall character of the demonic influence behind the people who had become thoroughly steeped in the utter wickedness of an occultic nature.[40]

Understanding the direct demonic connection to the word "Chaldean" clarifies our use of the terms "spirit of Babylon" and/or "Chaldean spirit" as we move forward in our study of Yahweh's Threshold Covenant.

It should, therefore, come as no surprise to the attentive student of God's Word that this Chaldean spirit is called the "Mother of Prostitutes" in Revelation 17. It is figuratively tied to Sodom, Rome, Egypt, and even Jerusalem—which, by taking into account the larger narrative of Revelation, we understand the demonic spirit spoken of is actually the spirit of Babylon/Chaldea.[41]

> And their dead bodies shall lie in the street of the great city [Babylon/Chaldea], which spiritually is called Sodom and Egypt, where also our Lord was crucified. (Revelation 11:8)

The book of Revelation warns that this evil spirit remains at work in the world right up to the end, and its purposes have not changed. Its ultimate attempt to duplicate Yahweh's Kingdom will be manifested during the last-days reign of the Antichrist kingdom, as outlined in Revelation 13 and following.

> Then the angel carried me away in the Spirit into a wilderness. There I saw a woman sitting on a scarlet beast that was covered with blasphemous names and had seven heads and ten horns. The woman was dressed in purple and scarlet, and was glittering with gold, precious stones and pearls. She held a golden cup in her hand, filled with abominable things and the filth of her adulteries. **The name written on her forehead was a mystery: Babylon [Chaldea] the Great, the Mother of Prostitutes, and of the Abominations of the Earth.** I saw that the woman was drunk with the blood of God's holy people, the blood of those who bore testimony to Jesus. (Revelation 17:3–6; emphasis added.)

"Fallen. Fallen is Babylon the Great." She has become a dwelling for demons and a haunt for every impure spirit, a haunt for every unclean bird, a haunt for every unclean and detestable animal. For all the nations have drunk the maddening wine of her adulteries. The kings of the earth committed adultery with her, and the merchants of the earth grew rich from her excessive luxuries."

By your magic spell all the nations were led astray. In her was found the blood of prophets and of God's holy people, of all who have been slaughtered on the earth. (Revelation 18:2–3, 23–24; emphasis added)

Without a doubt, this evil, Satanic empire of the Chaldean "special forces" spirit will be the main focus of the outpouring of God's wrath in the very last days. As you just read, Revelation calls that Antichrist kingdom "Babylon (Chaldea) the Great" and specifically links it to the vilest of all demonic activity—a curse that eventually touches every nation on the planet on a wide scale.

Next, let's look at some of the most pronounced ways this is already happening globally.

chapter ten

DEMONIC REDEFINING OF THRESHOLDS

Satan understands the thresholds that confront us; we, too, must have a clear understanding of those divine boundaries and thresholds.

Think of the Chaldean spirit of demolition that is running rampant right before our eyes—throughout all the nations of the world. Their focus involves nothing less than tearing down every single threshold God has established among humanity from the beginning. The Chaldean spirits are seeking to redefine biblical institutions and principles, each of which is built upon the foundation of God's own heart, each defined by a specific and divine doorway and the threshold defining that doorway. And each of those thresholds has been purchased by the blood of the Lamb, Yeshua.

Examples of those thresholds include the heavenly definitions of marriage, home, family, manhood, womanhood, childhood, the boundaries of individual sexuality, the womb, the fruit of the womb, and gender—as well as government, law, courts of proper justice, and civil order.

Do you see what that demonic assault is up to? The Chaldean forces are marauding the earth at Satan's direction. They are redefining, trampling down, and laying waste to every God-ordained threshold on the planet. And it's happening now, in plain sight, and telegraphed 24/7 through ramped-up and never-before-seen global communications and information technologies.[42]

The Marriage Connection

Consider for just a moment the God-ordained institution of marriage. We know from the Word of God that Yeshua's collective Kingdom people are called His Bride. But Satan is degrading and perverting the very nature of that earthly relationship that begins with the divine Groom carrying His blood-bought Bride across a threshold—God's Covenant Threshold—and into His household![43]

Ephesians 5 presents this truth in plain language:

> "Therefore a man shall leave his father and mother and hold fast to his wife, and **the two shall become one** flesh." This mystery is profound, and I am saying that **it refers to Christ and the church.** However, let each one of you love his wife as himself, and let the wife see that she respects her husband. (Ephesians 5:31–33, emphasis added)

God will allow the influence of that Chaldean spirit to go only so far, and only for His ultimate and divine purposes. For example, that same depraved demonic spirit destroyed the people of Sodom and Gomorrah, enslaved the children of Israel, and entered King Nebuchadnezzar of Babylon to destroy God's Temple and Jerusalem and corrupt the young men and women with the Chaldean ways.

The Chaldean spirit entered Haman, prompting him to plot to destroy all the Jewish people under Persian rule, as well as King Herod, in

Yeshua's day, compelling the king to track down and attempt to destroy the baby boy who had just been born in Bethlehem. That child was suspected, within the halls of Satan, to be the one sent from Heaven to destroy him.

It didn't stop there. The Chaldean spirit's trail of destruction cut a wide swath through Nazi Germany, when Hitler and many of his closest cohorts immersed themselves in the occult along with sexual perversion and drug abuse, inextricably tying their destinies to the Chaldean spirits that sought to take what did not belong to them. The evil force carries out its devastating exploits by tempting fallen humanity through impure activities and attachments until they are finally under satanic control. These demonic principalities run rampant through the underbelly of the illicit drug world; the sex-trafficking trade; the porn industry; the human slave-trade industry (most frequently involving women and children); the anti-God curriculum; the entertainment industry; the halls of government, where insatiable power, lust, and greed are present; and all manner of addictive activities.

No place on earth is safe from being hijacked by the spirit of the Chaldeans. No message is protected from being infected by its counterfeit. Observe yet again the Apostle Paul's reminder of this profound spiritual phenomenon:

> The Spirit clearly says that in later times some will abandon the faith and follow deceiving spirits and things taught by demons. (1 Timothy 4:1)

As we draw ever closer to the end of the age, I am convinced the Lord is allowing the Chaldean spirit increasing freedom, with more diversity to its activities. Once again, He's using that dark kingdom as a tool, a sifting agent, to separate the chaff from the wheat. However, the Lord has effectively put His hooks into the jaws of these impure entities, sealing their fate in the soon-coming final judgment.

Despite Satan's limitations, because of not being privy to God's full plan, the fallen one understands the thresholds that confront us; we, too, must have a clear understanding of those divine boundaries and thresholds.

Satan's Revenge

Satan hates the concept of the threshold because he knows that once we enter God's Threshold Covenant, he's all but done. He tries everything possible to keep us from it, throwing forgery after forgery in the way of believers and unbelievers alike. He hopes we will lose sight of the significance of God's ordinances and structures by stumbling over the mountain of tradition surrounding false gods, rabbinical laws, empty religious traditions, nonbiblical participation in mere "churchianity," and even practicing remnants of ancient paganism.

When people chatter about the Old Testament having nothing to do with us in this age, they need to recognize they have become mere puppets of Satan. In the same way wooden dolls have no awareness of being manipulated by a puppeteer, people who are desensitized to the manipulations of the spirit realm often have no understanding of how they, too, are being swayed by the Chaldean spirit.

In reality, the thresholds of the Old Testament have everything to do with Messiah Yeshua. He never abolished the First Covenant; instead, He fulfilled it. He said:

> Do not think that I have come to abolish the Law or the Prophets;
> I have not come to abolish them but to fulfill them. (Matthew 5:17)

Every divine threshold agreement we face in this world rests on the foundation of our blood covenant with Yeshua. He alone is our once-for-all sacrificial Lamb.

He alone can make the eternal and ultimate blood alliance.

Part IV

Vital Perspectives

And he said, "Go, and say to this people: 'Keep on hearing, but do not understand; keep on seeing, but do not perceive.' Make the heart of this people dull, and their ears heavy, and blind their eyes; lest they see with their eyes, and hear with their ears, and understand with their hearts, and turn and be healed."

Isaiah 6:9–10

chapter eleven

THE THRESHOLD PORTAL

*Salvation has always been offered by way of
a divine interdimensional threshold.*

As we embark upon the next several chapters, let me first explain what we'll be doing.

I want to show you several biblical and historical examples of the importance of the "threshold" theme found throughout both Testaments of the Scriptures—that is, if you know what you're looking for. Once you see them, you will much more readily discover them as your study of God's Word progresses.

The following will most likely prove to be revelations you've never fully understood in light of the discoveries we've made in our journey thus far. So, as you enjoy the next nuggets of biblical truth, remember that we will soon get into some exceptionally practical applications of what we've been learning. I'm convinced that, by the time we reach that point, you'll be fairly shocked by what you see. Most importantly, you'll then understand *why* you see it, and what we have to do to correct the deceit that has infiltrated God's earthly Kingdom work!

The Threshold of the Lamb

Most believers, when asked what Jesus fulfilled on Golgotha's tree[44] (the cross), often reply something like: "He achieved our salvation." While that certainly is a part of His precious gift to us, it's not all He accomplished.

In truth, our eternal salvation was the *outcome* of what He fulfilled. But what He actually did was firmly establish the ultimate Threshold Covenant once and for all. Never doubt that our own *salvation* was the outcome of it all, to be sure. But to partake of that salvation, we must first be made alive in the Spirit of God; we have to be *born again*. That supernatural rebirth only happens when we cross over the threshold, where the properly and divinely applied blood of the Lamb has been placed, and thereby enter the Father's house. Every part of the original Passover's experience and significance foreshadowed the Lamb's threshold for all eternity!

> For Christ also suffered once for sins, the righteous for the unrighteous, that he might bring us to God, being put to death in the flesh but made alive in the spirit. (1 Peter 3:18)

> Jesus answered, "I am the way and the truth and the life. No one comes to the Father except through me." (John 14:6)

> And likewise the cup after they had eaten, saying, "This cup that is poured out for you is the new covenant in my blood." (Luke 22:20)

No More "Unknown" God

In the book of Acts, we see Paul witnessing in the Athens marketplace, where a group of Epicurean and Stoic philosophers began to debate with him. The apostle was reasoning with them regarding their false worship of *other gods*. He asked what gods they were venerating. As you'll see in a moment, an accurate translation reveals that Paul was actually talking about the posturing of the Athenians before the spiritual thresholds of their gods—the known ones as well as the unknown.[45]

Then Paul went on to preach about Yeshua, the boundaries of our earthly life, the threshold requirements for entering His presence, and our access to the very real dimension of eternity in Paradise.

So Paul, standing in the midst of the Areopagus, said: "Men of Athens, I perceive that in every way you are very religious. For as I passed along and observed the objects of your worship, I found also an altar with this inscription: 'To the unknown god.' What therefore you worship as unknown, this I proclaim to you.

"The God who made the world and everything in it, being Lord of heaven and earth, does not live in temples made by man, nor is he served by human hands, as though he needed anything, since he himself gives to all mankind life and breath and everything. And he made from one man every nation of mankind to live on all the face of the earth, having determined allotted periods and the boundaries of their dwelling place, that they should seek God, and perhaps feel their way toward him and find him.

"Yet he is actually not far from each one of us, for 'In him we live and move and have our being'; as even some of your own poets have said, 'For we are indeed his offspring.' Being then God's offspring, we ought not to think that the divine being is like gold or silver or stone, an image formed by the art and imagination of man." (Acts 17:22–29)

Pagan Thresholds

The people understood the concept of boundaries and thresholds from the ancient worship customs of their idols. They sometimes had strange and superstitious ways of determining where the thresholds to the so-called gods might be. At times, they would actually employ a ritual of releasing black and white sheep into the streets in times of plague, famine, or natural disaster. Through this procedure, they hoped to supernaturally find out where the thresholds to the unknown gods were located so they might be able to deliver the people from the calamities that had befallen them.[46]

How would the people locate those thresholds by using those roaming sheep? The ritual required that they slaughter a sheep wherever it finally chose to lie down to rest. They believed that very spot was the threshold they were to use to enter a covenant with that unknown god. The blood of the lamb was left at that place as a covenant agreement with that god, and an altar (a threshold monument) was erected.

Meyer's NT Commentary:

> It is related that Epimenides put an end to a plague in Athens by causing black and white sheep, which he had let loose on the Areopagus, to be sacrificed on the spots where they lay down… to the god concerned (yet not known by name), namely, who was the author of the plague; and that therefore one may find at Athens altars without the designation of a god by name. From this particular instance the general view may be derived, that on important occasions, when the reference to a god known by name was wanting, as in public calamities of which no definite goal could be assigned as the author, in order to honour or propitiate the god concerned by [a blood] sacrifice.[47] (See endnote for more commentary on this historical phenomenon.)

GOLGOTHA

The one true God had already established His threshold, and by so doing, He opened the door of invitation for all the world to see! It was established at the Golgotha sacrifice of Yeshua and punctuated by the Resurrection, so all could approach the cross of forgiveness at the God-designated place He had appointed as the entryway to His Kingdom. This is the message Paul was attempting to get across to the largely pagan Athenians.

Many of the apostle's listeners rejected his words, but some understood what he was saying and wanted to hear more. Others ultimately believed and were saved. By doing so, they participated in the Threshold Covenant through the blood of Yeshua…the *Lamb* slain and resurrected before the foundation of the world.[48] Paul said to the Athenians:

> "The times of ignorance God overlooked, but now he commands all people everywhere to repent, because he has fixed a day on which he will judge the world in righteousness by a man whom he has appointed; and of this he has given assurance to all by raising him from the dead."
>
> Now when they heard of the resurrection of the dead, some mocked. But others said, "We will hear you again about this." So Paul went out from their midst. But some [men and women] joined him and believed. (Acts 17:30–34)

But did the requirement of coming through Golgotha's "portal" for eternal salvation mean that they—or *we*—would have to travel to the literal location of Golgotha to cross the threshold properly? Absolutely not.

Salvation has always been offered by way of a divine *interdimensional threshold*. We might call it a "spiritual threshold" or a portal from the earthly dimension into the eternal one—*Paradise*. Our salvation does not depend upon our being in a certain place. The Threshold Covenant Yahweh demands is made in our inmost parts, then that blood covenant with Yeshua is sealed within our hearts.

chapter twelve

THE INWARD PARTS

We now realize what these words mean, especially when we comprehend just how intricate the Threshold Covenant really is.

The Orthodox Jewish people and, often, even a number of born-again believers who also follow the customs of the Jews fasten small Scripture boxes—*mezuzahs*—to their doorposts.[49] In so doing, they think they're fulfilling the letter and the law of scriptural declarations:

> Write the words of God on the gates and doorposts of your house. (Deuteronomy 6:9)

> Fix these words of mine in your hearts and minds; tie them as symbols on your hands and bind them on your foreheads. (Deuteronomy 11:18)

While nothing is wrong or sinful about attaching these Scripture boxes to physical doorposts, the problem is that these verses are meant to be more deeply understood and practiced in the *spiritual sense*, not necessarily in a merely literal fashion. The commandments about these matters speak of the need for God's Word to be written on our hearts and on the doorposts of our souls. They actually refer to the fundamentals of God's Threshold Covenant truths.

Keil and Delitzsch Biblical Commentary on the Old Testament:

> "Upon thine heart:" i.e., the commandments of God were to be an **affair of the heart**, and not merely of the memory (cf. Deuteronomy 11:18). [These words] were to be enforced upon the children, talked of at home and by the way, in the evening on lying down and in the morning on rising up, i.e., …everywhere and at all times…. As these words are figurative, and denote an undeviating observance of the divine commands, so also the commandment which follows, viz., to write the words upon the doorposts of the house, and also upon the gates, are to be **understood spiritually.**[50] (Emphasis added)

Jamieson-Fausset-Brown Bible Commentary:

> It is probable that Moses used the phraseology in Deuteronomy 6:7 **merely in a figurative way**, to signify assiduous, earnest, and frequent instruction; and **perhaps he meant the metaphorical language in Deuteronomy 6:8 to be taken in the same sense** also.[51] (Emphasis added)

DOORPOSTS

The word "doorpost" in Hebrew is *mezuzah*. The *mezuzah* doesn't refer to just a little box or even the literal posts and frames outlining the doorway into a house. It is pointing to a much larger picture. To put God's Word on the doorpost infers that the *entire structure of the house* will be protected; it has the power of being the very underpinnings that will keep the building—including doorposts, gates, and the thresholds—from collapsing. These structures are the portals into the rest of the house and into the *hearts of the family* who resides there.[52]

Unfortunately, the ancient rabbis didn't understand the meaning because they didn't have what believers in Yeshua now have: the ever-indwelling presence and guidance of the *Ruach HaKodesh* (the Holy Spirit) illuminating their understanding.

When people read Scripture in the absence of the revelation of the Holy Spirit, they often invent something to make it logical and then convince themselves they've arrived at the proper conclusion. Sadly, that's the origin of the *mezuzah*. Today we still have believers who are doing all they can to be "authentic Christians." They think they'll somehow become more genuine in their faith by mimicking ancient Jewish traditions originally invented through the rabbinical application of extrabiblical rituals and commandments. I hope this doesn't sound too harsh; I just want you, dear reader, to see the subtleties of how the Chaldean obfuscation works in our midst.

Since the completion of Heaven's genuine blood alliance at Golgotha's cross and the subsequent resurrection of Yeshua, the meaning of Jeremiah 31:33 was meant to become intimately personal and interdimensional. This is most pointedly true in reference to the *doorposts of our hearts*:

> But this shall be the covenant that I will make with the house of Israel; After those days, saith the LORD, **I will put my Law in their inward parts, and write it in their hearts**; and will be their God, and they shall be my people. (Jeremiah 31:33, KJV; emphasis added)

Around two-thirds of English translations do not use the words "inward parts" in that verse, while those closest to the original Hebrew include those *exact* words. This unfortunate circumstance is most often due to language difficulties and translation variances that are the result of converting one difficult language (ancient Hebrew) into other difficult languages.

For instance, Jeremiah 31:33 contains an extremely important reference to the threshold of the heart, identified as the "inward parts." Some translators appear to have missed the truest nuance of this phrase and have simply left it out, inserting words with much less significance.

For example, compare the English Standard Version with the King James Version:

> For this is the covenant that I will make with the house of Israel after those days, declares the Lord: **I will put my Law within them, and I will write it on their hearts.** And I will be their God, and they shall be my people. (Jeremiah 31:33, ESV; emphasis added)

> But this shall be the covenant that I will make with the house of Israel; After those days, saith the Lord, **I will put my Law in their inward parts, and write it in their hearts**; and will be their God, and they shall be my people. (Jeremiah 31:33, KJV; emphasis added)

The phrase "inward parts" refers to the *threshold of our hearts*—the entrance that actually leads to the heart. The reality is that we can't get to the heart without going through the "inward parts," because even the heart—the epicenter of Yahweh's connection and communication with us—has a threshold! Now, look at the following passage from Romans. You may never see it the same way again after understanding the threshold connection we just made!

> But what does [the Word of God] say? **"The word is near you, in your mouth and in your heart"** (that is, the word of faith that we proclaim); because, if you confess with your mouth that Jesus is Lord and believe in your heart that God raised him from the dead, you will be saved.
>
> **For with the heart one believes and is justified, and with the mouth one confesses and is saved.** For the Scripture says, "Everyone who believes in him will not be put to shame." For there is no distinction between Jew and Greek; for the same Lord is Lord of all, bestowing his riches on all who call on him.

For "everyone who calls on the name of the Lord will be saved." (Romans 10:8–13, emphasis added)

The spiritual implications of true salvation are becoming clearer. And they are all connected to the concept of the Threshold Covenant, the blood agreement we make with our Creator through Yeshua.

In the above passage, the *mouth* is the doorway, the entry point, the place of declaring one's desire to enter the covenant-keeper's house.

The *heart* is the holy altar, the spiritual place where the blood is divinely honored—the Holy of Holies. But we can't get to that altar without first crossing through the "inward parts." They are the essentials of true salvation. Those elements are biblically laid out as being: an agreement with His properly interpreted Word (His "contract and conditions"); a confession of faith; genuine repentance; and a biblical understanding of the covenant of obedience and love one is about to enter. This is the threshold where the blood of the sacrifice is first applied.

So, we approach the door. We see the blood. We see the basin. We know the Lamb has been offered. We know a serious covenant agreement is being offered. Now we have to decide:

- Am I willing to pass through the inward parts that make up the covenant and agree to the complete contract—or not?
- Will I declare (with my mouth) my desire?
- Will I fully enter that covenant and an agreement that requires my total heart belief—a faith that lives in my innermost parts—and not only with a superficial, mental acceptance of memorized biblical facts?

Those are the eternally significant questions. Sadly, many fail to see this most important truth.

chapter thirteen

THE MISSING NUANCE

Our Threshold Covenant with God is not simply a matter of keeping laws, joining a church, or saying a quick little prayer to be saved. It's a matter of the involvement of the whole "house" of our being.

For years, when quoting Jeremiah 31:33, I only referred to the heart. I never used the phrase "inward parts."

Then I believed that the Holy Spirit was directing me to go back and look closer at the Hebrew wording. After I examined it again, much more thoroughly, I said, "Wait a minute! There's something here that's not made very clear in many [almost two-thirds] of the English translations."

When I finally understood what was missing, or at least what was slightly obscured, I was floored. I found only sixteen translations—out of almost fifty of the most scholarly ones—that include the exact words from the Hebrew text "inward parts."[53]

Then I wondered why the Hebrew word for that term[54] had so often been replaced with more ambiguous phrases. Almost all other translations use "within their minds," "within them," or "inside them" instead. That's unfortunate, because "inward parts" is meant to denote the various components of the genuine Threshold Covenant and the blood alliance it demands.[55]

Important Words

Please understand that I'm not trying to be too tedious with my words here. It's just that I know what a biblical Threshold Covenant is, and I understand it from a Hebrew perspective. I suppose the other translations are fairly satisfactory. Again, I'm not condemning other translators for the verbiage they choose. However, I am keenly aware that words and their grammatical nuances, especially of the original-language words, have *meaning*. Sometimes those meanings are almost irreplaceable. This is why, on an issue as eternally important as this one, I want to make sure we understand what Yahweh is actually saying.

For example, if the translation simply says "inside them" or "within them," the larger picture does not come into its proper focus. But when the translation says the "inward parts," we are made aware of some sort of *structure* that's involved; we realize actual *parts* are associated within that structure, and it's not just some vague undefined "thing" inside us.

Inward Parts of a House

The entire structure of a house is built around, on top of, and supported by its *inward parts*. The dwelling is literally joined together by its foundation, walls, inner walls, joists, cornerstones or posts, support beams, ceiling components, floor structures, screws, nails, and other fasteners, as well as the doorways and thresholds comprising the lintels and doorposts that hold the doors and thresholds in place. Those are the true "inward parts" of the whole house. For the house to safely support itself and protect its occupants, it has to be properly connected to the "inward parts"; otherwise, it will eventually collapse. This is why it's important to understand the words the Holy Spirit used when the Word was originally given: "inward parts."

As indicated earlier, that Hebrew phrase, in its most literal understanding, can denote the entrails of an animal or human.[56] In order to get access to the beating heart of a person, a surgeon must traverse through myriad inward parts and their surrounding structures—the flesh, vessels, arteries, nerves, sinew, lungs, skeletal system, and the protective inner layers of tissue. There's really no confusion when those words are recognized, especially in their spiritual sense, and in light of the fact that Jeremiah 31:33 is speaking about God making a New Covenant with His people. He is most interested in a person's "heart" being changed…and that calls for us to understand that this organ is ultimately supported and protected by the "inward parts."

And, of all things, the supreme importance of the "inward parts" command is foreshadowed in the Threshold Covenant of the Passover:

> Then they shall take some of the blood and put it on the two doorposts and the lintel of the houses in which they eat it. **They shall eat the flesh that night**, roasted on the fire; with unleavened bread and bitter herbs they shall eat it. Do not eat any of it raw or boiled in water, but roasted, its head with its legs **and its inner parts**. (Exodus 12:7–9, emphasis added)

Why was this command included with the Passover *blood alliance* God was making with His people? The following commentary gets right to the point:

Keil and Delitzsch Biblical Commentary on the Old Testament:

> Through the unity and integrity of the lamb given them to eat, the participants were to be joined into an undivided unity and fellowship with the Lord, who had provided them with the meal.[57]

The Threshold Covenant Yahweh promises is centered around the ancient custom of going into the house and enjoying access to all the life within it that this concept represents: unbroken unity, fellowship, and loyalty. Now we realize what the phrase "inward parts" means, especially when we comprehend just how intricate the Threshold Covenant really is.

> But this shall be the covenant that I will make with the house of Israel; After those days, saith the LORD, I will put my Law in their **inward parts,** and [then] write it **in their hearts;** and will be their God, and they shall be my people. (Jeremiah 31:33, KJV; emphasis added)

> **In my Father's house are many rooms.** If it were not so, would I have told you that I go to prepare a place for you? And if I go and prepare a place for you, I will come again and will take you to myself, that where I am you may be also. (John 14:2–3, emphasis added)

The meaning is now clearer. When we enter the eternal *blood alliance* with Yahweh—our Creator—through *Yeshua Ha Mashiach,* we become a new creation in all of our "inward parts." Then, penetrating farther into our heart and soul, we arrive at the inner sanctuary of our being.

Our Threshold Covenant with God is not simply a matter of following laws, joining a church, or saying a quick prayer asking to be saved. It's a matter involving the whole "house" of our being…all our inner parts, as well as our hearts and minds—everything! None of it can be accessed unless by way of the Threshold Covenant.

This truth applies to everybody—Jews and Gentiles alike—under the blood of Yeshua.

> Not everyone who says to me, "Lord, Lord," will enter the kingdom of heaven, but the one who does the will of my Father who is in heaven. (Matthew 7:21)

Satan and his Chaldean demons will do everything they can to keep people from knowing these truths, to keep them from doing the *will of the Father.*

But now…*you* know, and can accurately live out this truth and share it with others.

chapter fourteen

THE ONE WHO KNOCKS

If we were to turn over the keys of our home to a guest knocking at the door and give them the deed to the house, we would no longer be the host; the house would then belong to the one who had knocked...and we would be the guests.

Now that we've come this far, let's illuminate yet another relevant perspective of the Threshold Covenant.

Many around the world struggle with disorders regarding their personal identity. Those maladies come in all types, more than we can imagine. Multiplied millions of wandering souls spend uncountable amounts of money trying to "find themselves"—trying to understand why they think what they think and do what they do. They feel lost and misunderstood, alone and empty. Sadly, exploding numbers of them are even suicidal.

It seems, for the most part, that their brains are struggling with a truckload of confusing messages—most having been demonically aimed at causing their total destruction. I am convinced a large part of this barrage of harmful communications is being imposed upon humanity by the Chaldean spirits—the gods (demons) of disorder and chaos. This is a global issue of massive proportion.

Within most of the battlefields in that universal spiritual war, many have yet to find their way past the seemingly unscalable wall of demonic interference and into the solid Word of God. I am not claiming that all who struggle with these matters are demon possessed, not at all. I'm merely pointing out the spiritual side of the impact this very real cosmic warfare is making upon multitudes of precious souls. Even within the daily struggles of a number of sincere believers, the Chaldean spirit is vile and relentless.

The National Institutes of Health Shock Report

To punctuate what is happening in the world, consider the following strange but "official" introduction to the problems related to self-identity and mental distress. It is from the National Institutes of Health (NIH) website, posted on their official NIH Journal webpage for its January–March 2017 edition. That piece was published three years *before* the 2020 global COVID-19 pandemic and the resulting fallout regarding the further increase in mental health issues worldwide.[58]

In the following, you'll see a telling reflection of what we already know from God's Word. The NIH officials apparently don't appear to have a clue as to what they're actually suggesting, biblically speaking. They tell of a growing global epidemic of mental disease, psychological disorders, and overall failing health. And they refer to this ever-perplexing phenomenon as the experience of the "hollow men."

Here is the title of that NIH article: "We Are the Hollow Men: The worldwide epidemic of mental illness, psychiatric and behavioral emergencies, and its impact on patients and providers."[59]

The first words of the article are lines reprinted from a portion of T. S. Elliot's poem titled "The Hollow Men":

> Those who have crossed
> With direct eyes, to death's other Kingdom

Remember us—if at all—not as lost
Violent souls, but only
As the hollow men
The stuffed men
This is the way the world ends
This is the way the world ends
Not with a bang but a whimper.

Right after those lines of the poem come the first words of the initial paragraph in the NIH study findings:

All across the world, patients are coming to their local Accident and Emergency Departments/Casualty Centers (EDs). They are in pain. Sometimes, their eyes scream out their suffering and other times they appear as cold, empty shells reflecting the hollowness the patient feels inside.

Then, note the ominous conditions the NIH acknowledged way back in 2017. As you read them, think of where the world must be *now*, considering these are still growing and vitally serious issues.

The World Health Organization has predicted that **by 2020, depression will be the second-leading cause of disease burden globally. Depression is set to outpace ischemic heart disease as the number one cause of disease burden worldwide by 2030.**
However, suicide is not just a "first world" problem...the **global suicide rate...[has] increased over 60% in the last 45 years.** One person commits suicide every 40 [seconds]...
The statistics are frightening. Many state hospitals are now closed, and community outreach programs are stretched to the breaking point. Chronically underfunded and perpetually overwhelmed, outpatient centers are simply unable to cater to the demand for their services. The mentally ill, are caught in the middle.[60] (Emphasis added)

It's as though they don't even know they are echoing the entire message of God's Word…the Gospel message…and the deliverance that awaits them on the "other side" after "crossing over" to Jesus Christ! They also seem to unwittingly acknowledge the end of the fallen world system that truly is on its way!

THE LIGHT OF THE WORLD

Jesus/Yeshua is a courteous gentleman. He's not going to push His way into anyone's life. He says in Revelation 3:20, "Behold, I stand at the door and knock. If anyone hears my voice and opens the door, I will come in to him and eat with him, and he with me." The entire exchange has to be mutual. He will not impose Himself upon anyone who doesn't want to be in covenant with Him.

Multitudes around the world are familiar with the *Light of the World* painting produced in the mid 1800's by William Holman Hunt. It's an allegorical work representing Jesus about to knock at a long-overgrown doorway. According to Hunt, "I painted the picture with what I thought, unworthy though I was, to be a divine command, and not simply a good subject."[61]

The door in the painting has no handle, and can therefore be opened only from the inside, representing "the obstinately shut mind."[62] The painting was often referred to as the "sermon in a frame." It was a widely traveled work of art, having been seen by millions of people in a 1904 world tour. It was even more famous than the works of the great masters of the Renaissance, as it seemingly reflected the innate hunger of so many for a true relationship with Jesus.

The ancient rules for cutting a covenant, killing an animal at the door, crossing the threshold of the abode of the one making the covenant, and sharing a meal are all components of the God/human covenant. Here, in the passage from Revelation that William Hunt's painting represents, Yeshua is saying if we open the threshold of our hearts to Him, He will come in and dine with us, and we will dine with Him.

Family-Table Fellowship

When we invite people into our homes as dinner guests, they're not entitled to wander throughout the private parts of our home. To break that unwritten rule would be considered rude and highly inappropriate. The guests dine with *us*. *We* are the hosts.

If, however, we were to turn over the keys of our home to a guest knocking at the door and give them the deed to the house, we would no longer be the host; the house would then belong to the one who knocked. At that point, *we* would become the guests! The dynamic around the dinner table would change as well. We would become the invitees and would eat with the new homeowner. The new owner would then be entitled to scrounge around in every drawer, filing cabinet, and closet as wished.

Revelation 3:20 speaks of the transfer of ownership of our souls: "I will come in to him and eat with him, and he with me." This happens only when we turn over the lordship of our lives to Yeshua—in our most *inward parts*—to the extent that we become *the guests* in our temporal lives and He becomes the owner. Then *we* dine with *Him*.

This is a compound theological truth, meaning it has applications for both now and the future.[63] This is because Yeshua truly is *the one who was, who is, and who is to come*. It also speaks of the dining that's connected to the Marriage Supper of the Lamb and of the eternal covenant with Yeshua, the final threshold.

> And the angel said to me, "Write this: Blessed are those who are invited to the marriage supper of the Lamb." And he said to me, "These are the true words of God." (Revelation 19:9)

Satan first entered humanity's heart threshold as a "thief"—in the Garden of Eden. He manipulated, lied, cajoled, slandered, and shoved his way through the door. He entered that door and belligerently trampled all over the threshold in order to steal what wasn't his. He wanted it for himself. At that point, "legally," it was given to Satan by the original "owners" of the house—Adam and Eve. In so doing, Satan brought the penalty of death with him...both physical and eternal.

That's when the cosmic war of the ages began. We are still caught up in it to this very day. But it's about to come to a screeching halt. Yeshua has won through the cross and Resurrection. A *renewed Threshold Covenant* was initiated through which a blood alliance is now offered to all who will come.

The language of the Word of God is always *covenant language*. Yeshua is the one lovingly and longingly standing at the threshold of our heart. If we respond to His call, He will cross the threshold of our *inner parts* and enter the heart of our very being. He'll dine with us in a completed Threshold Covenant. At that moment, He "legally" becomes the restored and loving owner of our lives, having bought us back by His own blood, which He willingly spilled at the threshold. What an amazingly beautiful picture of Yeshua's love for us.

chapter fifteen

THE NEW "RENEWED" COVENANT

"Behold, the days are coming," declares the Lord,
"when I will make a new covenant with the house of Israel."

Nothing is wrong with calling the New Covenant the "New Testament." I refer to it that way all the time, but it's important to know what the original says and means. Again, this is not an issue of trying to get overly technical, it's just a matter of understanding the foundations of our faith and the Hebrew word distinctions that help to correctly illuminate God's truth.

"Behold, the days are coming," declares the Lord, "when **I will make a new covenant** with the house of Israel and the house of Judah, not like the covenant that I made with their fathers on the day when I took them by the hand to bring them out of the land of Egypt, my covenant that they broke, though I was their husband," declares the Lord. (Jeremiah 31:31–32, emphasis added)

It's important to know the original Hebrew language calls the New Covenant the "renewed covenant." Remember, Yeshua didn't do anything *completely new* in making this covenant. After all, He is the "Lamb slain from the foundation of the world" (Revelation 13:8).

Dr. Joseph R. Nally[64] explains this as follows:

> Both the Hebrew *chadash* (Jer. 31:31) and the Greek *kainos* (Heb. 8:8) words for "new" may be more properly translated "renewed" as opposed to "new" or "brand-new" in certain contexts. *Chadash* may mean new in quality, not new in time (1 Sam. 11:14; 2 Chron. 15:8; 24:4, 12; Job 10:7; Psa. 103:5; 104:30; Isa. 61:4; Lam. 5:21). **It may also mean to "renew" or "repair".** For instance, in Psalm 51:10 David says, "Create in me a clean heart, O God; and renew a right spirit within me." David uses the same word as in Jeremiah 31:31 (*chadash*). **David was not asking for something brand-new but was asking for a renewal of what he had previously.** In 2 Chronicles 24:4, 12 we see the use of the terms repair and restore (root, *chadash*) with the already existent house of the Lord. So, in all these verses, there is a renewal, a repairing, a restoration of that which was already in existence. The same is true for Jeremiah 31.[65] (Emphasis added)

When Yeshua went to the cross to refresh and renew our opportunity to freely come back to Him, it wasn't an afterthought. It was planned before Adam drew his first breath! So how could it be "new"? It wasn't. It was *refreshed* and *renewed*—and at just the right time.

> So also, when we were children, we were enslaved under the basic principles of the world. But when the time had fully come, God sent His Son, born of a woman, born under the law, to redeem those under the law, that we might receive our adoption as sons. (Galatians 4:3–4, BSB)

Even when God says in Revelation 21 that He makes *all things new*, it's not new in terms of being utterly different; it's new in the sense that the cosmos and the earth have been refurbished to their original state of perfection. He is restoring everything that was ruined with the Fall of man. In the same way, the New Covenant is not completely different; it's *renewed*...in the deepest sense of meaning.

In the same way, Yeshua renews *us*! For that to happen, though, we have to be *born again*, renewed from our inward parts out. God didn't come up with some *brand-new* deal and call it a New Covenant. He makes all things new in terms of the complete restoration of the original. He simply reinstated everything that was lost when humanity fell. He restored the original covenant and called it the "Renewed Covenant."

The original covenant was not broken by God. *He* does not break covenants; *humanity* breaks them. Scripture tells us very clearly the original covenant He made with the house of Israel was broken by *them*—not by Him.

Yeshua, and only Yeshua, renews us. No earthly power, no otherworldly power, no governmental power, not even the strictest observance of the "law" can renew us! Yeshua says we must be born again...born from above.

> Now there was a man of the Pharisees named Nicodemus, a ruler of the Jews. This man came to Jesus by night and said to him, "Rabbi, we know that you are a teacher come from God, for no one can do these signs that you do unless God is with him."
>
> Jesus answered him, "Truly, truly, I say to you, **unless one is born again, he cannot see the kingdom of God.**" Nicodemus said to him, "How can a man be born when he is old? Can he enter a second time into his mother's womb and be born?" Jesus answered, "Truly, truly, I say to you, **unless one is born of water and the Spirit, he cannot enter the kingdom of God.**" (John 3:1–5, emphasis added)

Yeshua was patiently showing Nicodemus the way to the genuine Threshold Covenant! He told Nicodemus: "If you want to live for eternity, you're going to have to cross the eternal threshold. Merely keeping the laws and traditions won't do it for you, Nicodemus!"

chapter sixteen

IT HAS ALWAYS BEEN ABOUT FAITH

Any other way of entering the presence of our Creator that is attempted by humanity is bound to eternal failure.

The way to salvation has never changed. It has always been about faith (Hebrews 11:1–40). It has always been about stepping over the threshold and making a covenant of obedience and relationship with our Creator Yahweh.

In the Old Covenant, the people of God were looking forward, long into the future, toward the offering Messiah would ultimately bring—the offering of Himself, His own blood. This looking forward was done in faith, and faith alone. It was faith in Yahweh's promises and His Threshold Covenant that saved the people of the Old Testament.

In the Renewed Covenant, we are saved through that same promise, but now it has been fulfilled in its most profound sense. God fulfilled the covenant in and through Himself! The blood of Yeshua was shed and poured out over the threshold. God, through the prophet Zechariah, even told the ancients how it would happen: interdimensionally![66]

> And I will pour out on the house of David and the inhabitants of Jerusalem a spirit of grace and pleas for mercy, so that, when they look on me, on him whom they have pierced, they shall mourn for him, as one mourns for an only child, and weep bitterly over him, as one weeps over a firstborn. (Zechariah 12:10)

> On that day there shall be a fountain opened for the house of David and the inhabitants of Jerusalem, to cleanse them from sin and uncleanness. (Zechariah 13:1)

But now, in our own day, we look back on what God did almost two thousand years ago…and we step over that Threshold Covenant completed in Yeshua! We do it in faith, exactly as our ancient forefathers in Yahweh did. Salvation has always been by faith in the Threshold-Covenant offer held out to us in love, mercy, and grace.

Think of it. Even Abraham had the Gospel preached to him—by Yahweh Himself! So, the realities of the New Covenant were already in motion during the operation of the Old Covenant! God was already saving individuals by grace and faith alone.

> For because God knew beforehand that the nations are made right by faith, he preached The Good News to Abraham beforehand, as The Holy Scriptures say: "In you shall all the nations be blessed." (Galatians 3:8, Aramaic Bible in Plain English)

This was God's way from the very beginning, as addressed in an earlier chapter, as seen when God clothed Adam and Eve with animal skins by the shedding of blood (Genesis 3:21).

However, there are distinctions between the Old and New Covenants, even though the two fit like a hand into a glove, until the two literally operate as one. The "hand" actually animates the "glove"! The two are deeply and inextricably dependent upon each other and have been so from the beginning.

These vital elements of the Old and New Covenants aren't two dramatic differences; rather, they are subtle distinctions, or improvements through ultimate fulfillment. The Apostle Paul, a former Pharisee and Orthodox rabbi, in the entire third and seventh chapters of Romans, categorically underscores the fact that the Mosaic Covenant was renewed, refreshed, invigorated, and ultimately fulfilled through God's mercy and grace in *Yeshua Ha Mashiach*. Paul makes it clear that God did this because of human sin.

Paul says the Law was used by God to convict us of our sin and to clarify our need for the completed Threshold Covenant that can only be attained through the blood of Yeshua. Any other way we attempt to enter the presence of our Creator is bound to eternal failure. It is a counterfeit. It is "unauthorized fire." It falls outside the boundaries of God's divinely ordained plan.

Ancient Boundaries

Along these same lines, consider this: Covenants also involve distinct boundaries, and all boundaries have thresholds.

> Do not move the ancient landmark that your fathers have set. (Proverbs 22:28)

Who are the fathers spoken of in that passage? The ancestors of Israel, as well as of our faith in Yahweh/Yeshua: Moses, Abraham, Isaac, and Jacob. The ancient boundaries were given by God Himself. Threshold Covenants were struck when Israel put the blood on the lintels, when Israel crossed the Red Sea, and when Israel went into the wilderness. God says the ancient boundaries are not to be moved.[67]

But now, in our own time, we can surely see the Chaldean spirit pushing back to prevent the ancient boundaries from being honored. Satan wants to move them. Satan wants Israel and anyone who supports Israel to be "removed from the land." He wants any born-again believer who has crossed the true Covenant Threshold to be debilitated and confused, if at all possible. The war is on! It's intense…and it's for keeps.

God says when we cross a threshold in an unauthorized manner, we could be killed. It's a matter of life or death. We read in Leviticus 10 of such an account involving the sons of the high priest Aaron, who was a foreshadowing of *Yeshua Ha Mashiach*.

> Now Nadab and Abihu, the sons of Aaron, each took his censer and put fire in it and laid incense on it and offered unauthorized fire before the Lord, which he had not commanded them. And fire came out from before the Lord and consumed them, and they died before the Lord. (Leviticus 10:1–2)

Aaron had two sons, Nahab and Abihu. They took some fire and added some incense to it, offering "unauthorized fire" before the Lord, contrary to what the Lord had commanded. Yahweh had been very clear about not moving ancient *boundaries*. Those boundaries were indicative of what was to come in Yeshua.

Nevertheless, these two took it upon themselves to operate according to their own ideas of how things *should* be done. It was, I believe, the spirit of the Chaldeans manipulating them even then.

Whatever their motivation, they chose to try to change the way God had ordained things to be done. So, fire came from the presence of the Lord and consumed them. God took out the sons of Aaron, the high priest, because they dared to move ancient boundaries…ancient thresholds…divine instructions.

When God ordains something, it's not to be taken lightly.

chapter seventeen

THRESHOLD CONSEQUENCES

Satan is no respecter of people. He'll do anything to stop the spread of the Gospel and to take people to the wrong door, threshold, or gospel.

In order to be sincerely obedient, we have to recognize what is required of us through covenant cutting with Yahweh. While many say several different roads lead to God, in John 14:6, Yeshua made the boundaries very clear:

> Jesus said to him, "I am the way, and the truth, and the life. No one comes to the Father except through me." (John 14:6)

ONE WAY, ONE THRESHOLD

No one can get to God except through belief and trust in the blood sacrifice and the subsequent death and resurrection of Yeshua. He is the threshold, and it's on loving obedience to Him alone that the Threshold Covenant has been established. There's no other way. Efforts to get to Him by being a good person, believing in Buddha or Mohammed, using New Age charms, following the teaching of the Hindu Veda, adhering to cultural constructs, embracing the newest political correctness, or simply being guided by one's own ideas are doomed to failure no matter how well-meaning they might be. Yahweh will accept no "strange fire" at His doorsteps and threshold.

Yeshua is the door. He is the threshold. He doesn't say He is *like* a door; He says He *is* the door to eternal salvation:

> I am the door. If anyone enters by me, he will be saved and will go in and out and find pasture. (John 10:9)

If we imagine Yeshua on the cross, we can see that His head, arms, and feet are saturated in His blood. Yeshua *is* the Word of God. He *is* the door. He *is* the lintel, the doorposts, and the threshold. His thorn-crowned head is the top of the door frame—the lintel of our door to eternity. His hands are the sides of the doorposts. His feet are the threshold. The entire door—Yeshua—was covered with His own blood.

> How beautiful upon the mountains are the feet of him who brings good news, who publishes peace, who brings good news of happiness, who publishes salvation, who says to Zion, "Your God reigns." (Isaiah 52:7)

By allowing Himself to be hung on a tree, Christ became a curse in our place and redeemed us from the curse of the Law.

> Christ redeemed us from the curse of the Law by becoming a curse for us—for it is written, "Cursed is everyone who is hanged on a tree." (Galatians 3:13)

All our efforts to attract the favor of God and attain eternal life through works signify nothing, because we can never do things with the absolute perfection required by righteousness. While it's true that faith without works is dead, works without faith are "deader"! They actually subject us to a curse:

> For all who rely on works of the Law are under a curse; for it is written, "Cursed be everyone who does not abide by all things written in the Book of the Law, and do them." Now it is evident that no one is justified before God by the Law, for "The righteous shall live by faith." But the Law is not of faith, rather "The one who does them shall live by them." (Galatians 3:10–11)

The burden of futile efforts at self-righteousness was removed. Yeshua took the seemingly impossible situation upon Himself.

> Christ redeemed us from the curse of the Law by becoming a curse for us—for it is written, "Cursed is everyone who is hanged on a tree"—so that in Christ Jesus the blessing of Abraham might come to the Gentiles, so that we might receive the promised Spirit through faith. (Galatians 3:13–14)

> When the sun had gone down and a [deep] darkness had come, there appeared a smoking brazier and a flaming torch which passed between the [divided] pieces [of the animals]. On the same day the Lord made a covenant [promise, pledge] with Abram, saying, "To your descendants I have given this land, from the river of Egypt to the great river Euphrates." (Genesis 15:17–18; AMP)

Abraham had a dream in which he saw a big line down the road, with animals that had been cut to pieces on each side. God walked through the pieces of sacrifice with Abraham and declared His covenant with his descendants—Israel. We, the born again in Yeshua, are Israel, the children of the promise! It was a spiritual covenant with us and it's also a physical covenant with the land of Israel today. No one, no matter how great the threat may appear, can destroy Israel—neither the *physical* Israel nor the *spiritual*.[68]

A Threshold of Trembling

God doesn't break covenants; fallen humanity is the destroyer of them. This is a foreshadowing of the Threshold Covenant because God walked through the pieces. No matter how much Hamas, Iran, Hezbollah, or anyone else may try to attack Israel, the land can never again be utterly destroyed by anyone but God on judgment day.

> Behold, I will make Jerusalem a cup of trembling unto all the people round about, when they shall be in the siege both against Judah and against Jerusalem. (Zechariah 12:2, KJ21)

We know this is a future prophecy. It's a prophecy of God's judgment. It says He will make Jerusalem "a cup of trembling." The Hebrew, however, most correctly indicates that God will make Jerusalem a *threshold of trembling*. This very important language distinction changes everything![69]

Pulpit Commentary:

> A cup of trembling; This Jerome explains to mean that anyone who crosses the threshold of Jerusalem in hostile guise shall totter and fall.[70]

Jamieson-Fausset-Brown Bible Commentary:

> Calvin with the Septuagint translates, "threshold of destruction," on which they shall stumble and be crushed when they attempt to cross it.[71]

Let's look back at God walking with Abraham through the pieces of the animal sacrifice. Why were the animals cut into pieces? Because if anyone dared to break the covenant, what was done to the animals would be done to them. In Zechariah 12:2, when God says He will make Jerusalem a "threshold of trembling," we see what happens to those who break the covenant:

> And in that day will I make Jerusalem a burdensome stone for all people. All who burden themselves with it shall be cut in pieces, though all the people of the earth be gathered together against it. (Zechariah 12:3, KJV)

What was done to the animals would be done to them. All the people who broke the covenant would be cut to pieces.[72]

So now we have a fresh insight into the demonic realm. We can understand why the Egyptians have images of gods on their entrances and why fake thresholds are given significance. It's all about spiritual warfare. Satan is no respecter of people. He'll do anything to stop the spread of the Gospel and take people to the wrong threshold, or gospel.

> Therefore, whosoever heareth these sayings of Mine and doeth them, I will liken him unto a wise man, who built his house upon a rock. And the rain descended, and the floods came, and the winds blew and beat upon that house; and it fell not, for it was founded upon a rock. And everyone that heareth these sayings of Mine and doeth them not, shall be likened unto a foolish man, who built his house upon the sand; and the rain descended, and the floods came, and the winds blew, and beat upon that house; and it fell, and great was the fall of it. (Matthew 7:24–27, KJ21)

Why does Yeshua use the example of a house in Matthew 7? Because a house has a threshold. If we don't have the correct threshold, which is Yeshua, our house is going to fall. Peter says our bodies are temporary houses, temporary dwelling places. Without the Threshold Covenant, without Yeshua, everyone within this fallen world would crumble into a dark and godless eternity.

But thanks be unto Yeshua for the chance He has graciously given us to step over that threshold…and into life!

Over the next several short chapters, I'll show you other enlightening examples of biblical threshold language. After that, we'll delve right into our own day and take a hard look at the vicious Chaldean playground of deceit that is firmly entrenched among us.

That deceit is aimed right at Yahweh's blood alliance with us.

chapter eighteen

OFTEN OVERLOOKED

*It is better that we weigh and judge our own words
before we speak them than to give them life
and be condemned by them.*

We are finally getting a much clearer biblical understanding of the concept of thresholds. Basically, they're places of choice, points of decision, altars of commitment, positions of alignment, and entryways into divinely appointed spiritual dimensions. We don't talk much about thresholds in today's congregations of believers, but the Scripture is full of references to them.

MOUTHS, EARS, AND EYES

Have you ever thought of your mouth as a threshold? Our ears and eyes are gateways to our minds, but our mouths form the threshold over which every uttered thought (that is given voice) has to pass. All our senses, of course, communicate responses to stimuli for processing decisions, perceptions, attitudes, and beliefs. But our eyes, ears, and mouths are portals that facilitate our interaction with the world around us.

In the same way we have to cross the threshold of a doorway, sounds enter our conscious minds only by crossing the threshold of our ears. To a great extent, we choose what crosses our thresholds of sound. Earplugs were invented to help our choice-making abilities.

Images of the world around us have to pass through the threshold retinas of our eyes in order to impact our brains. Again, to a great extent, we choose what crosses our thresholds of sight. Despite the current pornographization of society,[73] for example, we choose whether to focus on destructive images that cross our sightlines or to turn away and replace thoughts of what we have just seen with healthy thoughts or memories of healthy images.

Our mouths are a different kind of threshold, because they are portals or thresholds for output of words.

> Set a guard, O Lord, over my mouth; keep watch over the door of my lips! (Psalm 141:3)

Psalm 141:3 refers to "the door of my lips." Our mouths are portals to our souls. No thought formed in the mind or heart escapes the silence of meditation except as words formed that must pass through the doors of our lips. Once words have been expressed, they reveal the condition and nature of the soul.

> Jesus called the crowd to Him and said, "Listen and understand. A man is not defiled by what enters his mouth, but by what comes out of it." (Matthew 15:11)

Every spoken word is the product of a journey over covenant thresholds. How it emerges from the depths of our souls is the audible evidence of the condition of the covenant we have made with God. It starts with the stimuli of our environment that we allow to cross the thresholds of our senses. The information is then processed for acceptance or rejection in our minds/souls, and from there, if we choose to give it life as a spoken word, it is formed by the tongue and emerges through the doors (thresholds) of our lips.

> Finally, brothers, whatever is true, whatever is honorable, whatever is just, whatever is pure, whatever is lovely, whatever is commendable, if there is any excellence, if there is anything worthy of praise, think about these things. (Philippians 4:8)

Are you familiar with a children's chorus by the Cedarmont Kids that speaks to this very subject?[74] Millions around the world have sung it as children. It was written to help little ones and their families know how to live properly and how to deal with the influences that try to push against the boundaries of their lives. It's a simple exercise for choosing what kinds of thoughts to entertain in order to give the soul healthy, God-honoring raw material for forming the meditations of our hearts that eventually become spoken words.

Here are a few stanzas of that song:

O be careful little eyes what you see / O be careful little eyes what you see
    For the Father up above / Is looking down in love
    So, be careful little eyes what you see.
    O be careful little ears what you hear / O be careful little ears what you hear
    For the Father up above / Is looking down in love
    So, be careful little ears what you hear.
    O be careful little tongue what you say / O be careful little tongue what you say
    For the Father up above / Is looking down in love
    So, be careful little tongue what you say.[75]

If our mouths are the doors from our souls, then our authentic relationship with Yeshua demands that the words we speak confirm the covenant we have with Him.

> Then the Lord put forth His hand and **touched my mouth**, and the Lord said to me: "**Behold, I have put My words in your mouth.** See, I have this day set you over the nations and over the kingdoms, to root out and to pull down, to destroy and to throw down, to build and to plant." (Jeremiah 1:9–10, emphasis added)

It's easy to speak carelessly and end up with regrets. But more than that—if our mouths are doors (thresholds), we can defile ourselves by breaking covenant through the words we speak. We cannot say "Yeshua is Lord" one minute and take His name in vain the next.

> You brood of vipers! How can you speak good, when you are evil? For out of the abundance of the heart the mouth speaks. (Matthew 12:34)

> This people honors me with their lips, but their heart is far from me. (Matthew 15:8)

> Death and life are in the power of the tongue, and those who love it will eat its fruits. (Proverbs 18:21)

> I said, "I will guard my ways, that I may not sin with my tongue; I will guard my mouth with a muzzle, so long as the wicked are in my presence." (Psalm 39:1)

It is over the threshold of our mouths that we join in agreement with God regarding salvation. Salvation happens in the heart when we believe on the Lord Jesus Christ, but our Threshold Covenant with our Savior is pledged when we speak words of acceptance of Him as our once-and-for-all-time sacrificial Lamb.

> If you confess with your mouth that Jesus is Lord and believe in your heart that God raised him from the dead, you will be saved. For with the heart one believes and is justified, and with the mouth one confesses and is saved. (Romans 10:9–10)

Yeshua said His words are "spirit and life":

> It is the Spirit who gives life; the flesh is no help at all. The words that I have spoken to you are spirit and life. (John 6:63)

We were created as spiritual beings with physical bodies and eternal souls. Our unseen spirits are manifested through the words we speak, as processed through our souls.

Word Power

Just as God spoke the world into existence, we, in large measure, speak ours into existence. We either speak words of life or death—words of affirmation of God's Word, or ways or words of unbelief, mistrust, and cursing.

Before a word escapes the portal or threshold of our spirit, it is processed through the mechanism of free will that is activated in our minds with the development of thoughts. If we decide to let our inward thoughts be made known, we form them into words and permit or enable them to cross the thresholds of our mouths.

The authenticity of our covenant with God will be tested on the day of judgment, when we will have to give an account for "every idle word":

A good man out of the good treasure of his heart brings forth good things, and an evil man out of the evil treasure brings forth evil things. **But I say to you that for every idle word men may speak, they will give account of it in the day of judgment.** For by your words you will be justified, and by your words you will be condemned. (Matthew 12:35–37, emphasis added)

It is better to weigh and judge our own words before we speak them than to give them life and risk being condemned by them. The guard we are to place over the doors of our lips is an assessment of their value. Are they true or false? Are they God-honoring or self-motivated? Are they necessary or idle? Do they—by their very nature, tone, and content—confirm the covenant we have made with Him?

chapter nineteen

ON OR OVER?

*All the people of Judah had to do was to accept the sacrifice,
cross over the threshold in the proper manner,
and be at peace with Yahweh—in His presence, in His salvation.
Instead...they trampled on the threshold.*

The early Israelites were accustomed to numerous references to thresholds in their daily lives. The ancient rituals of the pagan gods were being practiced all around them, as were the thresholds they claimed they controlled.

The religion of the ancient Greeks and Romans, much like many belief systems today, had gods for almost everything. Poseidon was the god of the sea. Apollo was the god of the sun, and then there was Venus, goddess of love and beauty.[76]

Although the two-faced Janus may be lesser known, he was worshiped as the Roman god of *doors and transitions*. He guarded the thresholds between the dimensions of philosophy and substance...like the transitions between life and death, youth and adulthood, war and peace, barbarism and civilization.[77]

Janus held the key to the door between what is and what is to come. According to Roman mythology, he was present at the creation of the world and was often invoked at public sacrifices as the overseer of planting and harvests. It was with heavy symbolism that the pagan god Janus was portrayed as having two faces: one faced the past and the other the future.[78]

So, what we've learned in our biblical and historical journey thus far is that there are *always* choices when we encounter thresholds: We can step *over* a threshold and *into* something; we can step *away* and avoid the invitation; or we can stomp *on it*, refusing to walk through to the path on the other side.

An Important Example

Now, let me illustrate how important the concept of the Threshold Covenant really is, and how Satan actively works to keep its truth hidden. We'll first look at Zephaniah 1:9, another Old Testament verse that includes the word "threshold." The instruction further illustrates the importance of our study. Note the subtle differences in several versions' translations of that verse. Believe it or not, the translation really does matter, as you'll soon see.

> In the same day also will I punish all those that **leap on the threshold**, which fill their masters' houses with violence and deceit. (Zephaniah 1:9, KJV; emphasis added)

> On that day I will punish everyone who **leaps over the threshold**, and those who fill their master's house with violence and fraud. (Zephaniah 1:9, ESV; emphasis added)

Many iterations of Zephaniah 1:9 speak of God's divine punishment that is coming to those who leap "on" the threshold. Still others translate that verse as those who leap "over" the threshold. The Hebrew word *al*, used in this verse, can mean either "over" or "on" in English, depending on the context.

So, which is it, here in Zephaniah 1? Should it be "on" or "over?" Everyone who understands English knows "on" and "over" don't mean the same thing. They have entirely different meanings. In the following pages, you'll see the verse in its full context, but for now, we'll focus on the varying translations of the words "over" and "on" used for that verse.

As an example of the difficulty people have with Zephaniah 1:9, sometime back, I asked a rabbi here in Israel about that verse and what it meant to step "on" the threshold Zephaniah was talking about. He replied, "Well, it means all those who don't keep the Sabbath will be punished by God."

I couldn't believe his answer. I was flabbergasted. I responded, "It doesn't say that at all! It's not even talking about the Sabbath. The Sabbath isn't even hinted at within the entirety of that text. It's talking specifically about thresholds and the covenants that are attached to them." At that, the rabbi didn't want to discuss the matter any further.

But those who understand the concept of the Threshold Covenant (like you!) immediately understand why the word "on" has to be the correct translation. It's very clear that God says He will punish those who step "on" the threshold.

The threshold *ultimately* represents Yeshua's blood, given at Golgotha, and the eternally finished/Renewed Covenant purchased with His blood. From the revelations of previous chapters, you now understand that if you step *on* the threshold, you take the blood of Yeshua for granted. In so doing, you profane God's only offer of salvation. Leaping *on* the threshold implies a person's wholehearted rejection of Yahweh's offered covenant.

Those who read Zephaniah 1:9 who don't understand the biblical/historical context of the Threshold Covenant or the entire surrounding passage can have no idea what this verse truly means. Because of this, the majority of readers often just skip over the words with a shrug of their shoulders. They sometimes assume that because it's in the Old Testament, it has nothing to do with them. This way of thinking is as far from the truth as it can be! The Chaldean spirit of deception loves that so many people miss it.

When a sacrifice was made and the blood was shed at the threshold, the person entering the agreement would be very careful to avoid stepping *on* the place where the blood had been shed. Instead, they would step *over* it.

God will never punish those who leap *over* the threshold, because it's evidence of their enthusiastic agreement with His covenant. It's the desire of His heart to see people leap exuberantly into covenant with Him.

Sadly, those who don't understand the context are vulnerable to the meddling of the Chaldean spirit. Some translators have incorrectly used the words "leap over" to advance their own interpretation. Others simply have not understood the depth of what you now understand and have chosen the words "leap over" because they seemed, at the moment, to make the most sense, according to their limited understanding. Whatever the situation, the matter has become a powerful playground for Chaldean interference.[79]

We need to take the original Hebrew at face value, without putting any personal spin on it. For instance, the New American Standard Bible inserts the word "temple" before "threshold" (as do several other translations, including the Septuagint)...except the word "temple" is *not* in the original Hebrew recording of that passage, and neither does the context allow for the word "temple" to be there![80]

And on that day I will punish all who leap on the *temple* threshold, who fill the house of their lord with violence and deceit. (Zephaniah 1:9, NASB)

The italics for "temple" are in the original translation—indicating the translators inserted the word in their version and that it is not in the original Hebrew manuscripts.

Let's take a look at the first eight verses of Zephaniah 1, which give a much fuller context to verse 9. Sorting out this important matter of translation will give us a clearer perspective.

chapter 20

Yahweh's Message to Zephaniah

What is required for salvation from the coming judgment is for the one who is subject to that judgment to step "over" the threshold.

In the first nine verses of Zephaniah 1, Yahweh announces through His prophet that the land of Judah has been profaned by idol worship, thus constituting a full-scale rejection of the original Threshold Covenant He held out to them. By stepping *on* the threshold, they have sealed the act of refusing the covenant.

> ¹ The word of the Lord which came unto Zephaniah…in the days of Josiah the son of Amon, king of Judah.
> ² I will utterly consume all things from off the land, saith the Lord.
> ³ I will consume man and beast; I will consume the fowls of the heaven, and the fishes of the sea, and the stumbling blocks with the wicked; and I will cut off man from off the land, saith the Lord.

⁴ I will also stretch out mine hand upon Judah, and upon all the inhabitants of Jerusalem; and I will cut off the remnant of Baal from this place, and the name of the idolatrous priests along with the [other] priests,

⁵ And them that worship the host of heaven upon the housetops; and them that worship and that swear by the LORD, [an indication of their unholy "double mindedness"] and that swear by Milcom[81] [Molech],

⁶ And them that are turned back from the LORD; and those that have not sought the LORD, nor inquired for him.

⁷ Hold thy peace at the presence of the Lord God: for the day of the LORD is at hand: for the LORD hath prepared a sacrifice, he hath bid his guests.

⁸ And it shall come to pass in the day of the LORD'S sacrifice, that I will punish the princes, and the king's children, and all such as are clothed with strange apparel.

⁹ On the same day also will I punish all those that leap on the threshold, which fill their masters' houses with violence and deceit. (Zephaniah 1:1–9, KJV)

THE CHALDEAN SPIRIT

In the first six verses of Zephaniah 1, we see what's happening: Idol worship among God's people has ruled the day. By and large, the people have rejected Yahweh and His Threshold Covenant.

They worship at the pagan thresholds of Baal, Molech, and even the stars and planets of the heavens. On top of that, they have become convinced they can also claim to worship the LORD of Heaven—at the same time they sacrifice their children to the fires of Molech! All of this depraved idolatry was formed by the design of the *Chaldean spirits*! We just can't get past the Chaldean spirit when it comes to the threshold sacrifice. Now you see why I so heavily emphasized this demonic presence earlier.

Jamieson-Fausset-Brown Bible Commentary (Zephaniah 1:1):

The prophecy begins with the nation's sin and the fearful retribution coming at the hands of the Chaldeans.[82]

Pulpit Commentary (Zephaniah 1:7):

The particular agents intended are not specified by the prophet, whose mission was not directed to any such definition. He has to speak generally of the judgment to come, not of those whom God should employ to inflict it. We know from other sources that the Chaldeans are meant.[83]

Jamieson-Fausset-Brown Bible Commentary (Zephaniah 1:7):

It enhances the bitterness of the judgment that the heathen Chaldeans should be sanctified, or consecrated as it were, by God as His agents.[84]

Gill's Exposition of the Entire Bible (Zephaniah 1:7):

The Lord hath prepared a sacrifice; the wicked among the Jews, whom he will sacrifice by the Chaldean's sword.[85]

Take a look at the last three verses of this section of Zephaniah. Now that the proper context has been so clearly illuminated, the biblical concept of the Threshold Covenant is coming into a much clearer view.

> ⁷ Hold thy peace at the presence of the Lord GOD: for the day of the LORD is at hand: for the LORD hath prepared a sacrifice, he hath bid his guests.

> [8] And it shall come to pass in the day of the LORD's sacrifice, that I will punish the princes, and the king's children, and all such as are clothed with strange apparel.
> [9] In the same day also will I punish all those that **leap on the threshold**, [those] which fill their masters' houses with violence and deceit. (Zephaniah 1:1–9, KJV; emphasis added)

The Lord Yahweh Himself prepares the blood covenant. He alone offers the true sacrifice, a way of forgiveness at the threshold to His presence.

All the people of Judah had to do was to accept the sacrifice, *cross over the threshold* in the proper manner, and be at peace with Yahweh, in His presence and salvation. Instead…they trampled *on* the threshold. They despised the ways of Yahweh…and they were left to the demonic forces of the Chaldean spirit waiting just outside the Father's house.

As a result, God's own people ultimately bowed down to Baal. That god's chief allurement was the promise of luxury and wealth.[86] Molech involved the sacrifice of infants and children in order to obtain further prosperity and coveted societal positioning.[87] Worshiping the stars came with great promises of powerful glimpses into the "future." Does any of this sound eerily familiar to our own day? Of course! The Chaldean spirits are still at work; they always have been. They just operate in more "sophisticated" ways and disguises.

Jamieson-Fausset-Brown Bible Commentary:

> Those that **leap on the threshold**—the servants of the princes, who, after having gotten prey (like hounds) for their masters, **leap exultingly on their masters' thresholds**; or, on the **thresholds of the houses which they break into**. Jerome explains it of those who walk up the steps into the sanctuary with haughtiness.[88] (Emphasis added)

Barnes' Notes on the Bible:

They are also the same persons, who "**leap on the threshold**," and who "fill their masters' houses with violence and deceit." … This relates…to plunder and goods unjustly gotten.[89] (Emphasis added)

Henry's Complete Commentary on the Bible:

In the same day will I punish those that **leap on the threshold**, a phrase, no doubt, well understood then, and which probably signified the invading of their neighbor's rights. Entering their houses by force and violence, and seizing their possessions, **they leap on the threshold**, as much as to say that the house is their own and they will keep their hold of it; and, accordingly, they make all in it their own that they can lay their hands on, and so fill their masters' houses with goods gotten by violence and deceit and with all the guilt thereby contracted.[90] (Emphasis added)

There can be no doubt: The Day of the Lord is approaching. His judgment is surely coming upon this world. The sacrifice has been made with the blood of Yeshua. It has been ladled into the *groover* of the threshold as an offer of salvation to all who will step *over* the threshold. In the meantime, the demonic realm wants the world to "leap upon" God's sacred threshold—to trounce it, profane it, step all over it! They want us to ultimately reject God's offer of grace and mercy, His Word, His covenants, and citizenship in His eternal Kingdom.

What is required for salvation from the coming judgment is for the one who is subject to that judgment to step "over" the threshold. Accept the covenant, including all of the "inward parts" and the *threshold of the heart*, then sit at Yahweh's table and dine with the Savior—thus sealing the covenant of blood.

After those days, saith the LORD, I will put my Law in their inward parts, and write it in their hearts; and will be their God, and they shall be my people. (Jeremiah 31:33, KJV)

If you confess with your mouth that Jesus is Lord and believe in your heart that God raised him from the dead, you will be saved. (Romans 10:9)

Sadly, most of the world will not do what the Lord has commanded. Instead, they trample "on" the threshold and leave themselves open to the judgment of the Chaldean spirits, who have come only to kill, steal, and destroy.

How much worse punishment, do you think, will be deserved by the one who has trampled underfoot the Son of God, and has profaned the blood of the covenant by which he was sanctified, and has outraged the Spirit of Grace? (Hebrews 10:29)

The Heaven-ordained obliteration of the demonic thresholds plaguing our current prophetic times is on its way. I do not set dates and times for its arrival. That information is squarely in the hands of Heaven's throne. But never doubt: that day is coming.

In the meantime, how did those same demonic spirits manage to penetrate the visible organization of the congregations of Yeshua today? As you might imagine, Yeshua clearly warned of that diabolical invasion.

Next, we'll look at one more quick example of the importance of stepping *over* the thresholds within the biblical narrative. Then we'll be ready to explore together just how insidious this demonic encroachment really is, most notably in our own day.

chapter twenty-one

THE FALL OF DAGON

Things did not go well in Ashdod when the Ark of God was hijacked and taken to the temple of Dagon.

In 1 Samuel 5 we find yet more dramatic evidence of God's intolerance for pagan worship and His refusal to share space or covenant benefits with false gods. This truth was brought to a stark reality among the Hebrews when the Ark of the Covenant was seized by their enemies, the Philistines, then taken into the shrine of their god, Dagon. Once again, in 1 Samuel, we discover the importance of the threshold concept and see another great illustration of the value Yahweh places on this matter.

THE FISH GOD

When the Philistines defeated four thousand Israelites at Ebenezer, the Israelites scrambled to save themselves from their enemies by having the Ark of the Covenant brought to their camp from Shiloh.

When the Philistines heard the holy vessel was there, they were terrified, because they knew the stories of how the God of Israel had struck the Egyptians with plague after plague until freedom was granted to the Israelites. They reasoned that if they could capture the Ark of the Covenant, they would remove the source of Israel's power and save themselves.

The Philistines (who were a part of the Canaanites) worshiped Dagon, Baal, and Astarte/Ashtoreth/Ishtar. Dagon was said by the Philistines to be the father of Baal.[91] *Dagon* means "fish-god."[92]

Despite their fear of the God of Israel, the Philistines had no concept of the sovereignty and exclusivity of Yahweh. They thought they could take the best of both worlds and exalt themselves as the spiritual elite by controlling Israel's Ark of the Covenant. Once they took possession of it, they put it in the temple of Dagon. Only then did they assume they had all of the gods finally covered in their cultic worship rituals.

Little did they understand that Yahweh of Israel was Lord over everything and would not tolerate any attempts to access His presence through pagan rituals. They would not be allowed to walk "over" His divine threshold and have a covenant relationship with Him in a false manner. Nor would He allow them to walk "on" His covenant threshold for the purpose of profaning His name and thinking they could somehow seize His power.

Following is 1 Samuel, chapter 5:

> ¹ When the Philistines captured the ark of God, they brought it from Ebenezer to Ashdod.
> ² Then the Philistines took the ark of God and brought it into the house of Dagon and set it up beside Dagon.
> ³ And when the people of Ashdod rose early the next day, behold, Dagon had fallen face downward on the ground before the ark of the Lord. So they took Dagon and put him back in his place.
> ⁴ But when they rose early on the next morning, behold, **Dagon had fallen face downward** on the ground before the ark of the

Lord, and the head of Dagon and **both his hands were lying cut off on the threshold.** Only the trunk of Dagon was left to him.

⁵ **This is why the priests of Dagon and all who enter the house of Dagon do not tread on the threshold of Dagon** in Ashdod to this day.

⁶ The hand of the Lord was heavy against the people of Ashdod, and he terrified and afflicted them with tumors, both Ashdod and its territory.

⁷ And when the men of Ashdod saw how things were, they said, "The ark of the God of Israel must not remain with us, for his hand is hard against us and against Dagon our god."

⁸ So they sent and gathered together all the lords of the Philistines and said, "What shall we do with the ark of the God of Israel?" They answered, "Let the ark of the God of Israel be brought around to Gath."

⁹ So they brought the ark of the God of Israel there. But after they had brought it around, the hand of the Lord was against the city, causing a very great panic, and he afflicted the men of the city, both young and old, so that tumors broke out on them.

¹⁰ So they sent the ark of God to Ekron. But as soon as the ark of God came to Ekron, the people of Ekron cried out, "They have brought around to us the ark of the God of Israel to kill us and our people."

¹¹ They sent therefore and gathered together all the lords of the Philistines and said, "Send away the ark of the God of Israel, and let it return to its own place, that it may not kill us and our people." For there was a deathly panic throughout the whole city. The hand of God was very heavy there.

¹² The men who did not die were struck with tumors, and the cry of the city went up to heaven. (1 Samuel 5:1–12, emphasis added)

Cut Off

Regarding "stepping on" or "leaping over" a threshold of sacrifice, the context now becomes crystal clear! Things did not go well in Ashdod when the Ark of God was hijacked and taken to the temple of Dagon. Interestingly, the Philistines knew better than to place the Ark at the feet of their god, Dagon. Instead, they put the Ark beside the idol, which makes the sequence of events all the more interesting, because when the idol fell, "Dagon had fallen face downward on the ground before the ark of the Lord."

Note that Scripture doesn't say Dagon fell beside the Ark, as would naturally have happened if the vessel was positioned beside it. Rather, it fell face down, as though prostrate before the Lord. Seemingly unyielding to the significance of their god falling down before the God of Israel, the men of Ashdod put Dagon back in his place beside the Ark.

The next morning it got really interesting. The Philistines discovered Dagon once more prostrate before the Ark of the Lord, but this time with *his hands and head cut off*—not broken off—and resting *directly on the threshold* of his own shrine in utter disgrace. The people were afflicted with tumors, having incurred the deadly wrath of God. Stepping *on* the threshold represents certain death.

The men of Ashdod, in consultation with the Philistine leaders, knew their god, Dagon, was no match for the God of Israel, so they sent the Ark to Gath, where the same conclusion became obvious.

However, Dagon toppling across the threshold of his own shrine is nothing in comparison to the eventual global, Heaven-ordained toppling of the false gods of today. They will collapse across the threshold of a black eternity, separate from the Creator of the universe—cut to pieces. Never doubt that day is coming.

In the meantime, how did these same demonic spirits manage to penetrate the visible organization of the Body of Christ today? As you might imagine, Yeshua clearly warned us of that diabolical invasion.

After all, we are living in Satan's fallen kingdom…but only for the time being.

Part V

Seizing the Kingdom

[Jesus said,] From the days of John the Baptist until now the kingdom of heaven has suffered violence, and the violent take it by force.

Matthew 11:12

chapter twenty-two

A Carnal Kingdom

In Rome, early Christianity and biblical Judaism
foundations were basically inseparable...
perhaps even until the middle of the second century.

Let me offer an important disclaimer—and encouragement—before we continue this part of our journey. From this point forward is where the proverbial wheel meets the road.

I do not make judgments upon individual people or their faith systems. My wife is a former Buddhist. I am a former Orthodox Jew. Almost all of my own immediate and extended family members are still Orthodox Jews. I also have dear friends and ministry associates who are former Muslims. All of us—former Jews-Muslims-Buddhists—have beloved family members or acquaintances who are still a part of those faith systems as well as several other avenues of belief. We understand what it means to walk in darkness—without, at times, even being aware of how deceived we had been.

In truth, I minister in one way or the other among *all* people and *all* faith structures, even within various denominations of Christianity.

This includes ministering to Roman Catholics as well as Protestants, in addition to various denominations of evangelical Christianity. I go wherever Yeshua directs for the sole purpose of trying to lead people across the genuine thresholds of salvation and into a true biblical understanding (1 Corinthians 9:19–23).

With the Lord's help, I am as considerate and caring as I can be to all people. However, I must respectfully speak as much biblical truth as I know. This is especially so when I am addressing the realities of the Chaldean spirit's work that attempts to destroy or hide Yahweh's Threshold Covenant. Sometimes, it makes those who are steeped in their own "religious" traditions very uncomfortable, both Jews and Christians.

But, at the end of it all, my only purpose in life and ministry is to exalt the name of Yeshua and lead all who will respond to come to Him in truth. Please read what follows within the context of this understanding as we continue our journey of spiritual archeology.

Divine Warnings

The Chaldean spirit has been trying to destroy or cover up the genuine entrance across the New Covenant and the Kingdom threshold since John the Baptist's appearance along the Jordan River. That demonic assault has bullied its way along the vile path of destruction right up until our own day. Its progress still escalates as it offers up one counterfeit after another, doing anything to keep humanity from crossing the true thresholds of Yahweh's blood covenants of salvation and fellowship offered in Yeshua.

Observe the scriptural evidence of Jesus' warnings about this very thing happening as soon as the Kingdom work got underway:

> [Jesus said,] from the days of John the Baptist until now the kingdom of heaven has suffered violence, and the violent take it by force. (Matthew 11:12)

Dr. Coffman's Commentary on the Bible says the following about Matthew 11:12:[93]

> Jesus here pictures the kingdom of heaven as a besieged city. The city is shut up, but the enemies which surround it, [Chaldean spirit] storm its walls and try to force an entrance [a false threshold]…
>
> The gates of Christ's kingdom [the true threshold] were not opened until the day of Pentecost (Acts 2); but men, hearing it was about to be opened, sought to enter it [the Kingdom threshold covenant] prematurely, not by the gates [true thresholds] which God would open, [the threshold covenant]…but by such breaches [demonically instigated] as they themselves sought to make in its walls [influenced by the Chaldean spirit!].[94] (See endnote for the complete commentary on this verse.)

Dr. Thomas L. Constable's Expository Notes (Matthew 11:12) explains that verse in much the same way:

> Jesus meant that the religious leaders of His day were trying to bring in the kingdom in their own carnal way [a false threshold constructed by the Chaldean spirit] while refusing to accept God's way [thus "trampling upon the blood" of the true threshold covenant!] that John and Jesus announced.[95]

The focus of Matthew 11:12 is echoed by Yeshua just two chapters farther into the same book. There, Yeshua reveals the spiritual power behind the attacks. He had just shared the parable of the wheat and tares (weeds) with a large crowd, and His disciples had asked for an explanation.

> Then he left the crowd and went into the house. His disciples came to him and said, "Explain to us the parable of the weeds in the field."

He answered, "The one who sowed the good seed is the Son of Man. The field is the world, and the good seed stands for the people of the kingdom. The weeds are the people of the evil one, and the enemy who sows them is the devil. The harvest is the end of the age, and the harvesters are angels. As the weeds are pulled up and burned in the fire, so it will be at the end of the age. (Matthew 13:36–40, NIV)

Yeshua's teaching on this matter couldn't be any clearer. Sadly, it seems that a good many of today's Christians are missing this key element of *ministry alertness*.

Now, let's plumb the depths of this life-changing understanding.

chapter twenty-three

Polluting the "One New Man" Threshold

They separate those who have come through the genuine threshold from those who have come by another entrance—like the thieves they are.

The major point of the *false threshold* upon which I'm now focusing refers to the religious aberration that evolved into its present form after the persistent manipulations of Flavius Valerius Constantinus (Constantine), the Emperor of fourth-century Rome.

Constantine began his reign almost two hundred years after the Resurrection of Yeshua. He initiated many of the consequent developments that infect Christian congregations and several of their convoluted biblical doctrines right until this very day.

Subsequently, we often blame Constantine for many of our current "religious" woes. These issues involve blending biblical truth with certain well-known and widely practiced pagan traditions of Constantine's time. This also contributed to the misunderstandings regarding Yahweh's Threshold Covenant of salvation, as well as the authentic fellowship with

Him this covenant holds out to all who will believe. What we will explore next is crucial and, perhaps, it might even make you a bit uncomfortable. But, as you will discover, the information we'll look at is reliably documented by respected scholarly sources. It is now time for us to face up to the truth.[96]

To be fair, while Constantine was undoubtedly responsible for many critical "adjustments" to God's Word, in reality, he was only one of the factors that led to turning the authentic practice of following Yeshua into a powerless likeness of what God desired. The Chaldean spirit was at work trying to steal hearts and souls away from Yahweh for thousands of years before Constantine was even born.

However, Constantine's true infamy was rooted in his ability to set the destructive efforts of the Chaldean deception in concrete for more than two thousand years, all of it backed up by governmental control and wealthy international power mongers. As we've just read, these are the very things Yeshua and the Holy Spirit-inspired writers of the New Testament warned about:

> But understand this, that in the last days there will come times of difficulty. For people will be lovers of self, lovers of money, proud, arrogant, abusive, disobedient to their parents, ungrateful, unholy, heartless, unappeasable, slanderous, without self-control, brutal, not loving good, treacherous, reckless, swollen with conceit, lovers of pleasure rather than lovers of God, having the appearance of godliness, but denying its power. Avoid such people. (2 Timothy 3:1–5)

Ellicott's Commentary for English Readers (2 Timothy 3:5):

> Having a form of godliness, but denying the power thereof. — Keeping up a show of observing the outward forms of religion, but renouncing its power and its influence over the heart and the life [the threshold elements of a covenant relationship!]...

These, by claiming the title of Christians, wearing before men the uniform of Christ, but by their lives dishonoring His name.... Here he describes the characteristics of a new Paganism, which went under the name of Christianity.[97]

MacLaren's Expositions (2 Timothy 3:5):

But even in the Apostolic Church there were an Ananias and a Sapphira, a Simon Magus, and a Demas. As years go on, and primitive enthusiasms die out, and the cause which was once all freshly radiant and manifestly heaven-born becomes an earthly institution, there is a growing tendency to gather round it superficial, half-and-half adherents.... [This is] why, "Christendom" is largely a mass of pagans masquerading as Christians.[98]

Constantine had become yet another face of the Chaldean spirit that threw early believers into horrendous situations and forever changed important elements of Christianity through his own ignorance and insincerity of heart. He eventually became the earthly puppet—holding a position of great human power—who was deceptively played by the Chaldean puppet masters of his day.

Now the Spirit expressly says that in later times some will depart from the faith by devoting themselves to deceitful spirits and teachings of demons, through the insincerity of liars whose consciences are seared. (1 Timothy 4:1–3)

While Constantine, Hitler, Mussolini, and myriad other destructive leaders are no longer with us, the Chaldean puppeteers remain. They have always been among us, pulling the strings of power players like the pope of Rome, an array of globalist movers and shakers, Protestant and evangelical denominational leaders, various religious institutions, governmental entities, and the prevailing ecclesiastical heads of all the bastions of religious authority. These demonically influenced authorities have always determined to hide the truth for their own pleasure, thus destroying the beautiful life Yeshua came to bring.

This truth is echoed in the words of Yeshua in the Gospel of John. You've most likely seen the following many times, but now you probably immediately notice the threshold language and recognize the reference to the demonic presence attempting to stop you from "crossing over" that divine threshold.

> [Yeshua said to them,] I am the door. If anyone enters by me, he will be saved and will go in and out and find pasture. The thief comes only to steal and kill and destroy. I came that they may have life and have it abundantly. I am the good shepherd. The good shepherd lays down his life for the sheep. (John 10:9–11)

Is all of this beginning to make more sense now—especially as we further examine the world in which we currently live?

THE ONE NEW MAN

Almost until the time of Constantine, Jew and Gentile believers, since the birth of the congregation of the redeemed in Yeshua, had largely worshiped together as the "one new man" described in Paul's letter to the Ephesians:

> For he himself is our peace, who has made us both one and has broken down in his flesh the dividing wall of hostility by abolishing the Law of commandments expressed in ordinances, that he might create in himself one new man in place of the two, so making peace, and might reconcile us both to God in one body

through the cross, [the true covenant threshold] thereby killing the hostility. (Ephesians 2:13–16)

Think of it: Yeshua Himself was a Torah-observant Jew. He faithfully practiced the Feasts of the Lord[99] and the God-ordained cycles, customs, and instructions of Jewish life as laid out in the contextually applied Word of God—as opposed to the false constructs of the rabbis and Pharisees. After all, those feasts and God-ordained worship laws were always all about Yeshua! Until He went to the cross in order to fulfil them, He observed them.

As a matter of fact, the Apostle Paul, a former Orthodox Pharisee and rabbi and the author of almost half of the New Testament documents, often planned his missionary trips around the feasts. He obviously assumed all the new believers in Yeshua would celebrate them as well. Why wouldn't they? They had been the very first witnesses to Yeshua's fulfillment of them all! They alone understood the finalized and prophetically revealed threshold connections. (See Acts 20:6–16 and 1 Corinthians 5:7–8).

Additionally, even the Gentiles who had become believers during and after the time of Yeshua knew they were participating in a belief system rooted in Judaism. They, too, observed the feasts—but in all their biblical breadth—as they, too, understood that those feasts had been fulfilled in Yeshua.

Further, on the first day of the week, in celebration of the Resurrection of Yeshua, the believers congregated to worship, eat, and take up love offerings for other groups of believers in need. There was no separation between believing Jews and believing Gentiles. They were one body united by the Holy Spirit.[100]

Dr. Mark Nanos, a respected Jewish historian and author of *The Mystery of Romans*, says:

> The Jewish Context of Paul's Letter asserts that in Rome, early Christianity and Biblical Judaism foundations were basically

inseparable…perhaps even until the middle of the second century. Furthermore, Jewish believers in Yeshua that were in Rome continued to be part of their Jewish communities and cultural life for a long time.[101]

Yeshua Himself often spoke of this unity between Jews and Gentiles under the Threshold Covenant made with His blood.

> I lay down my life for the sheep. And I have other sheep that are not of this fold. I must bring them also, and they will listen to my voice. So there will be one flock, one shepherd. (John 10:15–16)

So, how did all that original "unity" eventually come to a grinding halt? We'll explore that topic next.

chapter twenty-four

THE CHALDEAN HOLY DAY

The best evidence we have indicates that the
word "Easter," as well as the entire concept of it,
carries overtly pagan attachments.

When Constantine came to power in the early AD 300s, a massive, government-sponsored persecution of Christians had been underway throughout the Roman Empire for several grueling decades. Eventually, as the efforts to destroy believers proved largely unsuccessful, Constantine switched the gears and befriended various congregations of the Empire's Christians. This ultimately paved the way for Christianity to finally be declared the Roman Empire's official state religion. In the process, Constantine claimed he, too, had become a Christian.

There is much controversy regarding Constantine's "conversion" experience. Arguments revolve around whether he truly understood the work of Yeshua, as well as the possibility that his actions might have been politically motivated. To this day, those questions remain points of frequent debate.[102]

Whatever the reality, Constantine effectively installed himself as the unofficial head of the then almost three hundred-year-old Christian community and set out to change almost everything about it. He eventually separated it from its most basic biblical Hebrew foundations and melded it with certain elements of paganism that were already rampant in the Roman religious culture at the time. Consequently, he replaced authentic, biblically prescribed worship and a personal relationship with Yeshua with a weak substitute, something that bore the name of Christ but was a far cry from the real thing.[103]

In short, Constantine took a metaphorical wrecking ball to the early Church, resulting in various biblical manipulations that mixed and/or replaced God's certain appointed times, principally the Feasts of the Lord, with various pagan customs and celebrations of his day.

But here was the problem: Each of the Feasts of the Lord represents divine Threshold Covenants God made with His people. As we've already explored, the first feast covenant was the blood alliance of Passover—the week of Yeshua's Crucifixion and Resurrection! And, as you'll read for yourself, that is one of the feasts Constantine went after with a vengeance.

A number of modern historians attempt to excuse Constantine's misdeeds by claiming he was actually trying to meld several Christian traditions into the culturally accepted pagan ones to unite the two factions into some sort of manufactured peace arrangement—all for the sake of more adequately managing the affairs of the Roman Empire. Apparently, this type of religious blending was an obsession of many of the Roman Emperors.[104] Of course, the Word of God is filled with strict commands against the type of things Constantine eventually pulled off. God's directives are filled with warnings for those who would dare cross *over* those unholy thresholds and thereby *step on* the genuine ones.

The Feast of Passover Becomes Easter

The most egregious of the Constantinian fusions were the pagan influences surrounding the week of the biblical Feast of Passover—the week of Yeshua's Crucifixion and Resurrection. I'm thinking specifically of what is commonly described as "Easter" and everything that now goes with it.

Those later-developed elements of Easter would include the Romanic-infused Lent; Ash Wednesday; Mardi Gras parades and the open celebration of debauchery;[105] bunnies, eggs, and Easter baskets; as well as several out-and-out Roman-era pagan superstitions, some of which involved overtly occultic associations.[106] Academically acclaimed historical sources attest that Emperor Constantine was the "gear" that officially set all this in motion.

Origins of Easter Practices

Bibleinfo.com sheds the following light on Easter's origin:

> Ash Wednesday has a non-Christian [pagan] origin and was accepted into the beliefs of the Catholic Church at the Council of Nicaea [in Constantine's reign and under his direction] in 325 AD. The council also settled upon the 40-day fast period as the standard length to celebrate Lent. During this time period the goal of Constantine was to combine pagans and Christians into a peaceable unit within the Roman kingdom.
>
> Even after the Council of Nicaea the beginning start date of Lent was still questioned. In 601 Pope Gregory moved the beginning of Lent from the fourth Sunday of the year to Ash Wednesday, 46 days before Easter [Passover week].... Pope Gregory also instituted the tradition of marking parishioner's foreheads with ashes in the shape of a cross.[107]

The best research we have indicates the word "Easter," as well as the entire concept, has overtly pagan attachments.

From *US News and World Report*, Bruce Forbes, a religious studies scholar specializing in early Christianity, says his "research shows that [the] dating of Easter goes back to the complicated origins of this holiday and how it has evolved over the centuries."

He continues:

> The naming of the celebration as "Easter" seems to go back to the name of a pre-Christian goddess in England, Eostre,[108] who was celebrated at beginning of spring. The only reference to this goddess comes from the writings of the Venerable Bede, a British monk who lived in the late seventh and early eighth century.[109]

Forbes then summarizes:

> Bede wrote that the month in which English Christians were celebrating the resurrection of Jesus had been called Eosturmonath ["Easter Month"] in Old English, referring to a goddess named Eostre. And even though Christians had begun affirming the Christian meaning of the celebration, they continued to use the name of the goddess to designate the season.
>
> It is important to point out that while the name "Easter" is used in the English-speaking world, many more cultures refer to it by terms best translated as "Passover" (for instance, "Pascha" in Greek)—a reference, indeed, to the Jewish festival of Passover.[110]

Make no mistake: The Roman "Easter spirit" truly did become entrenched into a large portion of the early Church, and it's still deeply established in the Church of our day. But its ancient beginnings are quite interesting—and are a part of one of the most covered-up schemes ever executed by the Chaldean spirit.

chapter twenty-five

THE EASTER SPIRIT

There can be little doubt: The word "Easter" has definitive, well-documented, and unarguably pagan roots; this is even rather hesitantly admitted by the Roman Catholic Church.

If you've ever questioned the possibility that Easter has pagan roots and just how insidiously it might have slithered into the relatively early body of believers in Yeshua, the next chapters will remove all of that doubt.

We'll begin with the following monumental admission of the Roman Catholic Church (RCC) itself. It is catalogued in (among other RCC resources) *The New Catholic Encyclopedia, 2003, Volume 5, (Easter and Its Cycle)*. In that edition, the RCC actually concedes that their tradition of Easter does indeed have ancient pagan attachments.

Remember, the ancient Roman Catholic Church and many of its subsequent ecclesiastical traditions were the resultant construct of the Nicene Council, which was headed by the heavily pagan-influenced Roman Emperor Constantine in AD 325.[111] We'll look at the history of that Council shortly.

Following is what *The New Catholic Encyclopedia* has to say:

Easter is the central liturgical season of the Church year... Since Bede the Venerable the origin of the term for the feast of Christ's Resurrection has been popularly considered[112] to be from the Anglo-Saxon Eastre, a goddess of spring.

Another ancient name that has become more common with the renewal of Biblical studies and the liturgy is Pasch, from the Greek transliteration pascal of the Aramaic word for the Hebrew pesach, Passover...gradually it was felt incongruous[113] that Christians should celebrate Easter on a Jewish feast, and unity in celebrating the principal Christian feast [Easter] was called for.[114]

The *New Advent Catholic Encyclopedia* affirms this:

The English term, according to the Ven. Bede (De temporum ratione, I, v), relates to Estre, a Teutonic goddess of the rising light of day and spring...[and the] Anglo-Saxon, eâster, eâstron;... April was called easter-monadh [month]. The plural eâstron is used, because the feast lasts seven days.[115]

Observe the following excerpt from an AD 325 letter Emperor Constantine addressed "to all churches concerning the date of Easter" very soon after the Nicene Council's conclusion. The discussion of Easter and the setting of its date were considered among the most important matters of business conducted by the Nicene Council.

At the council we also considered the issue of our holiest day, Easter, and it was determined by common consent that everyone, everywhere should celebrate it on one and the same day. For what can be more appropriate, or what more solemn, than that this feast from which we have received the hope of immortality, should be kept by all without variation, using the same order and a clear arrangement?[116]

The Easter spirit of the Chaldean confusion was now legally embedded in the official "Christian" church of the largely pagan Roman Empire.[117]

Even in the staunchly leftist ABC.net.au, we read further affirmation of the *Eostre*/Easter connection, a pagan link that traces back long before the Christ event:

> Easter actually began as a pagan festival celebrating spring in the Northern Hemisphere, long before the advent of Christianity.... "Since pre-historic times, people have celebrated the equinoxes and the solstices as sacred times," University of Sydney Professor Carole Cusack said.... "People mapped their whole life according to the patterns of nature."
>
> "In the first couple of centuries [during Constantine] after Jesus's life, [biblical] feast days in the new Christian church were attached to old pagan festivals," Professor Cusack said.
>
> In 325 AD the first major church council, the Council of Nicaea, determined that Easter [properly the Feast of Passover] should fall on the Sunday following the first full moon after the spring equinox.
>
> ...Easter takes its name from a pagan goddess from Anglo-Saxon England... "Eostre was a goddess of spring or renewal and that's why her feast is attached to the vernal equinox," Professor Cusack said.
>
> Rabbits and hares are also associated with fertility and were symbols linked to the goddess Eostre.... During the Middle Ages, people began decorating eggs and eating them as a treat following mass on Easter Sunday after fasting through Lent.[118]

More than a century ago, the 1910–1911 *Encyclopedia Britannica Eleventh Edition (Easter)*, also verifies this apparently well-known fact.

> [The festival] is applied to the Jewish Passover. It is called Easter in the English, from the goddess Eodre, worshipped by the Saxons [ancient Briton] with peculiar ceremonies in the month of April.[119]

A 1915 book, published in London by historical researcher and author Ethel Lucy Urlin, also attests to the truths we are uncovering. The book is titled *Festivals, Holy Days, and Saints' Days: A Study in Origins and Survivals in Church Ceremonies & Secular Customs*:

> The Western Church adopted the first Sunday after the first full moon, after the Vernal Equinox, as the date of Easter, but some churches did not fall into line in keeping it, for centuries after. Gregory Nazianzen styles it, "the queen of days, and festival of festivals."
>
> On this greatest of Christian festivals, several survivals occur of ancient heathen ceremonies. To begin with, the name itself is not Christian but pagan. "Ostara" was the Anglo-Saxon Goddess of Spring. The Latin nations more correctly call the festival Pascha; a Greek form of the Jewish Passover.[120]

There can be little doubt that Easter has definitive and well-documented pagan roots, as admitted by the Roman Catholic Church and scholarly sources the world over. Those pagan foundations link directly to ancient Great Britain, a fact that will become hugely important in the next couple of chapters. Are you seeing the extent to which the Chaldean spirit of doctrinal pollution will travel?

> Now the Spirit expressly says that in later times some will depart from the faith by devoting themselves to deceitful spirits and teachings of demons. (1 Timothy 4:1)

We're not yet finished settling this matter. There is an even wider and more insidious connection to *Eostre* and the nearly unfathomable depths of the Chaldean deceit that surrounds it.

chapter twenty-six

THE ASTARTE/ISHTAR CONNECTION

This fact would seem to directly connect to what we've already discovered concerning the early British acceptance of the pagan goddess Eostre.

It is always my endeavor to provide my readers with the most reliable scholarship and historical accuracy I am familiar with at the time of writing. Accordingly, I must emphasize another significant aspect of Easter: its connection to the ancient fertility goddess Ishtar.

Through a casual Internet search, one might surmise that the word "Easter" did *not* originate from the ancient term "Ishtar." For example, GotQuestions.org, a generally respected Christian online commentary site, states succinctly:

> There is absolutely no conclusive connection between the pagan goddess Ishtar and the Christian celebration of Easter. Any theory that Easter is named after Ishtar is pure speculation. There is also

no proof that Ishtar was ever associated with eggs or rabbits as symbols. In fact, Ishtar's sacred animal seems to have been the lion.[121]

Further, Crosswalk.com, also a much relied-upon Christian commentary site, notes the following:

> Is Easter named after Ishtar? In short, no. The names do share a similar resemblance, but not overly so. Where we run into an issue is with Eostre.… Although Easter and Ishtar share name similarities, and symbols of fertility, the roots of Easter's name are more likely to stem from Eostre.[122]

In spite of arguments such as these, there is actually a plethora of reliable scholarship making the case for a connection between "Easter" and "Ishtar." And the links are far from inconsequential. Let's have a look at the facts.

A Legitimate Connection?

Let's begin with a controversial figure: Alexander Hislop (1807–1865),[123] a Free Church of Scotland minister and researcher known for his bold criticisms of the Roman Catholic Church. He was also the author of eleven books of detailed historical research.

Hislop was one of the classical scholars who drew a direct connection between Ishtar and Easter. Moreover, his argument is so pointed that several Internet sites operate for the sole purpose of vehemently attempting to discredit Hislop's acclaimed work. You'll soon see why.

But first, let's consider the following quote from Hislop's most famous book, *The Two Babylons*, which was written in the mid-1800s and documented with the best historical sources of Hislop's day.[124]

> What means the term Easter itself? It is not a Christian name. It bears its Chaldean origin on its very forehead. Easter is nothing

else than Astarte [Ishtar], one of the titles of Beltis, the queen of heaven,[125] whose name, as pronounced by the people Nineveh, was evidently identical with that now in common use in this country. That name, as found by Layard on the Assyrian monuments, is Ishtar. The worship of Bel and Astarte was very early introduced into Britain, along with the Druids, "the priests of the groves."

...The unequivocal traces of that worship are found in regions of the British islands...and it has everywhere left indelible marks of the strong hold which it must have had on the early British mind.

...If Baal was thus worshipped in Britain, it will not be difficult to believe that his consort Astarte was also adored by our ancestors, and that from Astarte, whose name in Nineveh was Ishtar, the religious solemnities of April, as now practiced, are called by the name of Easter--that month, among our Pagan ancestors, having been called Easter-[month].[126]

Did you notice Hislop indicates a connection to the *Chaldean spirit*? That's an interesting correlation indeed, based upon what we've already learned in preceding chapters. No wonder that demonic spirit doesn't like Hislop's bold unveiling of the Easter ruse!

Also, we can't help but notice Hislop's attestation that the Ishtar connection left indelible marks of the "stronghold which it must have had on the early British mind." This would seem to link directly back to what we've already discovered concerning the early British acceptance of the pagan goddess of spring *Eostre* and its incursion into the ancient Roman Empire, and finally into the Romanized version of the "Church."

But from where might that term *Eostre* have originally come within the primeval days of the islands of ancient Britain? Join me as we trace the Ishtar connection to Britain, then into Rome, then as it becomes infused into the early Church.

chapter twenty-seven

Digging Deeper

To worship Yeshua in "truth" means to worship Him in the contextual truth of His Word.

Once I read about the connection Alexander Hislop's book *Two Babylons* made between Ishtar and Easter, I became curious. I had to find out for myself whether his assertions were historically validated. What I discovered alarmed me, most notably in relation to all the current Internet insistences that Hislop was somehow mistaken. In short, I can assure you, he was not.

In my independent research, I studied more than a dozen trustworthy resources. It might appear a bit tedious to list most of these resources right here in the text, but I believe it's important to share exactly what I explored, especially considering that the topic is so contentious within the halls of modern Christianity. Even though I'll provide a brief summation of the startling conclusions of my research, I urge you to eventually go back and have a look at each of the quotes from the material I've provided at each source's endnotes.

The materials I used as references are: *The Origins and Practices of Holidays: Beltane and the Last Day of Ridván* by Dhruti Bhagat (2019), accessed through the Boston Public Library;[127] *Watson's Biblical and Theological Dictionary*;[128] *Irish Druids and Old Irish Religions (Beltane)* by James Bonwick (1894), accessed through the National Library of Australia;[129] and *The Embassy of Lebanon in the United Kingdom* (2022, Britain and the Phoenicians).[130]

Furthermore, I examined the *English Bible Dictionary*;[131] the *Jewish Encyclopedia*;[132] the Metropolitan Museum of Art—New York (The Phoenicians);[133] "The Antiquities of Ancient Britain Derived From the Phoenicians" by Aylett Sammes (circa 1636), accessed through the University of Michigan Library;[134] as well as Ancient Roman History at UNRV;[135] the *World History Encyclopedia* (2021)—"Baal";[136] the *Encyclopedia Britannica*—"The Phoenicians and the Formation of the Western World;"[137] and *Oxford Bibliographies*—"Canaanites."[138]

I also referenced a very helpful book written by Edward Lipiński titled *Gods and Goddesses of the Phoenician and Punic Universe Orientalia* (1995).[139]

Additionally, I raked through numerous sections of the renowned work, *Phoenician Origins of Britons, Scotts, and Anglo-Saxons*, written by the celebrated British scholar and University lecturer L. A. Waddell (1924)[140]

And finally, I explored the acclaimed work of George Rawlinson, Camden professor of ancient history at the University of Oxford. His book is titled *The History of Phoenicia—1889*, published in London.[141]

Thank you for looking over those academic sources with me. Through them, I was able to make similar connections to what Alexander Hislop's *Two Babylons* had uncovered—and even more. Following is the synopsis of what I unearthed.

Finding the Truth

The worship of the connected Beltane/Baal/Astarte/Ashtoreth/Ishtar/Eostre gods and goddesses collection can be traced through its earliest pagan roots directly into the British Isles by way of the Phoenicians of biblical antiquity.[142]

This is a vital piece of information, because the Phoenicians appear to be the originators of the ancient Baal cults that are mentioned in the Bible! And that pagan cultic worship group includes the Baal-connected worship of Astarte/Ishtar.[143]

As a matter of fact, in their home region of the Levant,[144] the Phoenicians were also known as the *Canaanites*.[145] As they traveled abroad by sea, they became known to the other nations of their ancient world as "Phoenicians." They mainly came from the biblical cities of Tyre and Sidon.[146]

THE NASCENT ROMAN WORLD

According to *Ancient Roman History*, the early Romans treasured the islands of Britain for their tin mines. Tin was a vital resource for manufacturing the weapons and armor of the vast Roman legions and for making the priceless purple dyes. But the Romans weren't the first to discover tin in the islands of Britain. It was the Phoenicians who, as plainly recorded in a number of trustworthy historical sources, were among the very first to discover that natural resource there.[147]

Thus, there appears to be documented associations between Baal, Ishtar, and Eostre/Easter in the islands of primeval Britain. These links are said to have been introduced there by the biblical Canaanites more than 1,500 years before the Christian era in Rome. The natural evolution of the entrenched correlations of the Phoenician occultic rituals eventually made their way into the already pagan-infused and brand-new Roman Empire.[148]

This historical piece of evidence logically explains why ancient Britain's Easter, and its pagan Phoenician roots, could have become so thoroughly entrenched in the second- and third-century early Christian Church. That Church was squarely situated within the Roman Empire, and apparently there was very little objection from the Church at large to that pagan encroachment.

It would also explain why the words "Astarte," "Ashtoreth," "Ishtar," ancient Britain's "Eostre," and the more modern English term "Easter" sound so much alike. Based upon my extensive research, I suggest it's because they possess a naturally intertwined and evolved linguistic relationship, one that has been around since early antiquity and includes, of all things, their potential Chaldean connections.[149] By now, we should not be surprised to see that demonic association pop up yet again.

THE BOTTOM LINE

Even if we pretended (because that's what we would *have* to do at this point) that none of my previously referenced research even existed, and even if all the "popular" online materials still claimed there is no connection between Ishtar and Easter (even though we've satisfactorily shown them to be woefully incorrect), we'd still have to make the next, and most vigorous, observation: Not one correctly interpreted statement in the Bible connects the Lord's Feast of Passover with the word "Easter." Not a single one.

Neither is there a biblical connection with Easter bunnies, Easter eggs, Easter candy, Easter baskets, Easter lilies, Easter egg hunts, Easter clothing, or the mixing of pagan festivals with the Lord's feasts, and the like.[150]

Additionally, there isn't a single biblical command about Lent or ashes being applied in the shape of a cross placed upon one's forehead. Nor is there an ounce of biblical inspiration concerning various superstitions and overtly occultic Easter rituals that have sometimes been practiced through the ages.[151]

Each of those concepts is contrived, and most are tagged with the profusely documented name of an ancient goddess of fertility, Eostre. That word academically appears to be deeply related to the worship of the Phoenician Astarte/Ishtar.

The Goddess of Gender-Swapping

Another point of vital consideration regarding today's "church" being immersed in the Easter spirit is emphasized by several other important resources. The following is an entry from Encyclopedia.com titled "Inanna-Ishtar."

> The goddess in Mesopotamia who embodied sexuality in all its aspects was known as Inanna (in the Sumerian language) and Ishtar (in the Akkadian language). Inanna/Ishtar was the manifestation of sex and eroticism—bride of brides, solace of married women, and patron of prostitutes.
>
> Inanna and Ishtar assumed various gender roles. The proper gender role of Inanna is a theme in various Sumerian narratives.[152]

The Jewish Egg of Passover

It might also intrigue our Jewish readers to discover the ancient Hebrews, perhaps since the earlier Middle Ages—for some unknown reason—also began to incorporate a hardboiled egg that is still used in the Passover Seder meal!

Israel's most prominent news publication, *Haaretz*, published the historical connections of this in a 2021 article titled, "Do Passover Eggs and Easter Eggs Have a Shared Origin?"[153]

Here's an excerpt:

> Passover and Easter are both holidays that involve eggs, in some form. The first records of actually eating Passover eggs, and giving eggs as presents on Easter, were both in medieval Germany. Could the use of eggs by adherents of the two religions have a common origin?
>
> Several sources say the earliest reference to actually eating eggs

at the seder is in commentary written by Rabbi Moses Isserles (1520–1572) on the code of Jewish law called "Shulchan Aruch." [Rabbi] Isserles didn't know how the custom arose.... However, the egg existed on the Passover table centuries before [Rabbi] Isserles.[154]

The *Haaretz* attestation of the Jewish hardboiled eggs being used at Passover Seders, by at least the AD 1300s and maybe long before that, puts the advent of both Jewish and "Christian" traditions squarely in the same period of history! And, strangely, *Haaretz* claims the Jewish people don't know why.

For years, I've inquired among my contacts within the Israeli Orthodox rabbinical community about the mysterious Passover egg. Collectively, they don't have a clear and historically verified answer, either.

In today's world, most Christians also don't know why they use eggs in celebrations. I can only pray the book you are now reading brings some light of truth to this biblically important matter.

As a person with a deeply Jewish heritage, as well as a believer in Yeshua, I am convinced these artificial constructs are demonic incursions at their very core, and are also clear attempts by the *Chaldean spirit* to compel God's people to willingly step through unbiblical thresholds and into disastrously dark places.

It is heartbreaking to see how many of today's churches and their congregants try to normalize the historically documented pagan attachments to their "celebrations" of the Crucifixion and Resurrection of Yeshua. This sentiment becomes most apparent when we consider the mountains of scholarly evidence that flatly condemn the inadequate justifications. In the meantime, the demonic realm and the unbelieving realm mock us.

SPIRIT AND TRUTH

Never forget: All of this pagan influence was heavily saturated into the third-century church and ultimately decreed into practice by the Roman

Emperor Constantine, regardless of the fact that Yeshua Himself told us what kind worship we should offer:

> But a time is coming and has now come when the **true worshipers will worship the Father in spirit and in truth,** for the Father is seeking such as these to worship Him. God is Spirit, and **His worshipers must worship Him in spirit and in truth.** (John 4:23–24, emphasis added)

To worship the Lord in "spirit" means we *must not worship Him in the flesh,* or in carnal ways, traditions, and settled-upon customs. Neither should we bring those practices and myths into our worship experience or daily relationship with our Lord and Creator. And we certainly shouldn't present Him with anything that has verifiable pagan roots.

To worship Yeshua in "truth" means to worship Him in the contextual truth of *His Word.* We must not allow unbiblical, pagan, and blatantly worldly, politically correct, and/or *socially constructed* elements into our lives and ways of thinking and then call it "living for Yeshua." And we certainly should not call it "worship." It is not true worship. All of what Yeshua instructed is in direct conflict with the Easter/Eostre/Ishtar infusion…which is nothing less than a false Chaldean threshold going all the way back to the ancient Canaanites.

Is this line of reasoning beginning to make even more sense? Next, we'll discover *why* and *how* the pagan festival of Easter was decreed to be the true "Christian" celebration of the Resurrection of Yeshua.

chapter twenty-eight

ANTI-SEMITIC CONSTANTINE

The consequences of Constantine's protests were so dire that the "one new man" described by Paul in Ephesians 2:15 appeared to be torn asunder.

What follows in this chapter is yet another monumentally important consideration. This is especially so when one understands the overall impact Roman Emperor Constantine had on the Christian Church from the AD 300s forward.

The matter is significant because Constantine is often held out as a hero, of sorts, in relation to Christianity. After all, he did finally put an end to the horrendous persecution of Christians that had existed in one form or another throughout the empire for more than two hundred years. By AD 325, according to numerous sources, more than two million Christians had been put to death for their faith. So, why wouldn't they have wanted an end to *that* atrocity and venerate the emperor who actually was instrumental in getting it done?[155]

The problem, however, is that history also proves Constantine actually "legalized" and directly encouraged the burgeoning chasm between the Jews and the non-Jews. Thus, the Gentile Christians, while they were then beginning to deeply hate the Jews of the Roman Empire, were claiming to be genuine Christians! Of course, that assertion is a brazen biblical oxymoron.

THE DILEMMA

Think of it: How can a genuine born-again believer hate the Jewish people—especially when the Bible is clear that Yahweh Himself chose the Jewish people as His own instruments of the coming salvation in Yeshua? The resultant conduit that was designed to bless the entire planet throughout all ages would prove to be the nation of Israel...birthed from the seed of Abraham.

Through the Jews of Israel, the Lord would eventually bring the entire Word of God (the Old and New Testaments were written by Jews),[156] as well as the prophecies of the coming Christ, the Savior who was foretold to *be a Jew*.

Not only that, but the Holy Spirit of Yahweh would also speak through the prophets of God—all Jews. Furthermore, Christ Himself would manifest in the flesh as a Jew. Also, don't forget the Gospel message of salvation was first given and cultivated by Jewish believers. Jewish believers in Yeshua also made up almost the entire membership of the early Christian Church for the first several decades of its existence.[157] Do you see the dilemma? Paul undeniably settled these biblical matters through his teachings found in Romans 11 and Ephesians 2.

The gravity of this relatively new predicament wasn't lost on a number of the early "Christians" in the Roman Empire, either. So, they had to be provided an official explanation for how they were to think concerning this "Jewish problem." Constantine eventually gave them the answers, as well as the official and authoritative voice needed to enforce the explanation. Those so-called solutions, and the movement of many "Christians" toward adopting them, actually laid the foundation for nearly two thousand years of horrific anti-Semitism. This travesty still rages throughout the planet today.[158]

THE "CONVERSION" OF CONSTANTINE

Constantine claimed to have converted to Christianity in AD 312, with his conversion motivated in part by a vision he supposedly experienced at the Battle of the Milvian Bridge in Rome that year. He is said to have reported seeing an image in a vision that contained the Latin words *In Hoc Signo Vinces*, meaning "In this sign, conquer."[159]

Much later, and reported only by a couple of Constantine's close confidants, it was then said he had actually seen the sign of the cross of Christ. Controversy still swirls around both the event and the image he purportedly saw, as well as the genuine nature of his "conversion."[160]

The following Edict of Milan in AD 312 issued by the "converted" Constantine, finally granted Christians throughout the Empire the approval they had long dreamed of—to finally meet in their assemblies freely and openly. Christianity had been "legalized" by a Roman Emperor.[161]

Overall, however, Christianity was now being considered just one more of the thousands of native cults scattered throughout the Empire. Roman emperors were well known to give allegiance of one sort or another to almost all of these factions in order to promote general peace within the Roman realm.

To this day, it is still suspected that the "Roman peace" was Constantine's deeper motivation for his heavenly vision. History heavily leans toward the postulation that it was the overall *political* considerations of Constantine, rather than the vast *theological* differences of the early Church, that were the most significant in the development of the emperor's anti-Jewish stances. He would merely use the religious divisions of his day to gain more power and influence over the entire empire.[162]

The Nicene Council

And so it was that by 324 CE, Constantine had defeated his rival for the throne, Licinius, and became the exclusive emperor of Rome. In that situation of absolute political power, he would ultimately impose the edict of "One God, One Emperor, One Church."[163]

Constantine's Nicene Council of AD 325 called for a gathering of bishops from all over the empire to resolve several theological predicaments. The most important was whether to observe the Crucifixion and Resurrection of Yeshua in conjunction with the Lord's Feast of Passover or, as preferred by the emperor and many other churches in the empire, on the settled date with the long-accepted Roman customs of the pagan-born Easter festival. The churches of various regions were holding their services within the context of these two contradictions, and it was causing great division. Constantine saw his chance to be the hero and overlord, and he pounced on it.

Constantine was blatantly anti-Semitic in his power-play manner of "settling" this issue. This is not a conspiracy theory. His own words make the case for us.

Consider the following samples (in context) from an AD 325 missive the emperor sent throughout the land addressed to "all the churches." Steel yourself; this isn't easy to read.

> Emperor Constantine to all churches concerning the date of Easter. (AD 325)
>
> At the council we also considered the issue of our holiest day, Easter, and it was determined by common consent that everyone, everywhere should celebrate it on one and the same day. For what can be more appropriate, or what more solemn, than that this feast from which we have received the hope of immortality, should be kept by all without variation, using the same order and a clear arrangement?

And in the first place, it seemed very unworthy for us to keep this most sacred feast following the custom of the **Jews, a people who have soiled their hands in a most terrible outrage**, and have thus polluted their souls, and are now deservedly blind.

Therefore have nothing in common with that most **hostile people, the Jews**.... We have received another way from the Savior. In our holy religion we have set before us a course which is both valid and accurate. Let us unanimously pursue this. Let us, most honored brothers, **withdraw ourselves from that detestable association.**

....On what subject are they competent to form a correct judgment, who, after that murder of their Lord **lost their senses** and **are led not by any rational motive, but by an uncontrollable impulsiveness** to wherever their innate fury may drive them? This is why even in this matter they do not perceive the truth, so that they constantly err in the utmost degree....

So first, it was desirable to change the situation so that we **have nothing in common with that nation of father-killers who slew their Lord.**

[We must then] unite in desiring whatever common sense seems to demand, and what has **no association with the perjury of the Jews.**[164] (Emphasis added)

Unholy Invectives

What you just read is only a portion of the outrageous contempt Constantine spewed out upon the Jewish people. He did this within his own treatise upon the Nicene Council's agreements about Easter, a purported Christian holiday that now officially bore the Roman-certified name of a pagan goddess.

Consider what Constantine actually demanded the early Church to believe. He insisted the celebration of the entire Christ event was to be divorced from its biblical foundation of the Feast of Passover—because of those "detestable" Jews.

The consequences of Constantine's protests were so dire that the "one new man" described by Paul in Ephesians 2:15 appeared to be torn asunder, effectively dividing Jews and Gentiles.

While the Gentiles eventually took to painting eggs and chasing bunnies on the now-decreed, and pagan-rooted, Easter service and its ancient extrabiblical traditions, the Jews were reviled and excluded from genuine biblical worship of Yeshua as Messiah. Their hearts became hardened and embittered toward all they perceived as Christians and Christianity. Many of those feelings and misrepresentations of the contextual truth remain entrenched in many Jewish hearts to this day.

The work of the Chaldean spirits really couldn't be more transparent.

chapter twenty-nine

SINS OF THE FATHERS

Consider the historical succession of evil men
and nations that then, down through Israel's existence,
were demonically driven to cleanse the planet of Israel.

One has to wonder if Constantine even knew much at all about history and its pervasive biblical context. Did he understand the breadth of the Exodus event and its picture of the fulfillment of the Passover in Yeshua? Did he even fully grasp the magnitude of our own salvation through God's blood covenant based upon the sacrifice of the Lamb of God, the covenant the New Testament so clearly lays forth?

Wasn't he aware that the early Church was almost entirely comprised of Jewish people or converts to Judaism for the first several decades of its existence, until about AD 60? Didn't he know that multitudes of early Jewish religious leaders had actually believed upon *Yeshua Ha Mashiach*—including priests, rabbis, and teachers of the Law?[165]

The *Encyclopedia of World History* attests:

> The evidence of Paul's letters (50s and 60s CE), the gospels, and the Acts of the Apostles indicate that Gentiles [eventually] rapidly outnumbered Jewish believers. Despite the decree, tensions between Jewish-Christians (those who advocated full conversion) and Gentile-Christians (those who held to the Council of Jerusalem) continued. Paul constantly raged against "false apostles" who traveled to his communities, preaching that Paul was wrong, and the Gentiles should convert (Galatians 1:6–8, parenthesis in original).[166]

Did Constantine somehow overlook the biblical affirmation that both Roman and Jewish authorities, as well as crowds of various races and ethnicities, called for Jesus' crucifixion? That event was not merely a "Jewish" thing; it was, without argument, a "human" thing.

Jews and Gentiles, the Sanhedrin and Rome, powerful people as well as common folks *all* stood condemned in their fallen sin nature at the foot of that cross. And, by that same divine blood alliance fulfilled on the cross of Yeshua, God's Threshold Covenant was being established and offered to everyone—Jews and Gentiles, prostitutes, sinners, tax collectors, the rich, the poor, males, females, the young and old, and even slaves and the free!

The flames of anti-Semitism were further fueled by the Catholic-led Spanish Inquisitions, then the Muslim hordes, followed by the World War II Nazi Holocaust, and now the currently prophesied hatred among coalitions of a specific group of nations (Ezekiel 38) that want the prophetically returned Israel to be destroyed. Even a number of "Christian" denominations and pulpits hold out renewed animosity toward God's foretold return of Israel. Do you see the vile, blatant, demonic progression? Do you now understand more fully why today's Jewish people are so hard to reach with the pure Gospel of salvation in Yeshua?

This is why a book like the one you are reading is so important. It is meant to wake up the congregations of those who are born again in Yeshua, as well as help today's Jewish people see the real picture of the demonic levels at work trying to keep them from finding, then crossing over, God's covenant threshold, covered in the blood of Yeshua—their only hope of authentic salvation.

Is there now any doubt remaining as to what might have at least lit the match for the subsequent Roman Catholic Inquisitions leveled upon the Jewish people? That horrific travesty was meaningfully addressed only in 2014–2015 by the Spanish government. Perhaps this initial spark of hatred was used by the demonic realm to eventually fan into flame the Nazi Holocaust. And what about the anti-Semitism that still exists to this very day among the "nations," and even within the halls and pulpits of certain churches and "Christian" denominations?[167]

THROUGH THE AGES

The rationale for the participation in and continuance of this horrific matter of mortal hatred for the Jewish people is so multifaceted that it is nearly impossible to trace it or explain in merely human terms. However, we can certainly track the beginning of the hatred all the way back to the Fall of humanity in the Garden of Eden. It was there that Satan became incensed with God's human creation, especially with the mysteriously prophesied woman who would one day bear a male child who would ultimately become the conqueror of Satan's stolen kingdom. That prophetic declaration was leveled upon Satan by Yahweh/Elohim Himself (Genesis 3:15).

From there we follow Satan's hatred and manipulation of humanity all the way up to the days of Noah. After the Flood, we watch Satan focus on the Hebrew sojourner Abraham and his seed. Abraham was promised by the Creator to be the bearer of that promised blessing to the nations— ultimately, the Messiah.

Moreover, we can't forget about Satan's involvement in the children of Abraham being enslaved in Egypt, then the eventual Egyptian edict to kill all the male children of the Israelites and the subsequent supernatural sparing of the infant Moses that emerged from that demonically inspired genocide attempt.

How about the previous enemy incursions of the Amalekites and Canaanites into Israel's camp in the wilderness, under demonic inspiration? Their plan was to kill the Israelites and wipe them from the face of the earth.[168] And that's not to mention the Balaam-Balak conspiracy designed to destroy the entire nation of Israel just as they were about to enter the Promised Land (Numbers 21–30).

Now, consider the historical succession of evil men and nations that then, through Israel's existence, were demonically driven to cleanse the planet of Israel: These were Shalmaneser V of the Syrians (2 Kings 17), Nebuchadnezzar of the Babylonians (Daniel), Haman of the Persians (Esther), and Antiochus Epiphanes of the Greeks (the four hundred years of history between Malachi and Matthew).

Then there was Herod of the Romans—the king who launched a murderous rampage throughout Bethlehem to kill the young child called "King of the Jews" (Matthew 2), followed by the efforts of successive Roman emperors to expel the Jews from the entire empire and destroy as many as possible from AD 70 on. Then came Emperor Constantine and his anti-Jewish tirades in the "name of the consensus of the Church."

Finally, in AD 380, Emperor Theodosius I decreed Christianity the official state religion. Here's what the United States Holocaust Memorial Museum notes concerning the eventual fallout of Rome's new state church—the Roman Catholic Church:

> By then, the earlier imbalance of population of Jews over Christians was a matter of distant memory, even if pagans in the empire still far outnumbered the favored newcomer. But the Jewish position became precarious with this declaration.
>
> The theological anti-Judaism of the Church fathers, repeated endlessly in medieval and Renaissance-Reformation preaching, was the far greater culprit. It was the continuing rationale for the indefensible Christian conduct of the Middle Ages onward that

was xenophobic and angry at Jewish resistance to absorption into the cultural mainstream. But because the Church's preaching and its catechizing had long shaped the popular mind, a new phenomenon was able to come to birth: modern anti-Semitism.

Can the mischief of eighteen-and one-half centuries be reversed? Catholics point to statements like section 4 of the Vatican II statement on non-Christian religions (Nostra Aetate, October 1965) which exculpated the Jews of all time of the charge of deicide ("killing God"), and warned Catholics against thinking that anything in their scriptures taught that Jews were a people accursed or rejected.[169]

HOLDING OUT HOPE

I applaud the Catholic people of today who "get it," and are working to make amends to the Jewish people. I truly do. I am deeply grateful for their collective efforts to undo centuries of atrocious hatred toward God's chosen people and nation. That much-needed peacemaking would certainly make my ministry here in Israel easier, especially among my Jewish brethren...including my own family!

So, I pray this genuine goodwill continues to spread far and wide. Perhaps, through this book and others like it, we can persist in restoring the larger Christian community of congregations to the authentic biblical underpinnings of the faith. These are the Threshold Covenants ordained from Heaven, given by Yahweh to restore earth's fallen humanity.

If you have not understood these things before this moment, do you now recognize the demonic progression of targeting the people and nation of Abraham's seed, starting from the Garden of Eden? Now you know who's behind it. Now you understand the demonic rationale for it.

The evil one, through the Chaldean spirit, is attempting to block the true way to salvation through God's holy thresholds. Satan's demonic horde is continually offering up fraudulent copies and out-and-out deceptions to both Jews and Gentiles…of all the earth's populations, and even among all the Christian denominations of the world.

Satan knows his time is short. He passionately hates Israel, as well as born-again believers—*both Jews and Gentiles*—because they are the congregation of the "one new man" of the last days spoken of in Ephesians 2.

The book of Revelation, God's final Word about *last things*, records this truth in a striking manner:

> Therefore, rejoice, O heavens and you who dwell in them! But woe to you, O earth and sea, for the devil has come down to you in great wrath, because he knows that his time is short!… Then the dragon became furious with the woman [Israel][170] and went off to make war on the rest of her offspring, on those who keep the commandments of God and hold to the testimony of Jesus. And he stood on the sand of the sea. (Revelation 12:12, 17)

"Another Way"

Before we close this chapter, let me draw attention back to some of the previously quoted words of Constantine in his AD 325 missive about Easter and the Jews:

> We have received another way from the Savior. In our holy religion we have set before us a [another] course which is both valid and accurate.[171]

Constantine declared "another way" to Yeshua. He also insisted that *they* had devised another "course." He even claimed this *other way* was decreed by Yeshua Himself! He basically admitted they had intentionally invented another Threshold Covenant—one *better* than Yahweh's! The extent of Satan's hubris is astonishing.

In the meantime, please pray for Israel. Pray for the Jewish people. Pray for the nations that hate Israel. Pray for the congregations that meet for the claimed purpose of worshiping Yeshua, when they do not do it in spirit and in truth.

Pray for those who have yet to understand they are standing at false thresholds, wondering why their lives and their services of "worship" are still empty and unsatisfying.

chapter thirty

CALENDAR CHAOS

In Jesus' time, during Passover week of a specific year, those dates precisely corresponded with Yeshua's entry into Jerusalem on the tenth of Nisan.

To this day, there rages a debate as to exactly when believers should celebrate the Resurrection of Yeshua. This is largely (but not totally) because of the "Easter-Roman Church" aberration brought in by the Nicene Council along with all of its historical baggage. And that undaunted influence has since spilled over into Protestant churches as well as a large number of Evangelical churches. When we add into the mix the very different Hebrew calendar system and the fact that even the Jewish people themselves are divided over the dating systems of the Hebrew calendar for determining the proper date of Passover, we have a real mess.[172]

Let me illustrate the "mess" I'm talking about. The debated formulas for dating Passover and Easter are a bit complex; however, they're simplified in an excerpt of a 2019 *Atlantic* article:

> There's a **basic misalignment between the Christian and the Jewish festival calendars.** Both holidays are supposed to fall on,

163

or near, a full moon in the spring. Passover always begins on the 15th day of the Hebrew month of Nisan. Because the Hebrew months are pegged directly to the lunar cycle, the 15th day of Nisan is always a full moon....

For a time, early Christians used the Jewish calendar as a reference, celebrating Easter on the first Sunday after Nisan 15. But at the First Council of Nicaea in AD 325, the Church decided to set **its own date for Easter, independent of the Jewish reckoning.** Today most Christian communities celebrate Easter on the first Sunday following the first full moon after March 21. But sometimes this full moon isn't the same as the Jewish one....

The lunar mismatch occurs because both calendars must grapple with the same underlying problem: **A lunar year is not the same length as a full solar year.** In fact, nothing is exactly the same length as a solar year, because **not all solar years are the same length. This challenge ails not only both religious calendars,** but also **every human attempt at timekeeping on Earth.**[173] (Emphasis added)

IT'S NOT ABOUT THE EXACT DATE

Let me offer a few suggestions for today's born-again believers in Yeshua. Remember, the exact date, as it aligns with today's various calendars of the world, is not nearly as important to honor as is the actual memorial celebration of Yeshua's Resurrection. We are not observing a *date* so much as we are commemorating the Yeshua Resurrection *event* and *season*, and its connection to the dates of the original Feast of Passover (also called the Feast of Unleavened Bread) as outlined in Exodus 12.

The most important dates are centered around choosing the Passover lamb on the tenth of Nisan, then slaughtering it on the fourteenth of Nisan. The fifteenth day would then be the official biblical Passover meal. Then, the sixteenth day would begin the Feast of Unleavened Bread—a seven-day event.

In Jesus' time, during Passover week of a specific year, those dates precisely corresponded with Yeshua's entry into Jerusalem on the tenth of Nisan, then His ultimate rejection by the mobs who cried, "Crucify Him!" on the fourteenth. This would also include the Passover meal eaten at sundown on the evening of that Crucifixion. That meal would officially begin the fifteenth of Nisan.

Then, of course, there was the seventeenth of Nisan in that year, the day of the Resurrection! And *on that third day* from the Crucifixion, in that specific year, fell *the first day of the week*...also the Feast of First Fruits—the day of Yeshua's Resurrection.

Following are the scriptural affirmations of the most important elements of the Resurrection event:

Yeshua is our Passover Lamb:

Cleanse out the old leaven that you may be a new lump, as you really are unleavened. For Christ, our Passover lamb, has been sacrificed. (1 Corinthians 5:7)

He rose on the first day of the week:

Now when [Yeshua] rose early on the first day of the week, he appeared first to Mary Magdalene, from whom he had cast out seven demons. She went and told those who had been with him, as they mourned and wept. (Mark 16:9–10; see also Matthew 28:1, Luke 24:1, and John 20:1)

He rose on the Feast of Firstfruits:

But in fact Christ has been raised from the dead, the firstfruits of those who have fallen asleep. For as by a man came death, by a man has come also the resurrection of the dead. For as in Adam all die, so also in Christ shall all be made alive. But each in his own order: Christ the firstfruits, then at his coming those who belong to Christ. (1 Corinthians 15:20–23)

He is the foundation of our faith:

And if Christ has not been raised, then our preaching is in vain and your faith is in vain.… And if Christ has not been raised, your faith is futile and you are still in your sins. Then those also who have fallen asleep in Christ have perished. (1 Corinthians 15:14, 17)

But the fact remains, Constantine's "Easter" should never be confused with the original Feast of Passover Resurrection event among God's born-again people. Admittedly, it will take loads of patience and a huge dose of biblical education for a believing congregation to make the necessary shifts into the scriptural realm of the Threshold Covenant and what that blood alliance really means.

But that's the reason this book was written in the first place…to give God's people a reliable teaching tool.

chapter thirty-one

ELIMINATING THE EASTER CONFUSION

So, here's what we have: A jam-packed, conservative Christian church congregation in the United States was presented a sermon mainly about Easter eggs and hunts.

In this chapter, I will suggest a few ways to bring a congregation of believers into the most biblically correct way to celebrate Yeshua's Resurrection.

At the very least, it would be best to avoid using the word "Easter" in any Resurrection celebration service. This also includes removing all vestiges of Easter's historically acknowledged pagan influences, including the Lent traditions, eggs, egg hunts, bunnies, baskets, and the like.

THE "EGG-HUNT SHOCKER"

Let me give an illustration of why these recommendations are important to consider. A trusted friend happened to be in the United States during

Passover/Resurrection week just a short time back. He called me a few days after Passover week, while I was in Israel, to tell me about several things he had observed while in the States. He also said he wanted to tell me about a conversation he'd engaged in regarding the matter.

My friend first told me of his shock at the widespread use of the term "Easter" by well-known American evangelical leaders and prominent congregations and their representatives. He saw them on television and billboards, heard them on radio advertisements, and saw them in other interview situations. He noticed signs openly advertising Easter egg hunts on the church grounds and at huge community Easter gatherings that had been planned and sponsored by Christian congregations. He was floored and brokenhearted by the pervasiveness of the Easter spirit.

Then he told me of a large, traditionally conservative, evangelical church that had heavily advertised its Easter services in the community he was visiting. Additionally, the church's highway sign unashamedly advertised the upcoming Easter festivities to all who passed by.

He then related how he happened to run into a woman from that church a day after the Sunday morning Easter services. Based upon what happened next, he told me he thought the Lord had actually ordained the meeting. He said that, after a brief introductory conversation, the woman began to dive into the topic of the pastor's sermon the previous day; she was filled with enthusiasm as she bubbled out the details to my friend.

The woman said the "amazing" sermon had been largely about the Easter egg, egg hunts, and egg-decorating parties. She said the pastor had made a big deal about how much "fellowship and fun" the Easter event usually provided "God's people" on that "special day." She claimed her pastor had dramatically emphasized that "we should enjoy those things about the day."

The pastor had also explained that, every now and then, someone might find an empty egg when they were on an Easter egg hunt or when they were coloring the eggs for hiding. He spoke of how a person would be "so surprised" to find an egg in that condition. It would be like finding a rare treasure, he explained.

Continuing her account of the message, the woman told my friend that the preacher had equated the imagined shock of finding an empty Easter egg with the surprise the women disciples must have felt when they first found Jesus' tomb empty "early on that *Easter* morning."

After the woman had finished sharing the details of the Easter sermon, my friend said he stood dumbfounded for a moment. Then he politely asked her a few questions.

"Since your pastor spoke of Easter egg hunts in his sermon," he began to probe, "did he happen to say anything about the actual history of *Easter*? Did he perhaps provide any explanation of the historical roots of the Easter traditions, or did he happen to speak of the Feast of the Passover, and how the first three Feasts of the Lord (Passover, Unleavened Bread, and First Fruits) related to Jesus' Crucifixion and Resurrection?"

She answered that her pastor hadn't spoken of *any* of those things. My friend said the woman acted as if she had no clue as to why, in the first place, those topics might even be important for an Easter service.

So, here's what we have: A large, jam-packed, conservative Christian church congregation in the United States was presented a sermon mainly about Easter eggs and hunts. Then they were finally told that *somehow, maybe, sort-of,* those eggs tie into the account of the Resurrection of Jesus.

Basically, an entire Resurrection/Passover week message was given without a word about the vital prophecies that Jesus' Passover, Crucifixion, and Resurrection had actually fulfilled. Therefore, much of the deepest meaning and biblical connections went unspoken at one of the largest gatherings of people the church would probably have that year.

That kind of oversight, my brothers and sisters, simply must be eliminated among God's congregations of believers.

Accommodate without Compromise

Along those lines, I also suggest that it would be wise for congregational leaders to preach and teach, at appropriate times throughout the year, about the biblical elements of *all* the Feasts of the Lord, especially the Feasts of Passover, Unleavened Bread, and Firstfruits. Most specifically, they should explain how all of the Feasts of the Lord were, and will be, completely fulfilled in Yeshua.

I understand that, in the larger "Christian world," there is such an absence of understanding on this topic that it might sometimes be necessary to temporarily accommodate the culture *without compromising* the Gospel of Yeshua. This could be accomplished by holding Resurrection Day services on the world's Easter, for the sole purpose of drawing in large numbers of people to whom we could graciously and powerfully advance the authentic message of Yeshua's Resurrection.

However, as I've already suggested, I would use *none* of the Easter language when promoting or presenting this message. This simple tactic, in and of itself, could become the anointed beginning of a genuine biblical teaching experience for the throngs of people in attendance. Such a service would perhaps reach many who have never heard the depths of the Resurrection truth.

In that service, a pastor might graciously explain the discrepancies between the various calendar systems and the difficulty in determining the date of the Resurrection almost two thousand years after the fact. It could also be emphasized that, although we might not be certain of the precise date in any given year, the focus of the celebration is Yeshua's Crucifixion and Resurrection and the resulting Threshold Covenant. Further, we celebrate those events within the very *season* in which Passover originally occurred, and on the very day of the week when the disciples discovered the tomb was empty.

Even if pastors and teachers aren't able to go into great detail on a Resurrection celebration day, simply eliminating all language about and vestiges of Easter and sticking to the unmitigated biblical message of the Resurrection would be a monumental beginning. In fact, in today's world, it apparently would be a rare type of Resurrection service. You might be instrumental in starting something eternally powerful for the Kingdom work in your area!

Regardless of the methodology a congregation might use, the following is our biblical foundation for approaching the matter in a way similar to what I've just suggested:

> For though I am free from all, I have made myself a servant to all, that I might win more of them. To the Jews I became as a Jew, in order to win Jews. To those under the law I became as one under the law (though not being myself under the law) that I might win those under the law.
>
> To those outside the law I became as one outside the law (not being outside the law of God but under the law of Christ) that I might win those outside the law. To the weak I became weak, that I might win the weak. I have become all things to all people, that by all means I might save some.
>
> I do it all for the sake of the gospel, that I may share with them in its blessings. (1 Corinthians 9:19–23)

Every time we meet in *spirit and in truth* for a congregational service of worship—regardless of the day of the week—the gathering is actually a celebration of Yeshua's Crucifixion and Resurrection, as well as of His promised Return. He is the Lamb who was slain to provide God's offer of the Threshold Covenant relationship. He is our Unleavened Bread—the Bread of Life. And He is our Firstfruits from among the realm of death—our promise of eternal life and destiny.

Let me be clear. I know of no congregation of true believers who purposefully plan to "worship" the Easter Bunny or Ishtar/Astarte/Ashtoreth. It would be ludicrous for anyone to suggest that. However, I'm certain you get the point we're exploring here.

The trappings of the Easter "spirit" are thoroughly pagan, overtly unbiblical, and pervasively spread among God's people the world over. Obviously, these things should have no place whatsoever in our message as we present the Gospel of salvation offered in Yeshua. That, after all, is our central mission, especially in these prophetically important times.

So, here's the bottom line. The fields are now "white unto harvest," perhaps like never before (John 4:35). The biblical Threshold Covenants are being blurred and hidden in an unprecedented manner, even among believers. Sometimes the messages about the Threshold Covenants are being blurred *by* believers who still, even after they learn the truth, insist on using the language of Easter and the Constantinian Roman Catholic trappings that stand squarely against the Lord's Feast of Passover.

The Chaldean spirit is hard at work in the Body of Christ. The spirit of Antichrist—the man of lawlessness—continually attempts to establish his blasphemous presence among the *ecclesia*[174] of the last days—which is the true Temple of God (Ephesians 2).

The Great Day of God's coming judgment upon this world is getting closer with each passing moment. We still have a lot of work to do. Let's do that work as excellently as possible, and with the anointing of the Holy Spirit of God upon us.

> We must work the works of Him who sent me while it is day; night is coming, when no one can work. As long as I am in the world, I am the light of the world. (John 9:4–5)

> Do your best to present yourself to God as one approved, a worker who has no need to be ashamed, rightly handling the word of truth. But avoid irreverent babble, for it will lead people into more and more ungodliness, and their talk will spread like gangrene. (2 Timothy 2:15–17)

Next, we'll examine another major diversion from the threshold teachings. It has also swept a large swath of the Christian world into a whirlwind of deception, and once again hides many treasures of our relationship with Yeshua. It is a divisive and insidiously emotional topic for many within today's Christian world.

PART VI

TEMPLE FRENZY

[Jesus said] I tell you that one greater than the temple is here.

MATTHEW 12:6–7

The priests shall offer his burnt offering and his peace offerings, and he shall worship at the threshold of the gate.

EZEKIEL 46:2

Author's note: I asked my long-time ministry associate Pastor Carl Gallups to coauthor this section on the "Temple Frenzy," as well as the one that follows—"Ezekiel's Temple." Carl is the senior pastor of a well-known evangelical Gulf Coast church and an eminent biblical researcher and Christian media personality, as well as an Amazon Top-60 bestselling author. Together, over the years, we have written and spoken about this controversial topic on several occasions.[175]

chapter thirty-two

THE THIRD-TEMPLE DIVERSION

> There is not one recorded word of Jesus flat-out insisting that a Third Temple would be rebuilt on the Temple Mount in the last days, just before His return.

A great deal of misunderstanding shrouds the truth of God's plans regarding the possibility of a rebuilt temple of the last days standing in Jerusalem on the Temple Mount. This, too, is a distraction manufactured by the Chaldean spirit to hide the importance of the Threshold Covenant. Now it's time to sweep away the rubble and find what really lies beneath the matter and why it's so important that we know the truth.

THE KOTEL SECRET

No doubt many are familiar with the Wailing Wall or the Western Wall (Hebrew: *kotel*) in Jerusalem's Old City. It is one of the most famous places on earth. For ages, countless multitudes of tourists have tucked scraps of paper containing the deepest desires of their hearts into whatever crevices they can find between the ancient stones, hoping God might see their pleas and respond. It is there where only a tiny number of Orthodox Jews sometimes gather to pray for the rebuilding of the Jewish Temple—the "Third Temple"—in the hope that they can once again fulfill the Old Covenant requirement of daily sacrifices.[176]

I can tell you there is a hidden fact regarding a rebuilt temple on the Temple Mount. Please recall that I am an authentic Jewish person who has deep familial and professional connections to the Israeli culture, the Orthodox and rabbinical community, the rabbinical courts, the military, and the government. In addition, I speak Hebrew as my original tongue. I know what I'm talking about regarding the truth of this topic. The well-hidden truth is this: Almost *no one in Israel* wants a rebuilt temple on the Temple Mount.[177]

There are a number of reasons why this is so, but the fact is indisputable and well documented. This is a well-known Israeli reality that is difficult for many Christians around the world to comprehend, especially in light of the misaligned teaching they have been accustomed to hearing for so many decades.[178]

THE WORD OF GOD

Does the Word of God affirm that a Third Temple edifice will eventually be constructed on the Temple Mount in the Old City of Jerusalem?[179] Most people would probably answer "yes." However, that simply is not true.

To discover the answers to two thousand years of questions surrounding this subject, we must dig for the truth and be willing to avoid speculative rhetoric, Constantinian meddling, Jewish and Christian myths, and outright misunderstanding of certain scriptural declarations. Instead, we must be willing to venture into the deeper realm of authentic biblical interpretation.

The proper protocol for this kind of spiritual archeology project also requires a correct understanding of Hebrew and Greek word usages, the complex nuances of those words, rules of proper (contextual) biblical interpretation, and the understanding of *compound prophecy*.[180] It also incorporates a willingness to discern what the Scriptures actually say rather than simply interpreting them to say what we want them to mean...and so much more.

The Most Important Consideration

Let me affirm from the outset that nothing in the Word of God emphatically requires the rebuilding of a stone-and-mortar Temple on the Temple Mount in the last days.[181]

By the time we've properly examined the few Scriptures that might *appear* to say this, you'll understand the truth of the previous statement. When we examine those passages with the fullest scrutiny of the biblical languages, most students of the Word of God are stunned by what they discover. What they *do* find simply does not align with a certain portion of the relatively modern popular ideas on the subject of the Third Temple. Thus, we begin to uncover the reason for so much confusion over this issue. And, as you might have guessed, it too, involves a stunning threshold revelation.

Let's now consider the following significant biblical truths:

1. Not a word from Yeshua: Not one recorded word of Yeshua *insists* a Third Temple will be rebuilt on the Temple Mount in the last days, just before His return.

Think about that for just a moment. If an event as monumental as a *rebuilt Temple* edifice on the Temple Mount was supposed to become a literal, end-time reality as well as a prophetic necessity, then why didn't Yeshua tell us about it—and in great detail? After all, He *did* foretell the impending *destruction* of the Second Temple, the one standing in Jerusalem at the time He was with His disciples. However, Yeshua spoke not a word about a stone-and-mortar Third Temple that would be reconstructed in the last days.

2. Not a word from the Gospel writers: There is not a single mention of the rebuilding of a Third Temple structure on the Temple Mount in the last days from any of the *Gospel writers,* either. Neither is it spoken of in Acts. Not a word! The four Gospels and Acts, which together provide the bulk of our understanding of the entire Christ event do not even contextually hint at the rebuilding of a literal Third Temple on the Temple Mount before the Second Coming of Jesus.

3. Not a word from Paul: Even the Apostle Paul, who wrote almost half of the New Testament, doesn't mention a Third Temple on the Temple Mount…notwithstanding the often-supposed exception of the mention of a "temple" related to the man of lawlessness found in the second chapter of 2 Thessalonians.

4. Not a word from the remaining writers: Furthermore, the *remaining writers* of the New Testament documents do not mention the subject, either—not Jude, Peter, the writer of Hebrews, Matthew, Mark, Luke, John's Gospel, or the book of James.

Neither is there an utterance of it in John's writings outside of his Gospel, with the exception of *one verse* in Revelation 11 wherein some interpreters claim that John "indirectly" refers to a Third Temple, on the Temple Mount, in the last days. But that is flatly not what John was revealing, as we will soon disclose.

One Potential Exception

That only leaves us with one more potential exception. It's most famously found in Matthew 24, wherein Yeshua is speaking of the "signs" of His return in the last days. In that address, He expresses a somewhat cryptic statement. The text of the passage even indicates that understanding the matter will take supernatural discernment when the prophecy begins to unfold:

> So when you see the abomination of desolation spoken of by the prophet Daniel, standing in the holy place (let the reader under-

stand), then let those who are in Judea flee to the mountains. (Matthew 24:15–16, parentheses in original)

You guessed it. We'll look at the context of that statement, and when we do, we'll discover several other surprising revelations.

Three Considerations

For now, here's what we're left with. In almost three hundred pages of New Testament writings, only three possibilities might appear to suggest there will be a literal Third Temple on the Temple Mount in Jerusalem. In the next several chapters, we'll closely examine those three passages.

So, *could* a person draw inferences from certain Scriptures in attempting to argue for a rebuilt Temple in Jerusalem? Yes, they could…and they often do.

However, can we point to *any verse* wherein that subject is clearly spelled out, in specific detail, and declared as a certainty? No, we cannot—from *any* of the writers or speakers in the New or Old Testaments. And that's the point. What would be the likelihood of there being no direct reference to such an important and supposed prophetic event as this?

What in the world are we missing?

chapter thirty-three

WORDS HAVE MEANING

There may be a Third Temple one day,
even on the Temple Mount, but 2 Thessalonians 2:4
is not the verse making that claim.

Within the Old and New Testaments, only a handful of verses are alleged to be speaking of a rebuilt Third Temple on the Temple Mount in Jerusalem. We must look closely at four precise words before we can reach proper conclusions about the passages. Two of those four words are Hebrew, and the other two are Greek.

The problem is those words almost always find their way into our English translations as the word "temple." Additionally, some English translations use the word "temple" when that word isn't even in the original text. On other occasions, the English word translated as "temple" begs for the subtlety of the original language to convey its fullest meaning.

These are sticky translation issues, indeed. These complications and a few others are usually the reason for our modern misunderstanding of the topic of the Third Temple. In the Greek language, two specific words are often translated as "temple" in New Testament documents: *hieron* and *naos*.

Hieron

The word *hieron* means the actual building itself, the entire complex as a whole. Therefore, the structure on the Temple Mount, along with the attached section of Solomon's Colonnade, is called the *hieron*.[182]

Following are examples of how *hieron* is used.

> Then the devil took him to the holy city and set him on the pinnacle of the **temple** [*hieron*]. (Matthew 4:5, emphasis added)

> Jesus left the **temple** [*hieron*] and was going away, when his disciples came to point out to him the buildings of the **temple** [*hieron*]. (Matthew 24:1, emphasis added)

> And [Jesus] was teaching daily in the **temple** [*hieron*]. The chief priests and the scribes and the principal men of the people were seeking to destroy him. (Luke 19:47, emphasis added)

That last reference, Luke 19:47, is a perfect example showing that the words "in the temple" are inclusive of the area of Solomon's Colonnade, and that the structure was indeed considered a part of the overall *hieron*. Jesus wasn't actually inside the four walls of the building while He was teaching. However, He was still considered to be "in" the Temple because He was in Solomon's Colonnade—the *hieron*.[183]

Naos

The Greek word *naos*—often translated as "temple" as well—means the *innermost Holy of Holies* located within the literal—*hieron*—building. It is an internal room or compartment that represents the presence of God Himself. This *naos* contained the Ark of the Covenant during the time of the Wilderness Tabernacle and Solomon's Temple, but not during the time of the Second Temple in Yeshua's day.[184] The fact remains, the *naos* was the inmost chamber in the *hieron*. It is an entirely different word from *hieron*. The two are *not* technically synonymous.[185]

Most often, however, throughout the entire New Testament, *naos* is used in its very important metaphorical sense to indicate the congregation of believers itself, or the individual Christian person, or the physical body of Jesus Himself. That's because this is how God, through Yeshua and the Holy Spirit, has chosen to "meet" with His people in the very last days. It is the ultimate last-days Holy of Holies.[186]

The Apostle Paul, throughout his New Testament writings, almost always uses the word *naos*. He only uses the word *hieron* to speak of the actual structure on the Temple Mount, and he uses that word only once in all of his writings—in the following:

> Do you not know that those who serve around sacred things eat from the things of the **temple** [*hieron*], and those who wait on the altar have their portion with the altar? (1 Corinthians 9:13, New Heart English Version, emphasis added)

However, Paul uses *naos* a total of nine times in his instructions to the churches. Unfortunately, most English Bible versions also translate *naos* as "temple."

Are you beginning to see where the misunderstanding comes into play? The confusion is not from the actual text, nor is it from the original language; the problems arise from the subtle differences between *hieron* and *naos* and how the English versions translate those words.[187]

Paul Defines It

Following are eight of the nine places where Paul speaks of the genuine last-days Temple of God.

> Do you not know that you are God's **temple** [*naos*] and that God's Spirit dwells in you? If anyone destroys God's **temple** [*naos*], God will destroy him. For God's **temple** [*naos*] is holy, and you are that **temple** [*naos*]. (1 Corinthians 3:16–17, emphasis added)

> Or do you not know that your body is a **temple** [*naos*] of the Holy Spirit within you, whom you have from God? You are not your own… (1 Corinthians 6:19, emphasis added)

> What agreement has the **temple** [*naos*] of God with idols? For we are the **temple** [*naos*] of the living God; as God said, "I will make my dwelling among them and walk among them, and I will be their God, and they shall be my people. (2 Corinthians 6:16, emphasis added)

> So then you are no longer strangers and aliens, but you are fellow citizens with the saints, and are of God's household, having been built on the foundation of the apostles and prophets, Christ Jesus Himself being the corner (stone), in whom the whole building, being fitted together, is growing into a holy **temple** [*naos*] in the Lord, in whom you also are being built together into a dwelling of God in the Spirit. (Ephesians 2:19–22, emphasis added)

Thus, in eight of the nine times Paul uses *naos*, he unambiguously declares that *born-again believers* are the new, and thus the "third" Temple of God. He does this by defining the meaning of the word he is using within the text itself. In this matter, Paul wants to make certain there is no misunderstanding of what he is revealing to God's people.

In Ephesians 2, Paul even emphasizes the "one new man" characteristic of this *Temple of God*—that "temple" is declared to be the believing Jews and Gentiles…under the blood of Yeshua. These have entered God's presence through the true Threshold Covenant. This, and this alone, is the authentic "rebuilt" Temple of God in the last days. And it is the only one the New Testament mentions in this literal regard. Paul was passionate about making this case for the early Church.

Destroy This Temple!

In addition to Paul's use of *naos* in his writings, we find that his usage matches precisely what Yeshua declared about the *naos*. Consider the connections between the following passages:

> **John 2:19–21:** Jesus answered them, "Destroy this **temple** [*naos*], and I will raise it again in three days." The Jews replied, "It has taken forty-six years to build this **temple** [*naos*], and you are going to raise it in three days?" But the **temple** [*naos*] he had spoken of was his body. (NIV, emphasis added)

> **Matthew 12:6–7:** [Jesus said,] "I tell you that one greater than the **temple** [*naos*] is here. (NIV, emphasis added)

Now observe how Paul translates these declarations of Yeshua concerning the "temple" and His "body" and the "body of Christ."

> **1 Corinthians 12:27–28:** Now you are the **body of Christ**, and each one of you is a part of it. (NIV, emphasis added)

> **Ephesians 4:11–13:** It was He who gave some to be apostles, some to be prophets, some to be evangelists, and some to be pastors and teachers, to prepare God's people for works of service, so that the **body of Christ** may be built up. (NIV, emphasis added)

Here's the main thing to remember: Did you notice Paul never once even hinted that a third *hieron*, a literal rebuilt Temple, would be constructed in the last days, before the return of Yeshua? But how could that be? How could the preeminent apostle/preacher/prophet of the New Testament have neglected to tell us about such a monumental prophetic happening?

The answer is that he didn't neglect it. He *knew* the destruction of the *hieron* in Jerusalem was coming soon, and it was never to rise again.[188] The new and "Third Temple" of the last days was the Body of Christ—the *naos*—the congregation of born-again believers! His direct revelations of this matter were plain, simple, and powerfully obvious…to those who have eyes to see.

Are you detecting the *Chaldean spirit* presence again—a demonic assault that is trying to force upon the world a counterfeit truth?

chapter thirty-four

THE THESSALONIAN DECLARATION

How did Paul define the word *naos* every time he used it, and in every book he wrote?

Let's now look at the ninth—*and last*—time Paul uses the word *naos*. Studied in its proper context, this ninth use of the word can have no other meaning than what it meant *every other time* Paul used it throughout his writings—and the clearly defined meaning in *every other instance* is "the congregation of believers."

> Let no one deceive you in any way, for [the coming of the Lord and our being gathered to Him] will not come until the rebellion occurs and the man of lawlessness—the son of destruction—is revealed. He will oppose and exalt himself above every so-called god or object of worship. So he will seat himself in the **temple** [*naos*] of God, proclaiming himself to be God. (2 Thessalonians 2:3–4, emphasis added)

There are only two questions to ask now that we've uncovered the biblical truths of the last chapter:

1. How did Paul define *naos* each time he used it? The answer is He used it to mean "the congregation of born-again believers." There's simply no way around this fact.
2. So, then, what does 2 Thessalonians 2:4 have to be talking about? It *has to mean* Antichrist and the Beast system will infiltrate and manipulate the Body of Christ—the congregations, the hearts and minds of true believers—in the last days. It also means he will insist he is the "god" and "lord" among them! That is to say 2 Thessalonians has nothing to do with a rebuilt Third Temple on the Temple Mount. *Nothing.*

I cannot overemphasize how important this is. I am amazed that a number of modern interpreters still insist on interpreting Paul's use of *naos* in 2 Thessalonians 2:4 as the holy place of a literal Third Temple on the Temple Mount in the last days. Apparently they have totally missed the fact that Paul has already, *seven times before this*, clearly identified how he used *naos* in all of his other writings.

A great number of renowned classical scholars agree with our word study of 2 Thessalonians and our conclusions. The following are just three, and I've listed the commentaries of seven more at the referenced endnote.[189]

Alford's Greek Testament Critical Exegetical Commentary:

[*Naos* was] used metaphorically by Paul in 1 Co 3:17: and why not here? [in 2 Thessalonians 2:4]. See also 1 Corinthians 6:16; Ephesians 2:21. From these passages it is plain that such figurative sense [applying to the Church, and not the Temple at Jerusalem] was familiar to the Apostle.[190]

Coffman's Commentary on the Bible:

Sitteth in the temple of God.... There can be no way that this is a reference to the Jewish temple. Paul, who wrote the Corinthians that "Ye are the temple of God," would never have made that...the "temple of God" historically. First, it means the church of Jesus Christ; but in context it means the apostate church of Jesus Christ, a deduction that is mandatory from the fact of the apostasy being Paul's subject in this paragraph. Therefore, whenever and wherever the "man of sin" appears it will be in the church apostate.[191]

The Pulpit Commentary:

It appears more correct to refer the expression metaphorically to the Christian Church. It is a favorite metaphor of Paul to compare believers in particular, or the Church in general, to the temple of God.[192]

There may be a Third Temple one day, even on the Temple Mount. And it might even be built and/or inhabited by Antichrist. But 2 Thessalonians 2:4 is *not the verse* making that claim. It is impossible to interpret Paul's use of that specific word in that manner, especially when we consider its appropriate context.

However, we still have two more places that might seem to say there will be a literal Third Temple on the Temple Mount. One is in Revelation 11 and the other is in the book of Daniel. Jesus Himself points us to the Daniel references in His discourse of Matthew 24.

chapter thirty-five

MEASURING THE REVELATION TEMPLE

He was measuring off the "wheat" from
the "tares" in the very last days.

In light of what we learned about the word *naos* and Paul's use of it, let's get right to the main features of this next and often-misunderstood passage of Scripture found in Revelation chapter 11:

> Then I was given a measuring rod like a staff, and I was told, "Rise and measure the **temple** [*naos*] of God and the altar and those who worship there, but do not measure the court outside the **temple** [*naos*]; leave that out, for it is given over to the nations, and they [the nations and people that reject Jesus] will trample the holy city for forty-two months. (Revelation 11:1–2, emphasis added)

I have no intention of getting into theological arguments about the book of Revelation as a whole, or even about the interpretation of Revelation 11 itself. What I will do, however, is set straight the meaning of Revelation 11:1–2 regarding the Temple. The answer should now be clear.

What is John told to measure? Clearly, it's not the Temple on the Temple Mount of John's day in downtown Jerusalem. The book of Revelation was written around AD 90. The Temple in Jerusalem had been destroyed by the Romans about twenty years prior to Revelation's writing.

Because of this, Revelation 11:1–2 becomes one of the three New Testament passages that are often molded into some type of statement "proving" there will be a rebuilt Third Temple in the last days. The argument goes something like this: *Why else would John be told to "measure the temple of God" when there's not one there? Obviously, he sees a rebuilt Third Temple in his vision!*

Considering what we now know about *naos*, the word John uses here, we understand what he is saying. He is talking about the congregation of born-again believers in the very last days.

There can be no doubt that this is what John is conveying, and here's how we know. Paul, whom John knew well, and who had been put to death some twenty-plus years earlier, had already defined the terms *naos* and the "temple of God" for the Christians of his day. And we know John had been referencing Paul's writings in ministering to his own congregations for more than twenty years.[193]

Why would John suddenly change the meaning of *naos*? Clearly he *wouldn't* have done so. If he had changed it, just for this verse, he would have needed to tell his audience what he had done; otherwise, he would have caused confusion. But John said no such thing.

In Revelation 11, John wasn't talking about a rebuilt Temple, he was referring to the Body of Christ—the *ecclesia*—the called-out ones, those who are born again. He used the word *naos* in the same way Paul *always* used it. Apparently, the first-century congregation of believers in Yeshua thoroughly understood the picture presented in Revelation 11.

The group of classically renowned scholars who were involved in penning the expansive *Pulpit Commentary* summed up the matter perfectly:

> [There can be no doubt] that **the temple is here figuratively used of the faithful portion of the Church of Christ.** The word is...

frequently found with this signification in Paul's writings, which were probably known to John.

Among the ungodly are even some who are nominally members of the Church, who are typified by the outer court. No one could be more conscious that **only a portion of the Church—"the elect"—was to be saved** than [the Apostle John] the writer of the Epistles to the seven Churches (Revelation 1–3.).

It therefore seems that "the temple" must be interpreted symbolically. It is the dwelling place of God, the place in which he is worshipped; that is, **the multitude of true believers, or the faithful Church.** John is bidden to measure it, in order to sustain the faith and hope of himself and his hearers. It is placed in antithesis to the outer court, the faithless portion of the visible Church of God, which is given over to the Gentiles—the type of all that is worldly.

"Them that worship therein" directs our thoughts to the **individual members of the one body which collectively is "the temple."** Revelation 11:1.[194] (Emphasis added)

The following observation is made by the three commentators of the highly respected *Jamieson-Fausset-Brown Bible Commentary*:

This temple was a type of the church under the New Testament, 1 Corinthians 3:17 2 Corinthians 6:16, and is so to be interpreted generally in this book: for the material temple at Jerusalem was destroyed by the Romans more than twenty years before this prophecy, never to be built more; not one stone was left upon another; so that John here was bid to measure the church.

And the altar, and them that worship therein; yet not the whole church, but that part of it which the inner court typified; the altar, and those that worshipped within that space where that was...and under the New Testament signified **those who were to be a holy priesthood, a spiritual house, those that should offer up spiritual sacrifices acceptable to God by Jesus Christ.**[195] (Emphasis added)

Barnes' Notes on the Bible, yet another esteemed resource, conveys the same truth:

> The language and the imagery are, therefore, taken from the temple, but there is **no reason to suppose that it had any literal reference to the temple**, or even that John would so understand it.... It is such language as John, educated as a Jew, and familiar with the temple worship, would be likely to employ if he designed to make a representation pertaining to the church...as applicable to the Christian church, the work to be done would be to obtain an exact estimate or measurement of what the true church was—as distinguished from all other bodies of people, and as constituted and appointed by the direction of God.[196] (Emphasis added)

John was told by "the voice from Heaven" to measure (take a survey of) the *naos* and to count, or "mark off," the worshipers who were there—the real Body of Christ in the last days. They were those who worship in "spirit and in truth" because they are truly born again. In Revelation 11, John was marking off the difference between the "wheat" and the "tares" in the very last days.

Britt Mooney, author and contributor to Crosswalk.com, a biblical commentary and contemporary online scholarship site, says:

> The short answer is that nowhere [in God's entire Word] do we see a physical Third Temple being built on this Earth.... So why would we make a physical Third Temple necessary? There is plenty in the New Testament to clearly explain that the Temple Christ has built (and is building) is an eternal one in the people of God.[197] (Parentheses in the original)

Next, we'll uncover the truth about Yeshua's reference to Scripture found in Daniel 9.

chapter thirty-six

Daniel and the Temple

Here again, in a number of translations, we find the word "temple" right in the middle of the English text.

We now know that *two* of the *three* scriptural possibilities concerning the "necessity" of a Third Temple in the last days absolutely *do not* make that declaration at all. This often comes as quite a revelation to a number of Bible students when they first see the evidence we've now explored together. So what do we do with Yeshua's references to the last-days "temple" in the book of Daniel?

Heykal and Miqdash

We were able to draw the preceding conclusions by studying the meaning of the Greek words translated as "temple" in the English. The Hebrew language has two words often translated as "temple" in English versions of the Old Testament as well, and they correspond to their Greek counterparts. The words are *heykal*[198] and *miqdash*.[199]

Heykal corresponds to the Greek *hieron;* both mean the literal, *block-and-mortar structure* of the actual building. However, *miqdash* and the

Greek *naos* both designate a place *within* the Temple—specifically, the Holy of Holies, where God chose to personally meet with His people. It was also the place where God *spoke to His people* through the high priest. In this manner, it could literally be called the "Holy Word Place."[200] The Holy of Holies contained the Ark of the Covenant, and only the high priest was allowed to enter it.

Neither the Hebrew *miqdash* nor the Greek *naos* denotes the entire building itself. Both have a literal as well as a spiritual meaning, in the same way we have already proven *naos* can also mean the individual believer and/or the congregation of believers.

THE FULLEST REVELATIONS OF PROPHECY

The New Testament is the *most expansive revelation* we have of the ultimate meaning of prophecies concerning the last days, as well as the most complete definitions of the words used in those predictions. This is true regardless of whether the words occur in the Greek New Testament or the Hebrew Old Testament.[201]

Accordingly, the two words *naos* and *miqdash*, when used in clearly end-time prophecies, would necessarily refer to the Greek *ecclesia* known as the congregation of born-again believers, Jew and Gentile—*the true ecclesia* of the last days.[202] *Naos* and *miqdash* are therefore synonymous when used in prophecies of the very last days.

JESUS AND DANIEL

With these insights in mind, a number of people still point to a specific utterance of Yeshua to support the idea that a Third Temple will be rebuilt before His return. However, just as in 2 Thessalonians 2 and Revelation 11 of the New Testament, you'll discover that the Old Testament prophet Daniel also does not speak of a rebuilt Third Temple before the return of Jesus.

Yeshua's mention of Daniel's end-time vision is found in Matthew 24.[203] In that passage, He gave a distinctive clue to several sweeping end-time revelations, just as the disciples asked:

> [Jesus said to them,] "So when you see the abomination of desolation spoken of by the prophet Daniel, standing in the holy place (let the reader understand), then let those who are in Judea flee to the mountains. (Matthew 24:15–16)

A Compound Prophecy

At the same time Yeshua is answering the pressing questions concerning the last days, He appears to be speaking in a *compound prophecy*.[204]

This potentiality is biblically logical. Since Jesus is God with us, He transcends the dimensions of our physical time. He is the one *who was, who is,* and *who is to come* (Revelation 1). Therefore, He knows what has been, what is soon to be, and what will ultimately be...at the culmination of all earthly things and throughout the ages beyond.

It then makes perfect sense that, in revealing the events of the *last days*, Yeshua would speak in a compound manner to illustrate to His contemporaries that, just as certain things had happened in the past, some of those same types of cycles would repeat within their own lifetimes. Furthermore, the cycles would also manifest well into the future, until the ultimate fulfillments of those foreshadowings are revealed in the end-time generation yet to come.

Antiochus

In His words recorded in Matthew 24, Jesus is first calling up memories of the horrible days in the annals of Jewish history—*the days of Antiochus Epiphanes*[205] in 168 BC. Those days indeed involved the appalling desecration of the Second Temple and the eventual cessation of all sacrifices, as well as the killing of multitudes of Jewish people. All of that ultimately led to the now-famous Maccabean Wars[206] and the current Jewish Feast of Hanukkah, also known as the Feast of Dedication (John 10:1ff). The very fact that Jesus quoted Daniel would have immediately evoked these images into the minds of His disciples. They would have been intimately familiar with almost all the details; those events were a huge part of their national heritage.

AD 70

Many scholars also see in Jesus' answer a further compounded prophecy of the soon-coming destruction of Jerusalem and the ruin of the Second Temple on the Temple Mount.[207] After all, Jesus had just predicted this coming atrocity. The disciples, understandably, had a hard time fathoming such a thing.

That prophesied destruction, which eventually happened in AD 70, ended the Jewish sacrificial system of burnt offerings; that discontinuance has now lasted for almost two thousand years...up to this very day. This last desecration of Jerusalem and the Temple was imposed upon the Jews by the Roman Legions of Vespasian and Titus.[208]

THE LAST DAYS

Then, most importantly, Jesus also spoke of a final fulfillment of these matters as it would be made manifest in *Antichrist of the very last days* and his ultimate attack on the blood-bought congregation of Yeshua during the days of apostasy and lawlessness. That part of the prophecy was later echoed by the Apostle Paul (2 Thessalonians 2:4).

Don't forget, it was the *very last days* and the culminating signs of His return the disciples had asked Yeshua to expound upon in the first place. Jesus continues, as we read in Matthew 24, to speak of the end-time signs, and He takes them right up to the "gathering of the elect" from all over the earth. That gathering would take place by the heavenly host, which He Himself will call forth to conduct that ominous mission.[209]

So, in Matthew 24, Jesus is obviously directing His disciples back to the book of Daniel in the *Tanakh* (Old Testament). This makes interpretation rather easy, because only three passages in Daniel refer to the "abomination that causes desolation": chapters 9, 11, and 12. Let's have a look.

A Shocking Discovery

Following is the Christian Standard Bible's translation of Daniel 9:27:

> He will make a firm covenant with many for one week, but in the middle of the week he will put a stop to sacrifice and offering. And the abomination of desolation will be on a wing of the temple until the decreed destruction is poured out on the desolator.

Here again, in a number of translations,[210] we find the word "temple" in the middle of this English text. But which Hebrew word is used here—*heykal* or *miqdash*? Knowing what we now understand, that would be a monumentally important piece of information.

However, there is a huge problem: The word "temple" is not even in this original Hebrew text of Daniel 9:27 *at all*! Neither *heykal* nor *miqdash* appear there. The word "temple" was *inserted* by the translators who assumed that's what the text meant. Several translations reflect that assumption.

However, the *English Standard Version*, as well as a number of others,[211] render the translation in the most literally accurate manner:

> And he shall make a strong covenant with many for one week, and for half of the week he shall put an end to sacrifice and offering.

And on the wing of abominations [instead of "temple"] shall come one who makes desolate, until the decreed end is poured out on the desolator. (Daniel 9:27, ESV)

But what is the word "wing" doing there, and what, precisely, does it mean?

chapter thirty-seven

THE WING

Three passages in Daniel speak of the abomination that causes desolation. Obviously, Jesus was pointing to one, or all, of these passages in His Matthew 24 discourse.

In Hebrew, the word for "wing" is *kanaph*. That word is used 109 times in the Old Testament. *Never* is it used in the Old Testament for the word "temple," nor is it used to even relate to the Temple.[212]

In a number of uses of the word in the Old Testament, *kanaph* speaks of the literal wing of a bird or an angel. Sometimes, however, it refers to the protecting presence of God Himself (He covers us with His wings; see Psalms 17, 36, 57, 61, and 63).

That word can also be used for the edges of a garment, most specifically a priestly robe (Ezekiel 5:3). In Isaiah 11 and 24, and in Job 37 and 38, *kanaph* is used for "the ends of the earth" or the "four corners of the earth." Additionally, the term is a metaphor indicating amazing speed or *rapidity*, as in Psalms 18, 104, and 139, "on the wings of the wind."

The *Cambridge Bible for Schools and Colleges* speculates upon the potential definition of the "wing" metaphor of Daniel 9:27:

In contrast to Jehovah, who rides upon the cherub (Psalm 18:10), the heathen foe will come…riding upon a winged creature, which is the personification of the forces and practices of heathenism. "Abomination" is often used as a contemptuous designation of a heathen god or idol, or an object connected with idolatrous rites: see e.g. Deuteronomy 29:17; 1 Kings 11:5; 1 Kings 11:7; Jeremiah 7:30.[213]

The Wings of Armies

But there is one other way the Hebrew word *kanaph* is used. It speaks of a rapidly approaching, conquering army. This is similar to what we've just observed from the *Cambridge Bible for Schools and Colleges*: "Winged creature, which is the personification of the forces…of heathenism." It sounds like *Cambridge* is getting awfully close to speaking of demonic forces from the unseen realms, as well as of literal and physical forces of armies and powers.

Have a look at the use of *kanaph/wings* in the prophecy of Isaiah 8:8:

> Now therefore, behold, the Lord bringeth up upon them the waters of the river, strong and many, even the king of Assyria, and all his glory: and he shall come up over all his channels, and go over all his banks: And he shall pass through Judah; he shall overflow and go over, he shall reach even to the neck; and the stretching out of his [*kanaph*] shall fill the breadth of thy land, O Immanuel. (Isaiah 8:7–8, KJV; emphasis added)

Now consider what the *Benson Commentary* says:

> More literally, And he shall be a desolator by the wing of abominations.… The wing, as well as the flood, is the Hebrew metaphor for great armies. Abominations, in the Jewish style, are idols.[214]

BLOOD ALLIANCE

ANOTHER COMPOUND PROPHECY

Even though various classical and modern commentators interpret the multitudinous and varied elements of Daniel's prophecy with some nuanced differences, almost *all* agree Daniel 9 is also a compound prophecy. Following is a sample reflecting that opinion.

Coffman's Commentaries on the Bible (Daniel 9):

> The destruction of Jerusalem is here plainly included in the seventy weeks; and we have interpreted this to mean that within that time, Christ indeed condemned the city to total destruction, a prophecy actually fulfilled nearly forty years after Christ spoke.... The further references to the destruction of Jerusalem, "the flood," and "the war," etc. are prophecies of the great tribulations that should overwhelm Jerusalem at the times when her doom was executed by the armies of Vespasian and Titus in the year 70 A.D.
>
> Jesus Christ interpreted [the abomination that causes desolation] as an event that would be openly visible to all, saints and sinners alike; he associated it with the destruction of Jerusalem; and **in the light of the fact that the destruction of that city was itself a type of the final holocaust on the eternal Judgment Day, and that many of the conditions existing in God's Israel prior to that event would also be manifested a second time in the New Israel prior to final Judgment, it appears that a second abomination of desolation shall occur in the final days of [the total of humanity's existence] on earth....**
>
> The abomination referred to the gross pollution of the "holy place," a reference to the temple sanctuary, or more properly, the Holy of Holies itself. This was to be the signal that indicated the approaching "desolation," thus it is said that the desolation was to come upon the "wing" of abominations (note the plural), indicating that the desolations would be a direct result of the gross pollution of the holy place.[215] (Emphasis added)

Coffman's understanding of Daniel 9 as a compound prophecy would certainly match up to Yeshua's similar compound prophecy in Matthew 24. *And it should.* After all, it was Yeshua who sent us to Daniel 9!

But then *Coffman's* understanding goes on to wrap up the culmination of Daniel's obviously dual prophetic utterance. That assessment lines up exactly with everything we've uncovered thus far in our New Testament word study:

> Almost certainly, here is the portion of this prophecy [Daniel 9:27] that may be applied to the end of all things culminating in the Final Judgment....
>
> In Christ's **multiple [compound] prophecy** of the end of the world (Matthew 24:9–11), He warned that.... When the time comes that the Church herself has forsaken the fundamentals of her faith in Christ, the abomination that makes desolate shall again appear in the "holy place," in the last instance of it, in the Church herself.[216] (Emphasis added)

In my opinion, *Coffman's* understanding of Daniel 9:27 is accurate. This is especially so in relating Daniel 9 right back to Jesus' prophecy in Matthew 24, as well as to Paul's teaching that the "temple" of the last days is none other than that of the *naos*—the Body of Christ that would be "desecrated" by the man of lawlessness.

However, as previously stated, three passages in Daniel speak of the "abomination that causes desolation." Obviously, Jesus was pointing to one, or all, of those passages in His Matthew 24 discourse.

The other two we'll examine are in Daniel 11 and 12. Each also mentions the cessation of offerings and sacrifices in conjunction with this "abomination" event.

chapter thirty-eight

THE TEMPLE AND THE LAWLESS ONE

If we take a position other than this, we are calling Paul a liar.

By now, we've settled the fact that the New Testament contains the most completely revealed truth regarding *any prophecies* of the last days. At this point, to say otherwise is to travel outside the boundaries of understanding the entire Word of God.[217]

With that in mind, we can acknowledge that the *miqdash/naos* of the last days is "the body of Yeshua," the *ecclesia*. It is the congregation of born-again believers, both Jews and Gentiles, under the Threshold Covenant of Yeshua's blood offering. The Apostle Paul allows no wiggle room at all concerning that fact, and neither do the general principles of contextual biblical interpretation.

So, if the New Testament gives a clear and final definition of a word, concept, or last-days doctrine, then we must interpret the Old Testament view of those last-days things in the same light as the New Testament revelation. The prophecies given in the Old Covenant and the ones given under the New Covenant cannot contradict each other regarding how the last days will unfold.[218]

The Christian Research Institute[219] affirms this as follows:

> While God spoke to Israel through various prophets in the past, the revelation that has come through Christ is more comprehensive because He is no mere prophet, but "the brightness of [God's] glory and the express image of His person."
>
> The New Testament is not a mere appendix added to the writings of the Old Testament prophets. It is a revelation of the new order in Jesus Christ, in whom all previous revelation finds its fulfillment, and through whom all previous revelation must be understood.[220]

Three Daniel "Abomination" Passages

As we wrap up this study, I want to settle a few other important interpretation issues that revolve around the principles I've just mentioned. Those issues concern Daniel 9, 11, and 12—the only three passages that speak of the "abomination that causes desolation." Have a look at each of them.

1. "And for half of the week he shall put an end to sacrifice and offering. And on the **wing** [*kanaph*] of abominations shall come one who makes desolate, until the decreed end is poured out on the desolator"[221] (Daniel 9:27, emphasis added).
2. "Forces from him shall appear and profane the **temple** [*miqdash*] and fortress, and shall take away the regular [daily][222] burnt offering. And they shall set up the abomination that makes desolate" (Daniel 11:31, emphasis added).[223]
3. "And from the time that the regular [daily][224] burnt offering is taken away and the abomination that makes desolate is set up, there shall be 1,290 days." (Daniel 12:11).[225]

The Temple Reference

From all we've learned thus far, we should immediately notice that *only one* of the three passages, Daniel 11, legitimately has a word in the original Hebrew text that could be translated as "temple." But that word is the Hebrew *miqdash*, and it corresponds directly with the Greek *naos*, "the Holy of Holies." According to the New Testament, last-days definition, "temple"/*miqdash*/*naos* has to be referring to the congregation of born-again believers in the final days, and not to some sort of rebuilt structure on the Temple Mount.

Remember, Antichrist is not profaning a *heykal*/*hieron* Temple. Rather, he will be profaning *the congregations* of born-again believers, as 2 Thessalonians 2:4 attests.[226]

The Same Antichrist Figure

Another enormous clue that connects Daniel's "abomination" prophecies to Paul's 2 Thessalonians 2:4 (and following) prophecy is found when comparing Paul's description of the Antichrist with what Daniel says in chapter 11.

Remember what Paul said of the last days in 2 Thessalonians 2:

> Let no one deceive you in any way. For that day will not come, unless the rebellion [*apostasy*, "turning from the truth"] comes first, and the man of lawlessness is revealed, the son of destruction, who opposes and exalts himself against every so-called god or object of worship, so that he takes his seat in the temple of God, [*naos*—the Body of Christ] proclaiming himself to be God. (2 Thessalonians 2:3–4)

Now compare the apostle's words in 2 Thessalonians with the words of Daniel 11:

And the king shall do as he wills. He shall exalt himself and magnify himself above every god, and shall speak astonishing things against the God of gods. He shall prosper till the indignation is accomplished; for what is decreed shall be done.... He shall not pay attention to any other god, for he shall magnify himself above all. (Daniel 11:36–37)

The similarities between those two passages are striking and are recognized by almost all scholarly commentators. Now we know why. Both prophecies, one from the Old Testament and one from the New, ultimately speak of *the very same thing.*

Keil and Delitzsch Biblical Commentary on the Old Testament (Daniel 11):

These words before us [Daniel 11:31–36] are expressly referred to Antichrist, and 2 Thessalonians 2:4.[227]

Jamieson-Fausset-Brown Bible Commentary (Daniel 11):

The willful king here, though primarily Antiochus, is antitypically and mainly Antichrist, the seventh head of the seven-headed and ten-horned beast of Revelation 13:1–18, and the "beast" of Armageddon (Revelation 16:13, 16; 19:19). …who will "plant his tabernacle between the seas in the holy mountain," "exalting himself above every god" (2 Thessalonians 2:4; Revelation 13:5, 6).[228]

Benson Commentary (Daniel 11):

Many of the things that follow may be applied, by way of accommodation, to antichrist, of whom Antiochus was an eminent type.[229]

Ellicott's Commentary for English Readers (Daniel 11):

The character of the northern king, on the contrary, finds a parallel in Paul's description of Antichrist (2 Thessalonians 2:4).[230]

By the time we read through Daniel 9 all the way to chapters 11 and 12, the three passages that refer to "the abomination that causes desolation," we finally see the culmination of the compound nature of Yeshua's prophetic declaration in Matthew 24:

Jamieson-Fausset-Brown Bible Commentary (Daniel 12):

Compare Daniel 12:4, 13; as Daniel 12:6, 7 refer to Daniel 7:25, that is, to the time of Antichrist.... The political resurrection of the Jews under the Maccabees is the starting point of transition to the literal resurrection about to follow the destruction of Antichrist by Christ's coming in glory. The language passes here from the nearer to the more remote event, to which alone it is fully applicable.[231]

Now that we've settled the subject of those prophecies, what about the *stoppage of the sacrifices and offerings* Daniel addresses in all three passages?

That answer is also right before our eyes, and once again, it speaks directly to the Threshold Covenants we make with our Creator.

chapter thirty-nine

OFFERINGS AND SACRIFICES

All this is connected to the threshold that moves
us from the Old Covenant to the New Covenant.

There's yet another observation we must examine when looking at Daniel 9, 11, and 12—the only passages that speak of the "abomination that causes desolation." Each refers to the Antichrist stopping the offerings and sacrifices in the last days. This is where so much modern teaching about a rebuilt Temple goes astray.

Some look at these passages and deduce that they must be referring to a rebuilt Third Temple, because how else could the Jews be performing continual sacrifices if there wasn't a new Temple on the Temple Mount in Jerusalem in the days of Antichrist?

Now you know the answer. Daniel is not seeing a Third Temple with animal sacrifices. He is seeing the *very last days*...the days of Antichrist. Jesus, Paul, and all the New Testament writings have given us the truth about those days—and about what those offerings and sacrifices designate within the context of the age of the ultimate *naos*.

The Apostle Paul said the true Temple/*naos* in the last days is the born-again congregation of believers. He also settled the issue of the "true" last-days "sacrifices" that would be required of the *naos* of the last days. These are the *daily sacrifices* the Beast system will attempt to shut down as the time of Yeshua's return draws closer and closer.

> I appeal to you therefore, brothers, by the mercies of God, to present your bodies as a living sacrifice, holy and acceptable to God, which is your spiritual worship. Do not be conformed to this world, but be transformed by the renewal of your mind, that by testing you may discern what is the will of God, what is good and acceptable and perfect. (Romans 12:1–2)

Meyer's New Testament Commentary (Romans 12:1–2):

> The apostle means quite strictly: your bodies… so that…the sanctification of the whole man distributed into its parts—that of the outer man (set forth as the offering of a sacrifice), and that of the inner (as a renewing transformation)…as a sacrifice which lives. For the…self-offering of the body is the antitypical of the ritual sacrificial service, in which the sacrifice dies; whereas that ethical sacrifice is no doubt also connected with dying, as to sin namely, in the sense of Romans 6:2, Romans 7:4 ff., Colossians 2:20; Colossians 3:5, Galatians 2:19.[232]

THE INNER PARTS, THE OUTER PARTS

Meyer's Commentary says our true worship is the "whole man distributed into its parts." Then it accurately, in Threshold Covenant language, explains the "inner parts" and "outer parts," further stating it is this worship through the New Covenant that brings us from death to life. The old rituals of sacrifice are gone—fulfilled in Yeshua.

We are now crossing over that threshold of the New Covenant. We now become "living sacrifices." The outer parts must come into covenant alignment with the inner parts. Only then will we finally come into full agreement with the blood alliance offered in Jesus Christ! Let me remind you of the striking New Testament pronouncement of this:

> If you **confess with your mouth** [outer parts] that Jesus is Lord and **believe in your heart** [inner parts] that God raised him from the dead, **you will be saved** [you will be in Threshold Covenant agreement with your Creator and Savior]. (Romans 10:9, emphasis added)

Do you now see how everything about our new life in Yeshua keeps coming back to the *Threshold Covenant*? Satan wants to keep this understanding from you. He and his demonic horde desire to hide it from the rest of the world by polluting and diluting it. Don't get caught up in a "rebuilt Third Temple" frenzy. That's a false threshold; it's another Chaldean demonic attempt to sidetrack you from your daily and powerful walk with Yeshua.

And, don't forget, Satan especially wants to keep this reality from the Jewish people! After all, they are God's chosen from the beginning, the ones who would eventually bring all the elements of the Threshold Covenants to the rest of the world through Yeshua.

One Last Perspective

With all of the foregoing artifacts of truth we've uncovered in our spiritual archeological quest, consider the following. When Yeshua, in Matthew 24, says Daniel speaks of the Antichrist "standing in the holy place" and then proclaims "let the reader understand," we now have a fuller picture of exactly what Yeshua was saying to His original disciples—*and us*.

When Yeshua spoke of the "holy place," He didn't use the Greek *naos*, nor did He use the Hebrew *miqdash*. He used the Greek word for "holy," *hagios*, that means "consecrated" or "set apart."[233] Then He used the Greek word *topos* for "place," which simply means any portion of space that is marked off, as in an inhabited area such as a city, village, district, or even designated region.[234]

It would have been simple enough for Yeshua to say, "When you see the abomination that causes desolation standing in a 'rebuilt' Temple (*hieron*)." Instead, He spoke of a "holy place."

The words "let the reader understand" appear to indicate a certain mystery was attached to Yeshua's declaration, and that the unveiling of that secret would come at a later date.[235] And now we understand that the mystery of which He spoke truly did come...*at a later date*.

What we know from Scripture and history is the "holy place" the Jews would have first thought of—the Temple on the Temple Mount—was eventually destroyed, never to rise again. Therefore, almost forty years after the Crucifixion and Resurrection, Yahweh *allowed* for the total destruction of the Old Covenant Temple, and for it to be completely removed from the Temple Mount. The old had been completely fulfilled in Yeshua's death and Resurrection, and the new had come!

And, through Paul's inspired writings, the "understanding" we needed had also finally arrived. The apostle proclaimed it without any misunderstanding about the context and its fullest meaning.

> Don't you know that you yourselves are God's temple and that God's Spirit lives in you? If anyone destroys God's temple, God will destroy him; for God's temple is sacred, and you are that temple. (1 Corinthians 3:16–17, NIV)

This is what Yeshua was ultimately talking about! The last-days body of born-again believers is the "holy place," the *naos*, or the "temple" of God. Thus, it is also what Daniel was talking about in chapters 9, 11, and 12 regarding the last days of the end time...*because Yeshua said so*. It's plain and simple. And all of this is connected to the threshold that moves us from the Old Covenant to the New Covenant![236]

Next, we'll explore the most mysterious depths of our spiritual digging site, now bathed in the biblical light of what we've already uncovered. What we find should illuminate the Word of God, the Threshold Covenant, and the reality of life in *Yeshua Ha Mashiach* like never before.

PART VII

Ezekiel's Temple Vision

Many would see Ezekiel's expansive vision of the Temple as encouraging a belief that there will be an end-time Temple matching Ezekiel's prophetic description. Yet a biblical theologian cannot approach this prophecy without noting the way in which this prophecy is understood by the New Testament writers.[237]

—Dr. Johnathan Menn

chapter forty

Ezekiel's Heykal

Understanding everything you've discovered in our previous chapters; you'll now see what Ezekiel saw.

With all of the exploration into the "Temple frenzy" and the corresponding Chaldean deception we've been through in the preceding chapters, how in the world do we interpret Ezekiel's vision of a seemingly new Temple that is often interpreted as one that will be standing in the very last days?

Let me first admit, along with almost the majority of classical commentators, that chapters 40–48 of the book of Ezekiel can certainly appear to be mystifying. This is especially true if one has never made the biblical and linguistic connections we've made in the foregoing chapters, as well as the ones we'll unearth in the next couple of chapters.

Those nine rather tedious chapters in Ezekiel, at first reading, appear to be describing a literal *heykal/hieron* that will be rebuilt sometime far into Israel's distant future. It seems to be complete with animal sacrifices, a very special high priest called "the prince," and almost all the trappings of the original Temple of Solomon—except this one looks to be a structure that's on steroids! It is grandiose in a humanly impossible sense.

However, because we are now snapping all of the language links together, we are finally equipped to take much of the mystery out of Ezekiel's vision.

Ezekiel tells us in the first five verses of chapter 40 that he has had a magnificently divine revelation. It was a journey that took him into an unspecified time in the distant future. His vision occurs twenty-five years after the exile of God's people began, and in the fourteenth year of the fall of Jerusalem and Solomon's Temple to Nebuchadnezzar of Babylon (the Chaldeans). Here's what Ezekiel saw:

> In the twenty-fifth year of our exile, at the beginning of the year, on the tenth day of the month, in the fourteenth year after the city was struck down, on that very day, the hand of the LORD was upon me, and he brought me to the city.
>
> In visions of God he brought me to the land of Israel, and set me down on a very high mountain, on which was a structure like a city to the south. When he brought me there, behold, there was a man whose appearance was like bronze, with a linen cord and a measuring reed in his hand. And he was standing in the gateway.
>
> And the man said to me, "Son of man, look with your eyes, and hear with your ears, and set your heart upon all that I shall show you, for you were brought here in order that I might show it to you. Declare all that you see to the house of Israel."
>
> And behold, there was a wall all around the outside of the **temple area**, [*bayith*] and the length of the measuring reed in the man's hand was six long cubits, each being a cubit and a handbreadth in length. (Ezekiel 40:1–5, emphasis added)

Word Nuances

Notice the Hebrew word *bayith* in brackets in the last verse of the above passage.[238] Almost all English translations insert the word "temple" there.

But neither of the Hebrew words for "temple"—*heykal* and *miqdash*—is in the original text. The Hebrew word used is *bayith*. And the most used translation of that word throughout the entire Bible, including a huge chunk of Ezekiel, is "house" or "household."[239]

This is an amazing connection to make in conjunction with Ezekiel's vision of the last-days Temple! Observe how the New Testament authors, and Yeshua Himself, use the term "house"/"household" in its fullest sense of the last-days *naos*, or "temple," of God.

> If I delay, you may know how one ought to behave in the **household of God**, which is the church of the living God, a pillar and buttress of the truth. (1 Timothy 3:15, emphasis added)

> [In Yeshua] So then you are no longer strangers and aliens, but you are fellow citizens with the saints and members of the **household of God**. (Ephesians 2:19, emphasis added)

> [Yeshua said,] In **my Father's house** are many rooms. If it were not so, would I have told you that I go to prepare a place for you? (John 14:2, emphasis added)

> But Christ is faithful over **God's house** as a son. And **we are his house,** if indeed we hold fast our confidence and our boasting in our hope. (Hebrews 3:6, emphasis added)

A Glimpse of Perfection

In short, Ezekiel is experiencing a *vision* of something that will be perfectly revealed in the future to all the people of God—Jews and Gentiles alike. I point this out because a *vision* is much different than a set of specific *instructions* given through a one-on-one encounter with God, as in the way Moses received instructions concerning the construction of the first tabernacle in the wilderness or how Noah received details about building the ark. The same was true with Solomon's directives about how to build the First Temple and regarding the Temple Mount.

On the other hand, Ezekiel is not directed to "build" anything. Instead, he is being shown something that has already been built. And he's shown it in a *symbolic* format. Ezekiel's vision is meant to be interpreted *spiritually*. It speaks of the culmination of all things, matters that tie directly into what we now know as the book of Revelation—a completed disclosure that was to come more than 2,500 years into Ezekiel's earthly future.

In Ezekiel's day, however, his vision served to comfort his people in the only way their ancient Hebrew minds could at least partially comprehend and spiritually look toward. After all, the entire Christ event was still far off, and the concept of the ultimate *Body of Christ* or the *household of God* as the genuine and final *naos* would have been impossible for the Jewish mind to comprehend in Ezekiel's day. So God was speaking "their language"—*temple language*—through Ezekiel's vision.

But what they were actually given in that vision was an account of the divinely perfected Temple of the last days, with the "prince," representative of Yeshua, offering perfect sacrifices (eventually completed in Yeshua) that were entirely pleasing to the Lord.

> It is for **the prince; the prince,** he shall sit in it to eat bread before the Lord; he shall enter by the way of the porch of that gate, and shall go out by the way of the same. (Ezekiel 44:3, emphasis added)

Ellicott's Commentary:

> The prince.—The Rabbis understood this to refer to the Messiah, and unquestionably the same person must be meant as by David in Ezekiel 34:23–24; Ezekiel 37:24. This gives another and a conclusive reason for regarding the sacrificial worship of Ezekiel 46 as symbolical.[240]

Barnes' Notes on the Bible:

The new system gives to the "prince" a privilege which he did not before possess; the prince, as the representative of the Messiah, standing in a higher position than the kings of old.[241]

Jamieson-Fausset-Brown Bible Commentary:

The Prince...represents Messiah, who entered heaven, the true sanctuary, by a way that none other could, namely, by His own holiness; all others must enter as sinners by faith in His blood, through grace.[242]

It is also apparent from Ezekiel's vision that this temple was to last forever! It would never be destroyed, and all who were a part of that "house" would always be with God; they would never go into exile again! All things would be made new within that idealistically presented "temple."

This genuine final Temple, or *naos*, as Paul and John called it, is presented as a huge and all-encompassing *household*, one that would stand throughout eternity...and located in the midst of a perfected "city."

On top of all of this, Ezekiel was given a glimpse of this future glory from a "high mountain" in Jerusalem...in the same way John was shown the vision of that same new "city of God" in Revelation 21.

Come, I will show you the Bride, [the ultimate household of God] the wife of the Lamb." And he carried me away in the Spirit to a great, high mountain, and showed me the holy city Jerusalem coming down out of heaven from God. (Revelation 21:9–10)

A number of trusted biblical scholars see the direct connection between Revelation 21 and Ezekiel 40–48.[243]

Scholarly Connections

Following is how a conservative online commentary site, Got Questions. org, states the substance of what we've uncovered in our exploration into Ezekiel's Temple.

> In the figurative view of Ezekiel's temple, the prophet's vision simply reiterates that God will once again dwell with His people in a perfect relationship. This relationship is described in the language that the people of the day (and especially for Ezekiel as a priest) would have understood—a Jewish temple of magnificent proportions, with regular, perfect sacrifices, with the Messiah presiding, and with the glory of God visibly evident.
>
> In later visions to other prophets, God revealed more about how He would accomplish this with the Messiah Himself replacing the temple, the sacrifices, and the land. The presence of God through the indwelling of the Holy Spirit would be more immediately evident than ever before.
>
> The fulfillment of Ezekiel's temple could thus be realized in the church age to some degree and, in the age to come, to perfection. The vision of Ezekiel's temple says that God has not forsaken His people and that His relationship with them will be restored and elevated to a new, never-before-conceived glory and intimacy. Present circumstances should never cause one to doubt the promises of God.[244] (Parentheses in original)

The *Jamieson-Fausset-Brown Bible Commentary* agrees with what we've laid forth on this topic. Following is a paragraph from it regarding Ezekiel's Temple. A much fuller rendering of the commentary entry is given at the endnote link.[245]

> In Revelation 21:22 "no temple" is seen, as in the perfection of the new dispensation the (elements) of place and form are no lon-

ger needed to realize to Christians what Ezekiel imparts to Jewish minds by the imagery familiar to them.[246] (Parentheses in original)

The *Jamieson-Fausset-Brown Commentary* also sees the direct link between the prophets John and Ezekiel, men of God who are separated by about 2,500 years. Those prophets saw that glorious city of God that is soon to come—that is, the heavenly city and the true Temple about which the stuff of hymns and praise songs are sung to this very day.

Dr. Jonathan Menn,[247] a contemporary biblical commentator and the author of *Biblical Eschatology (Ezekiel's Vision of a New Temple: Ezekiel 40–48)*, summarizes this topic as follows:

> The integration of the apostles together with the tribes of Israel as part of the city-temple's structure [Revelation 21:12–14]... confirms...that the multiracial Christian church [Jew and Gentile—one new man] will be the redeemed group who, together with Christ, will fulfill Ezekiel's prophecy of the future temple and city. This is in line with other NT passages in which the whole covenant community forms a spiritual temple where God's presence dwells (1 Cor. 3:16–17; 6:19; 2 Cor. 6:16; Eph. 2:21–22; 1 Pet. 2:5)
>
> Many would see Ezekiel's expansive vision of the Temple as encouraging a belief that there will be an end-time Temple matching Ezekiel's prophetic description. Yet a biblical theologian cannot approach this prophecy without noting the way in which this prophecy is understood by the New Testament writers.
>
> Ezekiel's imagery of the river flowing from the Temple (Ezek. 47:1ff) reappears twice in the New Testament. In John 7:37–39 the "rivers of living water" flow from Jesus himself; meanwhile in Revelation the "river of the water of life" flows through the middle of the New Jerusalem (Rev. 22:1ff).
>
> These two [books—John and Revelation] have consciously drawn upon Ezekiel's prophecy and applied it to Jesus and the

heavenly Jerusalem. As a result, they were presumably not expecting Ezekiel's prophecy to be fulfilled literally at some future point in a physical Temple. Instead this prophecy became a brilliant way of speaking pictorially of what God had now achieved in and through Jesus.

Paradoxically, therefore, although Ezekiel's vision had focused so much upon the Temple, it found its ultimate fulfillment in that city where there was "no Temple", because "its Temple is the Lord God Almighty and the Lamb" (Rev. 21:22).[248] (Parentheses in original)

Next, we'll explore how the Ezekiel-Revelation relationship comes into a much more enhanced view and understanding.

chapter forty-one

THE REVELATION-EZEKIEL LINK

> Ezekiel saw the ultimate household/Temple under the
> lordship of the ultimate Great High Priest: Yeshua.

In Revelation 21, John the Revelator finally gets to lay his eyes upon Ezekiel's "city" and "temple," or "household." He even mentions the conspicuous absence of a literal Temple in the city's midst.

John sees something far more glorious than what he could have imagined. He sees what Ezekiel saw, but now John can describe the essence of Ezekiel's mystical vision in light of its fullest revelation. That revelation is found in the crucified and resurrected Yeshua *Ha Mashiach* alone.

> And he that talked with me had a golden reed to measure the city, and the gates thereof, and the wall thereof....And I saw no **temple** [*naos*] **therein: for the Lord God Almighty and the Lamb are the temple** [*naos*] **of it.** (Revelation 21:15, 22; emphasis added)

Notice John sees the city, the wall, and the gates—and the consummation of what the "temple" actually *means*. Notice also he uses the Greek word *naos*, not *hieron*, in Revelation 21. In fact, as noted before, John *never* uses the word *hieron* throughout the book of Revelation. Now you know why! These prophetic elements were all the same things Ezekiel saw. Ezekiel used these "temple-styled" descriptions to comfort the people who were living in the Chaldean/Babylonian exile…and who had experienced the horrifying destruction of Solomon's Temple.

The Bigger and Grander Picture

Think of this next point. If the Temple had *always* represented everything about the Messiah who was to come—as the New Testament clearly reveals—from the sacrifices to the role of the Great High Priest and the Holy of Holies itself, then what did the *destruction* of Solomon's Temple and the Second rebuilt Temple represent? This next revelation ought to take your breath away.

Based upon all we've connected thus far, here is the link: Solomon's Temple did indeed represent the Messiah who was to come in Yeshua. But that first and glorious Temple was destroyed by the Chaldeans. See the connection?

Why did God allow it to be destroyed by the Chaldeans? Because His people, the Jewish people, had turned from Him and made a mockery of the Temple—*which ultimately represented Yeshua*—and its sacrificial rituals (see Ezekiel 9). And, of all things, the wrath of God began at the threshold of the very Temple they were defiling with their sin.

> Then **the glory of the God of Israel ascended from the cherub** on which it had been, **to the threshold of the temple.**… So they went out and struck the city. And while they were striking, and I was left alone, I [Ezekiel] fell upon my face, and cried, "Ah, Lord God! **Will you destroy all the remnant of Israel in the outpouring of your wrath on Jerusalem?**" (Ezekiel 9:3, 7–8; emphasis added)

So, the marauding Gentiles (the Chaldeans under Nebuchadnezzar) and the idolatrous and unrepentant Jews, together, were eventually responsible for destroying the Temple.

Destroy This Temple...

All of this was very similar to what happened under the Roman Empire during Yeshua's earthly ministry. But then it was reaching its culmination in *Yeshua Ha Mashiach*. The Jewish Sanhedrin, along with the rabbis, scribes, and elders, joined with the Roman authorities and literally caused the "destruction" of God's perfect earthly Temple...the physical body of Yeshua the Messiah.

In the destruction of Yeshua's flesh-and-blood body, both Jew and Gentile stood condemned for profaning God's genuine Temple. The Messiah had been sacrificed. The Lamb had been slain. The blood of the Lamb was now poured into the Threshold Covenant "groover." All who would *cross over* it would be allowed to come inside and dwell with their Creator in perfect union and fellowship...in His *household*. However, all who stepped *on* the threshold and rejected Yahweh's offer were cut off from the Father's house—they had trampled on the blood of Yeshua (Hebrews 10:29).

Don't forget the pointed words of Yeshua Himself regarding this matter:

> Jesus answered them, "**Destroy this temple** [*naos*], and **I will raise it again in three days.**" The Jews replied, "It has taken forty-six years to build this temple, and you are going to raise it in three days?" But the **temple** [*naos*] he had spoken of was **his body.** (John 2:19–21, NIV; emphasis added)

> [Jesus said.] I tell you that one greater than the **temple** [*naos*] is here. (Matthew 12:6–7, NIV; emphasis added)

Now have a look at classical scholar Charles John Ellicott's comments on the preceding information, as he also understands the links with Ezekiel's Temple vision.

Ellicott's Commentary for English Readers:

And I saw no temple therein…for the Lord God the Almighty is her temple, and the Lamb.

In Ezekiel's vision the vast and splendid proportions of the Temple formed a conspicuous part: its gigantic proportions declared it to be figurative (Ezekiel 48:8–20); but the present vision passes on to a higher state of things. "I saw no temple:"

Ezekiel's vision declared that the literal temple would be replaced by a far more glorious spiritual temple.…

Tongues, prophecies, knowledge, may pass away (1 Corinthians 13:9; Ephesians 4:11–13); [church buildings and denominations] will disappear, absorbed in the one glorious [Body of Yeshua]; ministries, missionary organizations, helps, governments, may cease.

There God is all. The Lord is there—the temple, the sanctuary, the dwelling-place of His people. (Comp. Ezekiel 48:35.) Every merely local aspect of worship is at an end.[249] (John 4:21–24).

None of the things we've unearthed so far have ever been hidden from God's people. The spiritual essence and sometimes even the specific details of these truths have been right before us in the Word of God for thousands of years. The only obfuscation of these facts has come through the demonic horde of the Chaldean incursion, and/or the rather shocking indifference of God's own people regarding how all of these biblical truths tie together.

King David Saw It, Too

In 2 Samuel 7, in an account of something that took place more than three thousand years ago, we read that God gave King David a glimpse of this coming glory, the glory that is the true and eternal Temple of God in *Yeshua Ha Mashiach:*

> When your [King David's] days are fulfilled and you lie down with your fathers, I will raise up your offspring after you, who shall come from your body, and I will establish his kingdom. He shall build a house for my name, and I will establish the throne of his kingdom forever. (2 Samuel 7:12–13)

God is promising that through David's "seed"—even beyond David's son Solomon—would come One who would finally build the house/household for Yahweh (see Psalm 89:29). His throne would be established forever! That One is none other than *Yeshua Ha Mashiach.* This is what Ezekiel saw as well. He saw the ultimate household/Temple, eventually to be under the lordship of the ultimate High Priest, Yeshua.

Coffman's Commentary on Revelation 21 mentions that passage in 2 Samuel 7 as being fulfilled in John's vision:

> The Lord God the Almighty, and the Lamb.... These are the temple thereof. Christ is the only true temple of God that this earth ever saw; and it includes also his spiritual body the church. This is the temple which God promised David that "his seed" would build. (2 Samuel 7:12, 13)[250]

Barnes' Notes on the Bible (2 Samuel 7):

> The words forever, emphatically twice repeated in 2 Samuel 7:16, show very distinctly that this prophecy looks beyond the succession of the kings of Judah of the house of David, and embraces the throne of Christ according to the Angel's interpretation given in Luke 1:31–33, where the reference to this passage cannot be mistaken.... This is also brought out fully in Psalm 89:29, Psalm 89:36–37. See also Daniel 7:13–14;

Isaiah 9:6–7; Jeremiah 23:5–6; Jeremiah 33:14–21; Ezekiel 34:24; Zechariah 12:7–8; Hosea 3:5… John 1:12; Ephesians 1:20–22; 1 Timothy 3:15; Hebrews 3:6; etc.; and Zechariah 6:12–13.[251]

Pulpit Commentary (2 Samuel 7):

We can scarcely, therefore, be wrong in the conviction that these promises pointed onwards to the establishment of Christ's kingdom, and that the great importance attached to the building of the temple finds its explanation in its relation to Him.[252]

With the foregoing discoveries in mind, let's now move to the book of Hebrews. Within the revelations of that New Testament book, we see the same things proclaimed in Hebrews that we observed through the words of Jesus, Paul, Ezekiel, and Daniel.

chapter forty-two

THE HEBREWS CONNECTION

In truth, Ezekiel's vision is of the last-days *naos* of God, the congregation of the Threshold Covenant-keepers—the true family of God.

Out of the twenty-seven books of the New Testament, the book of Hebrews contains the third-greatest number of Old Testament quotes and references. Revelation is number one in this regard, and the book of Matthew holds the second-highest count of quotes from the Tanakh.[253]

However, Hebrews offers the broadest picture of the ultimate Temple and Yeshua's identification with it that is presented in a single New Testament book.

An article from the Christian Research Institute, "Making Sense of Ezekiel's Temple Vision," highlights the connections between the book of Hebrews and the prophecy of Ezekiel 40–48.

> Biblical scholars acknowledge that the temple vision, which occupies the last nine chapters of Ezekiel, presents special challenges

in its interpretation. Some have even described it as the most difficult passage in the Old Testament....

Hebrews 1:1–3 affirms that, while God spoke to Israel through various prophets in the past, the revelation that has come through Christ is more comprehensive because He is no mere prophet, but "the brightness of [God's] glory and the express image of His person." ...Christ opened the understanding of His disciples so that they "might understand the [Old Testament] scriptures" (Luke 24:45).

This being the case, it would be foolish for us to seek a meaning of the prophets [including Ezekiel 40–48] contrary to that which Christ and the apostles taught. It is their witness that provides the strongest objections to any literalistic interpretation of Ezekiel 40. In Christ's new order (which, unlike the old order, is permanent), the temple, priesthood, and sacrifices are likewise spiritual (1 Peter 2:5).

...The new revelation in Christ encourages us to see its pattern as having been fulfilled in Jesus Christ Himself, who is the final atoning sacrifice and the eternal high priest of God's people.[254]

A Revelation for the Jews

The introductory verses of Hebrews declare that Yeshua is the personification and the indisputable fulfillment of *all things* regarding the Messiah and the ancient Temple sacrifices. The book begins by attesting that Yeshua is God with us and the Creator of all things:

> Long ago, at many times and in many ways, God spoke to our fathers by the prophets, but in these last days he has spoken to us by his Son, whom he appointed the heir of all things, through whom also he created the world. He is the radiance of the glory of God and the exact imprint of his nature, and he upholds the uni-

verse by the word of his power. After making purification for sins, he sat down at the right hand of the Majesty on high. (Hebrews 1:1–3)

The writer of Hebrews continues by making it clear that, as the Creator and Savior of all humanity, *Yeshua* is far superior to any "angelic being." Yet He is "honored" to call us His "brothers"—that is, those of us who have willfully chosen to participate in the new (Threshold) Covenant (Hebrews 1–2)…Jew and Gentile:

For he who sanctifies and those who are sanctified all have one source. That is why he is not ashamed to call them brothers. (Hebrews 2:11)

THE HOUSEHOLD CONNECTION

And, of all things, Hebrews 3 attests that Yeshua is the head of "God's house," and that the born-again congregation of believers is that house (3:4–6). Moses is called the "builder" of the house, but Yeshua is called the Son who is "over" the house.

For every house is built by someone, but the builder of all things is God. Now Moses was faithful in all God's house as a servant, to testify to the things that were to be spoken later, but Christ is faithful over God's house as a son. And we are his house, if indeed we hold fast our confidence and our boasting in our hope. (Hebrews 3:4–6)

We've already seen in the last chapter that Ezekiel's Temple is literally identified by the Hebrew word *bayith*…the "house" or the "household" of God, and is expressed in a glorified vision in a *temple format* given especially for the ancient Jewish mind. But, in truth, Ezekiel's vision is of the last-days *naos* of God, the congregation of the Threshold Covenant-keepers—the true family of God.

Dr. Peter Pett[255] is a popular contemporary biblical scholar. In *Pett's Commentary on the Bible* concerning Ezekiel's vision of chapters 40–48, he shares the following insight. Note he also connects Ezekiel to the book of Hebrews in the New Testament.

> Ezekiel is in fact here speaking of an everlasting sanctuary (Ezekiel 37:26; Ezekiel 37:28). This is no earthly Temple with earthly functions. There is no suggestion anywhere that it should be built, indeed it was already there and could be measured. It is an everlasting heavenly Temple of which the earthly was, and will be, but a shadow....
>
> A fuller picture of the heavenly temple is given throughout the Book of Revelation. And this temple was now 'seen' to be established in the land even before a physical temple was built. God had again taken possession of His land, and awaited the return of His people for the ongoing of His purposes....
>
> But a further point, putting these verses firmly in its context, is that this will make them [the Jews in exile] realize...they will be able to enter the eternal rest promised them by God, for His heavenly, everlasting temple was here so that He could dwell among them in an everlasting sanctuary. This was thus putting in terms that they could understand the heavenly future that awaited His people. It was a fuller and more perfect sanctuary (Ezekiel 37:26–28; Hebrews 9:11).[256]

This household family of God, spoken of in Ezekiel's vision and the book of Hebrews, is the last-days *naos* the Apostle Paul revealed in the book of Ephesians...the only Third Temple that was to come in the last days. That Temple is now here in *Yeshua Ha Mashiach*—the Body of Christ, the congregation of born-again believers, the household of God... the *true Temple*. Here is how Paul puts it:

> But now in Christ Jesus you who once were far off have been brought near by the blood of Christ...that he might create in himself one new man in place of the two, so making peace, and might reconcile us both to God in one body through the cross, thereby killing the hostility.
>
> So then you are no longer strangers and aliens, but you are fellow citizens with the saints and members of the **household of God**, built on the foundation of the apostles and prophets, Christ Jesus himself being the cornerstone, in whom the whole structure, being joined together, grows into a holy temple in the Lord.
>
> In him you also are being built together **into a dwelling place for God** by the Spirit [a new *household*[257]]. (Ephesians 2:19–22, emphasis added)

Notice Paul's distinctive Threshold Covenant language and imagery. He speaks of being brought into God's *house* by the blood sacrifice of the true Lamb, Jesus Christ. To lawfully come into any "house," one must first step over a doorway threshold, and this must be done in complete agreement with the owner's stipulations.

Then, invoking the language of Ezekiel's vision of chapters 40–48, Paul describes the joining together of Jew and Gentile under that new blood alliance as a "temple" (Greek: *naos*). Paul even employs the specific language Ezekiel used to describe that completed dwelling as a "household" (Hebrew: *bayith*).[258]

As stated earlier, the Threshold Covenant language is found throughout the Word of God, in both the Old and New Covenant imagery of the last days. You can never again un-see it once you know what you are looking at and why the link to it is biblically stated over and over again.

Part VIII

Remember the Sabbath

For the Son of Man is Lord of the Sabbath.

—Matthew 12:8

chapter forty-three

THE SABBATH THRESHOLD

Immediately we observe that God set the example for us.

The topic of the Sabbath has been quite controversial for ages, and with good reason. There is a ton of distorted information out there that we must wade through to reach the biblical understanding of the Sabbath and the genuine heart of the Sabbath law. The confusion, as you might imagine, is another diabolical exploitation by the Chaldean spirit, which is hiding yet another divine aspect of the Threshold Covenant God has so graciously opened. It's what the Chaldeans do best! I pray these next chapters will set the matter straight.

Always remember: Mere feelings, perceptions, personal preferences, or even honest misinformation do not negate the unadulterated truth of God's Word. Neither do they cancel out what Yeshua Himself asserts about the subject. At the end of it all, Yeshua's opinion is really the only one that counts!

Let me remind you what the Christian Research Institute[259] expresses about this fundamental truth:

While God spoke to Israel through various prophets in the past, the revelation that has come through Christ is more comprehensive because He is no mere prophet, but "the brightness of [God's] glory and the express image of His person."

The New Testament is not a mere appendix added to the writings of the Old Testament prophets. It is a revelation of the new order in Jesus Christ, in whom all previous revelation finds its fulfillment, and through whom all previous revelation must be understood.[260]

In the Beginning

Think of this question for just a moment: Why did God give us the Sabbath in the first place? We find the answer in the second chapter of Genesis. There, we are told what the Lord Himself did on that very first *seventh day*:

> And on the seventh day God finished his work that he had done, and he rested on the seventh day from all his work that he had done. So God blessed the seventh day and made it holy, because on it God rested from all his work that he had done in creation. (Genesis 2:2–3)

Immediately, we observe that God set the example for us: He "rested." I put that word in quotes, because God does not *need* rest the same way we do. He is not human. He has no physical need to recuperate from His labor. Literally, the Hebrew word for "rest" means He "ceased" His creative activities and just enjoyed Himself by glorying in what He had created![261]

The Lord's Delight

Perhaps He feasted His eyes upon the beauty of the trees and oceans, sunrises and sunsets, horses racing across plains, turtles lumbering across the sands of beautiful beaches, and the roar of pounding and receding waves. And, most of all, He surely would have taken His greatest delight in observing the beings He had made in His own image…the beautiful, perfect specimens of humanity walking majestically through creation.

However, notice Yahweh did not call for a worship meeting on that first Sabbath. Nor did He "demand" one to be held by the heavenly host. There was not a *required* gathering of the heavenly beings to mark the last day of Creation. Yet the angels surrounding Him on that monumentally glorious occasion voluntarily, as an internally conceived act of worship, broke into jubilation. In that moment, they literally shouted for joy… and they sang!

> [The Lord spoke unto Job,]Where were you when I laid the foundation of the earth? Tell me, if you have understanding. Who determined its measurements—surely you know! Or who stretched the line upon it? On what were its bases sunk, or who laid its cornerstone, when the morning stars sang together and all the sons of God shouted for joy? (Job 38:4–7)

Note however, that the adoration of Yahweh by the heavenly host was spontaneous, as it certainly should have been. Think of what they had just witnessed!

But it is also important to consider that there was no *divine command* for a communal worship service to be held on that first Sabbath, or on any other day. Instead, the whole event was bathed in a loving relationship, one combining the admiration God had for His new creation with the angelic beings' impulse to praise Him and thank Him for what He had done in their presence.

Once again, in case you think I'm nitpicking the words of Scripture, I'm not. We still have much more to disclose.

Right now, I'm merely reminding you of what God's Word actually says and *does not say*. In doing this, we are setting a foundation for the proper interpretation of every revelation that will soon follow.

Now…have you ever thought about the fact that we never see *anything* in the Bible about a Sabbath requirement until *several thousand years* after Creation,[262] and not until the children of Israel have finally been freed from slavery in Egypt?

chapter forty-four

THE CODIFICATION OF THE SABBATH

Yahweh said, "Stop! Stop and rest." He is saying,
through the Sabbath: "Honor what I have done for you."

Several thousand years from the first seventh-day rest the universe had ever experienced, the Lord emphasized the importance of taking a Sabbath day by carving it into stone. In so doing, He gave His people what we now know as the Fourth Commandment.

Consider the following significant, yet often missed, perspective penned by Dr. J. B. Coffman, author of *Coffman's Commentary on the Bible*:

> There is no sabbath commandment in Genesis; there is not even an indication that Adam knew anything about God resting on the sabbath day (Genesis 3:2).
>
> In Genesis, Moses was merely stating, generations and millenniums after the fact, what God had done in the remote ages long

before Moses wrote Genesis. Historically, the very first revelation of any such thing as the sabbath came not to Adam, but to Moses.

"Thou camest down also upon Mount Sinai, and spakest with them from heaven, and gavest them right judgments, true laws, good statutes and commandments: And madest known unto them thy holy sabbath…by the hand of Moses thy servant" (Nehemiah 9:13–14, KJV).

Conclusion: The sabbath observance did not antedate the Law of Moses; the sabbath was unknown prior to Moses, else God could not have revealed it to him.

Significantly, the reason God assigned for requiring Israel to keep the sabbath was not prior existence of the institution but their deliverance from bondage.[263]

The first time Scripture records that the actual *Sabbath law* was given was to God's "called-out" people at Sinai. They were those who had come out of Egyptian slavery under the Threshold Covenant of Passover. Remember, as we read in Leviticus 23, the Passover covenant that brought them out of Egypt and freed them from slavery began with an ordinance that was ultimately pointing to its final fulfillment in *Yeshua Ha Mashiach*! It is the same great truth we born-again believers celebrate every single Passover week concerning the Crucifixion and Resurrection of Yeshua. That great truth is crucially important to the entire matter of Sabbath law.

The Egyptian "refugees" were also the people who would eventually comprise the divinely designated nation of Israel. This would be the nation promised to Abraham through the first biblically recorded covenant-cutting.

Little did they know at the time they would also become the nation through which Yahweh would bring the Tanakh (the Old Testament), the prophecies of the coming New Covenant (Jeremiah 31), and the Messiah of God Himself (Genesis 3:15, Psalm 22, Isaiah 7:14, Isaiah 9, Isaiah 53, Zechariah 12, Micah 5, Malachi 3, etc.). Nor did they know all these elements would eventually be used to construct the Threshold Covenant of God's offer of salvation to the entire planet.

And don't forget, it would be primarily through the Jewish people that the first Old Covenant Gospel of salvation would also be preached. The Passover faith proclaimed, "Get under the blood of the Lamb! Cross over the threshold of Yahweh and make covenant with Him. Do this by your unbridled faith in Him alone, and then you and your families will be saved. You will be passed over from God's wrath!"

Those people were the called-out ones to whom the Sabbath law was first given. To the Jews first, and then to the Gentiles—all were under the same blood-bought covenant of the properly sacrificed Lamb of God. They didn't come out of Egypt under a law—they came out by their *faith in the blood alliance* they had "cut" with Yahweh, as given to them by Moses.

Following is that Fourth Commandment issued at Sinai. Notice what it says and, like we've done before, especially notice what it *does not* say:

Remember the Sabbath day, to keep it holy [reverently separate]. Six days you shall labor, and do all your work, but the seventh day is a Sabbath to the Lord your God.

On it you shall not do any work, you, or your son, or your daughter, your male servant, or your female servant, or your livestock, or the sojourner who is within your gates.

For in six days the Lord made heaven and earth, the sea, and all that is in them, and rested on the seventh day. Therefore the Lord blessed the Sabbath day and made it holy. (Exodus 20:8–11)

In that commandment, God said He created the Sabbath as a time of *rest* for both humans and beasts of burden. This rest was not set aside as some sort of supreme test of their love for Him. It was given as an act of love *to them*...from Him!

When Yahweh eventually put on flesh and tabernacled among us in the person of Yeshua, He punctuated that truth with these words:

And He said to them, "The sabbath was made for man, not man for the sabbath. So the Son of Man is lord even of the sabbath." (Mark 2:27–28)

Knowing how most fallen humans are prone to go after things of the world—like acquiring wealth and laboring away on the stuff of life they love until they drop—Yahweh said, "Stop! Stop and rest." He is saying, through the Sabbath: "Honor what I have done for you. Acknowledge what I have given you! Take a breath, and rest. In this way, you are also identifying with Me, and I with you."

The *Pulpit Commentary* states the matter beautifully:

> The Sabbath was instituted for the benefit of man, that he might refresh and renew his body, fatigued and worn by six days' labor, with the restful calm of the seventh; and that he might have leisure to apply his mind to the things which concern his everlasting salvation; to consider and meditate upon the Law of God; and rouse himself, by the remembrance of the Divine greatness and goodness, to true repentance, to gratitude, and to love. The force of the argument is this: The Sabbath was made on account of man, not man on account of the Sabbath.
>
> Therefore Christ was justified in permitting to his disciples a little labor in plucking these ears of corn on the Sabbath day, in order that they may appease their hunger. For it is better that the rest of the Sabbath should be disturbed, though but a little, than that any one of those for whose sake the Sabbath was instituted should perish.[264]

I know what you may be thinking at this point: "But doesn't it say somewhere in the Scriptures that a 'holy convocation' should be held on the Sabbath? Isn't that a command to collectively worship on that day as well?"

Yes. The Scriptures do say there should be a "convocation" or "assembly" on that day. But what does "convocation" even mean? And how was it historically practiced?

chapter forty-five

THE HOLY CONVOCATION

How could any "authority" insist upon such an assembly once they were in the Promised Land, and once the several million original people who left Egypt multiplied into millions more?

Everything we've said so far has been confirmed in Scripture. The context, and therefore the proper meaning, until this point, is awfully hard to dispute.

But what about passages that speak of the Sabbath requirement of a "holy convocation" or a "holy assembly" to be held by God's people?[265] Doesn't that cancel out what we've said thus far about no direct command in the Word of God requiring us to gather for an ordered service of worship?

THE SCRIPTURE

First let's look at what God's Word says about this convocation. The first of the following passages speaks of the "special sabbaths" that begin and end the week of Unleavened Bread (Passover). The second regards the actual weekly occurrence of the *seventh-day Sabbath*.

1. Regarding the Feast of Unleavened Bread

> This day shall be for you a memorial day, and you shall keep it as a feast to the LORD; throughout your generations, as a statute forever, you shall keep it as a feast. Seven days you shall eat unleavened bread...
>
> On the first day you shall hold a holy assembly, and on the seventh day a holy assembly. No work shall be done on those days. But what everyone needs to eat, that alone may be prepared by you. (Exodus 12: 14–16)

2. Regarding the weekly Sabbath

> Six days shall work be done, but on the seventh day is a Sabbath of solemn rest, a holy convocation. You shall do no work. It is a Sabbath to the LORD in all your dwelling places. (Leviticus 23:3)

These convocations were traditionally called to attention with the sounding of trumpets/shofars.

THE REHEARSAL

Let's make certain we understand the nuances of word meanings in these two passages and others like them. The Hebrew word for the noun "convocation" is *miqra*, which does speak of a sacred assembly. Even more intimately, it is also defined as a "rehearsal."[266] Now that's interesting!

The idea of *miqra* is much the same as a rehearsal before a wedding. That occasion could also be thought of as a "holy convocation." In this illustration, the wedding rehearsal itself is indeed an important event, and often it's passionately celebratory, but it's not the "real" thing. The actual marriage comes only with the completion of the marriage ceremony when the vows are exchanged between husband and wife. This is usually done much more formally, and in front of witnesses, then continues with the couple living as husband and wife.

By the way, that marriage relationship is also a covenant relationship. It usually involves crossing a *threshold* that is both spiritual and physical. In the spiritual realm, the two people become "one." In the physical realm, the husband often carries the bride across the threshold. That's quite a biblical picture as well, wouldn't you say? It is actually a picture of Yeshua and His Bride—the congregation of born-again believers. (See Ephesians 5:21ff.)

MAKE IT FAMOUS!

Even more surprising about the word *miqra* is its verb form, which is the Hebrew *qara*. That term means "to preach, to call out," or "to make famous, or to be famous."[267]

We've already learned the Sabbath is designated by Yahweh Himself as "a holy convocation." So, considering the shades of meanings of *miqra* and *qara*, Yahweh is telling us something very important. He is already hinting that the Sabbath day is a convocation of *rehearsal* for something much grander, something that involves an infinitely greater revelation and a future fulfillment that is much more important than the actual commandment itself.

We can also deduce that when this "greater Sabbath fulfillment" finally blossoms, the genuine purpose of *that day* will then be made "famous"! It is a day God Himself has set aside and called a "holy rehearsal." Very soon, in the following chapters, we'll discover exactly what this rehearsal is really about. And we'll discover what will be "made famous" in its fulfillment.

Common Sense

Let's consider for a moment the logistical and historical facts surrounding such an assembly among the Exodus people. First, there would have been around two million people in that Exodus crowd.

Exodus 12:37–38 tells us there were more than six hundred thousand Jewish men who came out of Egypt. That number did not count the women and children—and, again, that number was just among the Jews. But we also read that a *mixed multitude* also came out with them. Those were the Gentiles, *the non-Jewish nations* that had also been in Egyptian captivity. That multitude would have been made up of men, women, and children as well. So now we're getting close to several million people.

It would, however, seem highly unlikely that several million people could/would have consistently gathered in one specific place for a prolonged service of worship or any other purpose. The logistical arrangements alone, to meet the massive number of needs involved in such a meeting, would be astonishingly overwhelming. And all of this would have to be repeated every single week—*forever*!

Also consider that, for a good while, the people of the Exodus didn't even have a working tabernacle in the wilderness. Then, it would be another several hundred years before they would finally have Solomon's Temple. Further, how could any authority enforce such an organized and routinized formal assembly during the wilderness journey? Those millions of people and their animals, plus all of their personal belongings, were almost always on the move!

And how could there be such a massive *required* assembly once they were in the Promised Land—especially considering the original people by then would have multiplied into many more millions and were now dispersed into their assigned tribal lands. Surely, they couldn't all meet in a single holy convocation.

What did they do, then? How did they most likely practice this great "rehearsal"?

chapter forty-six

THE PURPOSE

Keeping the Sabbath was never meant to be a legalistic requirement for somehow earning God's favor.

The bottom line is that, of the dozen or more times the phrase "holy convocation" is used in the Old Testament, those passages give no specific directives as to *where* or *how* the several million people should assemble on the seventh day of every single week—not counting the other gatherings of the special Sabbaths that accompanied the Feast Days. Nor do the directives say *what* should be done in those convocations.

Very few historical records give us any great detail about these matters. However, the best sources indicate these kinds of gatherings were largely relegated to immediate families, and sometimes to small communities of local families.

Once the wilderness Tabernacle and (eventually) Solomon's Temple were in consistent operation, the priests would exercise a local holy convocation on the Sabbath at the entrance of the Tabernacle/Temple. That priestly duty involved offering certain sacrifices on behalf of the people who were able to attend, as well as the other people they represented—regardless of where those people were living throughout the land. These gatherings included music (the playing of instruments and singing) and prayer.

In Your Dwelling Places

We get a biblical hint of these practices as we conduct a closer examination of Leviticus 23:3:

> Six days shall work be done, but on the seventh day is a Sabbath of solemn rest, a holy convocation. You shall do no work. It is a Sabbath to the LORD **in all your dwelling places.** (Emphasis added)

The Hebrew word for "dwelling places" has a double meaning: 1) a community or region where someone resides; or 2) one's actual home.[268]

The following observations bolster the academic credibility of what we're considering.

Keil and Delitzsch Biblical Commentary on the Old Testament:

> [It is] wrong in identifying the "holy convocation" with a journey to the sanctuary, whereas appearance at the tabernacle to hold the holy convocations (for worship) was not regarded as necessary either in the law itself or according to the later orthodox custom, but, on the contrary, holy meetings for edification were held on the Sabbath in every place in the land, and it was out of this that the synagogues [eventually] arose.[269] (Parenthesis in original)

Jamieson-Fausset-Brown Bible Commentary:

> Six days shall work be done: but the seventh day is the sabbath of rest. The Sabbath has the precedence given to it, and it was to be "a holy convocation," observed by families "in their dwellings"; where practicable, by the people repairing to the door of the tab-

ernacle; at later periods, by meeting in the schools of the prophets, and in synagogues.[270]

The Pulpit Commentary:

It is not to be observed solely where the tabernacle is pitched or the temple is built, but in every town and village of Canaan—in all your dwellings.

In the sanctuary itself the peculiar characteristics of the sabbath were a holy convocation, the renewal of the shewbread, and the burnt offering of two lambs with their meat and drink offerings (Numbers 28:9, 10); elsewhere it was observed only by the holy convocation and rest from all labor. It commenced at sunset on Friday evening, and continued till sunset on Saturday evening.[271]

The Jewish Virtual Library offers additional insight on the Sabbath:

The Sabbath and the other holy days of Israel's calendar have played an immeasurable role in developing and ennobling Israel's worship...the idea of the Sabbath in the scriptural context is a unique institution, meant to articulate divine sovereignty over time....

From one point of view, [the Sabbath] was Israel's answer to the Egyptian bondage; any human being, even a slave, needs rest. Not only humans, but also animals require recuperation from toil (Ex. 23:12; Deut. 5:12–15). In the Exodus version of the Decalogue, the Sabbath assumes cosmic significance; it becomes a memorial to the story of Creation (Ex. 20:8–11; cf. Gen. 2:1–4).[272]

CONCLUSIONS

The words "holy convocation" certainly could have incorporated elements of community worship. Obviously, no command anywhere in the

Scriptures *forbids* the worship of Yahweh at any gathering! That would be ridiculous. We know God's people often did use these meetings to worship, even since the most ancient of times.

We later learn that "synagogue worship" on the Sabbath eventually grew out of the people's desire to meet in local communities. The Hebrews understood that what they were doing in those meetings was never in response to a specific commandment of God. It was originally born out of their *desire to worship* together on that day. It appears, therefore, that the people had certain freedoms in how they would *keep* the Sabbath. We were never intended to be "slaves" to it.

Historically, the Egyptians had demanded that the Israelite slaves work whenever commanded. Often the Israelites labored every day of the week—frequently under seemingly impossible conditions. On occasion, they were even worked to death—literally.

Instead, with Yahweh as their Lord, the covenant people of God were receiving a gift from Him via the Sabbath instruction. He was presenting them with a guaranteed day of rest, relaxation, and time for personal and family reflection upon God's grace and goodness. In this way they were joining Him, in spirit, in doing the same thing He did on the very first *seventh day*.

What we then discover is that, mostly, the practice of the "holy convocation" of ancient biblical times meant a local *gathering of one's family*. It was primarily a day of planned rest. That much is clearly defined in the Scripture, and is borne out by well-known historical practices and traditions. Therefore, the term "holy convocation" at least would have included the importance of that family time and, yes, *worship* as well. The Sabbath worship would most likely have been a natural outcome of such a family or communal gathering. How could it not have been?

And don't forget what we've previously learned. That is, the entire event of the Sabbath was a *rehearsal* of something much greater to come!

chapter forty-seven

Traditions, Laws, and Servitude

Sadly, the Jewish people had now accepted, and even embraced, the strict ritualism that accompanied their daily faith by the added decrees of tradition and "laws."

I'm biblically certain the Sabbath was *not* meant to be a day upon which one might be compelled to obey a plethora of ridiculous, manmade (rabbinical Talmudic) rules and regulations in order to be "properly obeying the laws" of the Sabbath. On the contrary, the actual biblical Sabbath commands were fairly straightforward.

Further, the Sabbath certainly wasn't meant to be a day when self-appointed religious overlords could, almost at will, bring down divine punishment upon a child of God, even if the supposed errant one was "officially determined" to not be strictly obeying those tedious, *manmade* rules and laws. That was the kind of corrupted Chaldean deception Yeshua continually railed against in His own confrontations with the rabbis, Pharisees, and Sadducees.

It was also the very way the Jewish ruling elite of Yeshua's day continually tried to get Him turned over to the Roman authorities to subject Him to the death penalty. Almost everything they "legally" held against Yeshua involved their humanly contrived "Sabbath law" violations. These tools were what gave them power, prestige, and almost unbridled control over the Jewish people.

- And [Yeshua] said to them [the rabbis and religious elite], "You have a fine way of rejecting the commandment of God in order to establish your tradition! ... thus making void the word of God by your tradition that you have handed down. And many such things you do." (Mark 7:9, 13)
- He went on from there and entered their synagogue. And a man was there with a withered hand. And they [the Pharisees] asked him, "Is it lawful to heal on the Sabbath?"—so that they might accuse him. He said to them, "Which one of you who has a sheep, if it falls into a pit on the Sabbath, will not take hold of it and lift it out? Of how much more value is a man than a sheep! So it is lawful to do good on the Sabbath." (Matthew 12: 9–12)

God had given His people a "threshold" of rest. But evil men, sometimes well-meaning at first, eventually turned it into a threshold of abject domination to advance their own malicious strongholds upon God's people.

It seems the Chaldean spirit of confusion, with its continual perversion of the Word of God, has been hard at work through the millennia. The deceptions have always been practiced to keep humanity—especially the Jews—from discovering Yeshua's loving Threshold Covenants of freedom, salvation, joy, and genuine life!

[Yeshua said to them,] The thief comes only to steal and kill and destroy. I came that they may have life and have it abundantly. (John 10:10)

The Synagogue

Many people ask about the advent of the synagogue tradition. The historical answer is that the time of the synagogue's beginning, with its related services of worship and instruction, is not precise. However, as previously noted, it most likely arose to satisfy various logistical considerations of the "holy convocation" language found in the Sabbath commands.

The *Encyclopedia Britannica* reveals the following insight:

> The oldest dated evidence of a synagogue is from the 3rd century [BC] but synagogues doubtless have an older history. Some scholars think that the destruction of Solomon's Temple of Jerusalem in 586 [BC] gave rise to synagogues after private homes were temporarily used for public worship and religious instruction.
>
> Whatever their origin, synagogues flourished side by side with the ancient Temple cult and existed long before Jewish sacrifice and the established priesthood were terminated with the destruction of the Second Temple by the Roman emperor Titus in 70 [AD].[273]

The prominence of synagogue life dramatically increased as the exiled Jews went through the Babylonian, Persian, Greek, and finally Roman domination of world affairs. By the latter part of the Greek period and the beginning of the Roman period, the Jewish people had the Second Temple in almost full-scale operation.[274]

Yet, the synagogues continued to flourish as well. This was largely because, for several hundred years, the Jews had been without a Temple and deprived of their sacrificial systems. They had gone through several new generations that basically ignored the Temple protocols. So, the religious elite eventually devised a way that declared "obeying the Law" was now the substitute "sacrifice." Keeping the Law was how they were to now make their "offerings" to God. Thus the synagogues became an integral part of ancient Jewish life.

This system worked fairly well until the new ruling class of the synagogue elite, the Pharisees and rabbis, began to contrive thousands upon thousands of their own interpretations of the Law. Eventually those interpretations became traditions. The traditions slowly became the new and codified nuances of the law. Eventually, the now-accepted traditions became laws that were vigorously enforced by the Pharisees and even, at times, the entire Sanhedrin Council. Before long, the Jewish people accepted the man-made laws/traditions as being equal to the Word of God itself.

The Roman World

By the turn of the first century AD, when the Roman Empire was unquestionably the dominant world power, the Sanhedrin was immersed in a heavy-handed and legalistic power grab over the Jewish population. Synagogues were everywhere, and the Pharisees and rabbis were in full control. At the same time, the Second Temple stood in Jerusalem upon the Temple Mount with a presence equaled only, perhaps, by Solomon's Temple itself. The Sadducees had a firm grip on that center of control over Jewish life.

Sadly, most of the Jewish people accepted and even embraced the strict ritualism that accompanied their daily faith. Under the Pharisees of the synagogues and the Sadducees of the Temple—with both groups in relatively strong cooperation—the Jewish people were once again subjugated to the suffocating presence of overlords. *Religious overlords.* Most of the Jews didn't even realize it, or, conversely, they simply tolerated it.

Yahweh's simple directive to enjoy biblical Sabbath "rest" had then become a conglomerated mess of more than three thousand Sabbath traditions, almost all of them demonically posing as His "laws." The people had become religious slaves to those laws and to their rabbis. The Sabbath itself had become the new slave owner, with the powerful elite in daily control of the Jewish servants. The Chaldean spirit had thoroughly corrupted what Yahweh had intended.

The Sadducees and the Pharisees controlled the Sanhedrin Council through a representative body—a Jewish ruling class officially sanctioned by the Roman Empire. The Sanhedrin had become an embedded government entity, and Rome made certain its own tentacles were firmly wrapped around that center of profound religious power.

About the only authority the Sanhedrin didn't have over the Jewish population of the first century was the ability to unilaterally impose the penalty of death. But there were ways around that, too, if they so desired. A fervent appeal to the Roman governor of Judea usually did the trick.

At Just the Right Time

It was into that world Yahweh Himself stepped. He came directly into the realm of earthly life—as a human being, born of a virgin (Isaiah 7:14, Micah 5), and wrapped in the flesh of *Yeshua Ha Mashiach* (John 1:1–14)...just as the prophets had foretold (Isaiah 9).

He had come with love in His heart but fire in His eyes. He was on a mission. He was in the earthly realm for the explicit purpose of setting a trap. It was a divine snare designed to destroy Satan's stolen earthly kingdom and ultimately restore Paradise (Ephesians 1:9; Genesis 3:15).

Yeshua was here to establish the final blood alliance with His people. The *groover* to that New Covenant threshold would be filled with blood, just like it had been on that original Passover evening. But, this time, the blood would be His own.

Never doubt this great truth: Through everything else He was doing, Yeshua also came to reestablish and completely fulfill the true sanctity of the intended Sabbath rest.

chapter forty-eight

ALL ABOUT YESHUA

The Sabbath Law...has always been about Yeshua's fulfillment of it, both now and in the Paradise to come!

By now, you've probably recognized the biblical pattern we've been tracking. That is, everything in the Tanakh, to one degree or another, is pointing to an ultimate fulfillment in Yeshua. *Everything.*

From the first verse of Genesis to the last verse of Malachi, we see that truth affirmed over and over. From one revelation to another, all, somehow, point to Him! History itself has *always, always, always* been about Yeshua.

The earliest called-out believers were fully aware of that truth. After all, they were living in the midst of much of its revelation!

- We also have the word of the prophets as confirmed beyond doubt. And you will do well to pay attention to it, as to a lamp shining in a dark place, until the day dawns and the morning star rises in your hearts. (2 Peter 1:19; Berean Study Bible)

- Concerning this salvation, the prophets who prophesied about the grace that was to be yours searched and inquired carefully, inquiring what person or time the Spirit of Christ in them was indicating when he predicted the sufferings of Christ and the subsequent glories. It was revealed to them that they were serving not themselves but you, in the things that have now been announced to you through those who preached the good news to you by the Holy Spirit sent from heaven, things into which angels long to look. (1 Peter 1:10–12)
- And Paul went in [to their synagogues], as was his custom, and on three Sabbath days he reasoned with them from the Scriptures, explaining and proving that it was necessary for the Christ to suffer and to rise from the dead, and saying, "This Jesus, whom I proclaim to you, is the Christ." (Acts 17:2–3; see also Acts 18–19)

Think of it. Starting with Genesis 1:1, the overall message has always been about the cross, the Resurrection, and the resulting blood alliance Yeshua bought and paid for to redeem us from a fallen creation.[275]

That redemption process was never about "Easter"; it has always been about Passover. It was never about worshiping or glorifying a certain day on a mixed-up calendar system. It has always been about worshiping *Yeshua Ha Mashiach*, who fulfilled every bit of the Passover week and all its rituals on Golgotha's tree and with an empty tomb. And the entire plan was all about the ultimate fulfillment of the Passover Covenant Threshold, when we are invited into the Father's House to eat the Passover anew in the Father's Kingdom. It has always been about Him…*from the beginning*!

And He said to them, "I have eagerly desired to eat this Passover with you before My suffering. For I tell you that I will not eat it again until it is fulfilled in the kingdom of God." (Luke 22:15–16)

In the same way, God's plan was never about a literal, brick-and-mortar Third Temple on the Temple Mount. It has always been about the

New Temple of the last days—the born-again congregation of believers, the household of God, Jews and Gentiles together, under the Threshold Covenant (Ephesians 2 and Romans 11). It's about the completed fulfillment of the Passover "rehearsal" of Exodus!

> [God has made] known to us the mystery of his will, according to his purpose, which he set forth in Christ as a plan for the fullness of time, to unite all things in him, things in heaven and things on earth. (Ephesians 1:9–10)

I reminded you of the foregoing to say this: The Sabbath Law itself, also, has always been about Yeshua's fulfillment of it, both now and in the Paradise to come.

The Sabbath Fulfillment

If I were to ask you if the Temple and all its sacrifices were ultimately about Yeshua, you would most likely say, "Yes." It's the same with the Seven Feasts of the Lord in Leviticus 23 and the office of the Great High Priest. Yeshua fulfills them all!

Likewise, if I asked: "Do we have to sacrifice lambs any more in order to have our sins covered?" Of course you would answer, "No." And you would be correct, again. Why? Because the true Lamb of God has been slain, in Yeshua. Therefore, the Temple sacrifices were literally "rehearsals" of something much greater to come. Yeshua satisfied the letter of the original law of sacrifice, and we now live in that fulfillment when we cross the Threshold Covenant that's "cut" with His blood. That was the whole point of the Feast of Passover and the Temple sacrifices from the very beginning.

By asserting these declarations about the Passover Feast and the blood sacrifices, we acknowledge they are all now fulfilled in Yeshua—every single one of them! They were *miqra*, "rehearsals"—holy convocations.

The Apostle Paul, a Messianic rabbi and formerly an Orthodox rabbi with an undeniably deep Orthodox lineage and heritage, assures us of the following biblical truth:

> Do you not know that a little leaven leavens the whole lump? Cleanse out the old leaven that you may be a new lump, as you really are unleavened. For Christ, our Passover lamb, has been sacrificed. Let us therefore celebrate the festival, not with the old leaven, the leaven of malice and evil, but with the unleavened bread of sincerity and truth. (1 Corinthians 5:7–8)

So, what if I told you Yeshua has also fulfilled the letter of the *Sabbath Law* as well? Meditate on that thought as you turn to the next page.

chapter forty-nine

Making the Biblical Case

The LORD gave those seven feasts to God's people.
And they all pointed to their ultimate fulfillment in Yeshua.

When we talk about the Sabbath, we're actually talking about the Feasts of the Lord. The two share a direct and startling connection.

How in the world can that be so? Where in the Bible is the direct connection between the Sabbath rest and the Lord's Feasts—except, of course, for the "special Sabbaths" that are built into a few of those feasts? We'll find the answers in this chapter.

Perhaps you are thinking the Sabbath commandment was meant to be applied in the same way it was originally given—that is, *forever and forever*. The command to "keep it" was meant to be *forever*. But the original giving of the Sabbath is not the ultimate *fulfillment* of it or how we are to always observe it. The genuine Sabbath has always been about Yeshua in the same way, for example, the laws regarding the sacrificial lambs in the Temple proceedings were always about the coming of the true Lamb of God.

265

The Feasts of the Lord

Let's approach the next stunning subject we'll examine step by step, beginning with the first two verses of Leviticus 23:

> The LORD spoke to Moses, saying, "Speak to the people of Israel and say to them, These are the appointed feasts of the LORD that you shall proclaim as holy convocations; [*miqra*: "rehearsals"] they are my appointed feasts. [Hebrew: *moed*][276] (Leviticus 23:1–2)

The remainder of chapter 23 profiles the ritual commands of the appointed Feasts of the Lord. These were initially given for the people who had come out of Egypt—both Jews and Gentiles. They were given these feasts through the Sinai encounter with God.

By the way, those holy feasts were always called the "Feasts of the Lord," and never the "Feasts of the Jews," as they are sometimes mischaracterized. Those feasts were Yahweh's ideas, not the concepts of the Jews or Gentiles who were with them in the Exodus.[277]

The feasts outlined in Leviticus 23 were designed to help keep God's called-out people focused on all He had done for them and how He would continually provide for their every need. Most importantly, they were meant to foreshadow all He would do for them in the future through *Yeshua Ha Mashiach*. In that way, the feasts were also meant specifically for us!

Many good books have been written about the Feasts of the Lord and how they were originally celebrated, as well as how they are still celebrated by most Orthodox Jews of today. The majority of those books also reveal the ultimate fulfillments of the Lord's feasts in Yeshua. The purpose of this book is not to simply reproduce that detailed information.

Since our focus is to consider the meaning of the Sabbath commandment, let's take a moment to scan through how each one of the seven major Feasts of the Lord has been, and/or will be, fulfilled in Yeshua. We will begin in this manner because the Sabbath commandment and the feast commandments are directly connected, as you'll see.

1. (*Pesach*): Yeshua is our Passover Lamb. He is our "once for all" sacrifice, the Lamb slain from the foundation of the world (1 Corinthians 5:6–8).
2. (*Chag HaMatzot* or *Pesach*): Yeshua is our eternal sustenance as we walk through this fallen wilderness world. He is the Bread of Life made without yeast (sin). He is our unleavened bread, offered in the Passover sacrifice as the one without sin (John 6:35, 48).
3. (*Tenufah* or *Shavuot*): Yeshua is the firstborn, and firstfruits, from the dead. He is our resurrection and our life. He is our promise of eternal life to come. His Resurrection on the very day of Firstfruits proves He has conquered death and the grave (1 Corinthians 15:20–22).
4. (*Shavuot*): This was the promised giving of the Holy Spirit to all believers—the birth of the born-again congregation of Yeshua—promised from the mouth of Yeshua Himself. To this day, among most Orthodox Jews, Pentecost also celebrates the giving of the Law at Sinai, resulting in the birth of the nation of Israel. Think of it: Pentecost celebrates both the birth of Israel and the birth of the Church. Here is yet another picture of the "one new man" and the true Temple of God in the last days (Ephesians 2, Romans 11).
5. (*Yom Teruah*): was the day of blowing trumpets throughout the land. It was the day of the *sound of warning* and preparation for Yom Kippur—the Day of Covering, or the Day of Atonement. It is also the sound of announcing Yeshua's return for His children (Matthew 24:31; 1 Corinthians 15:52; 1 Thessalonians 4:16; the seven trumpets of Revelation 8–11).
6. (*Yom Kippur*): Yeshua is our perfect, without sin, Great High Priest. He is the One who has now made the perfect sacrifice for all who will "cut a covenant" with Him through His shed blood. Once we are under that blood, we are under His "covering." Our sins are atoned for. We are His (Romans 3:25; Hebrews 2:17; and Hebrews 9:5). If we are not under His blood, that day becomes a day of the outpouring of God's Wrath (Revelation 15–18).

7. (*Sukkot*): This feast celebrates God's immediate dwelling (tabernacling) among His people in the wilderness. But it ultimately celebrates the first coming of Yeshua and His dwelling (tabernacling) among us in the flesh (John 1:1–14). Ultimately, it represents our final dwelling (tabernacling) with our Creator/Elohim in the recreated Paradise (Revelation 21 and 22).

THE HEAD FEAST

Many of God's people today fail to notice that, in Leviticus 23, at the *head* of all the feasts that follow stands the *Sabbath rest*. It, too, is called a feast (*moed*) of the Lord![278] The purposed reintroduction of the Sabbath rest, in conjunction with the seven Feasts of the Lord, is God's way of saying, "All of these feasts ultimately represent *Yeshua Ha Mashiach*…yet they are all literally *embodied* in one grand feast—the Day of Sabbath."

Look again at the first three verses of Leviticus 23, which begins with the words, "These are my appointed feasts." The first proclaimed is not the Feast of Passover, but the *weekly Sabbath*! Therefore, there are *eight* Feasts of the Lord![279] But they *start* with the Sabbath, and for good reason.

> The LORD spoke to Moses, saying, "Speak to the people of Israel and say to them, These are the appointed feasts of the LORD that you shall proclaim as holy convocations; [rehearsals; they point to Yeshua] they are my appointed feasts.
>
> "Six days shall work be done, but on the seventh day is a Sabbath of solemn rest, a holy convocation. [also a rehearsal, pointing to Yeshua!] You shall do no work. It is a Sabbath to the LORD in all your dwelling places." (Leviticus 23:1–3)

Then, verse 4 begins by describing the next feast—Passover, the ultimate revelation of the atoning work of Yeshua and the first "special" Feast of the Lord that was to start Israel's new year of feasts:

These are the appointed feasts of the LORD, the holy convocations, which you shall proclaim at the time appointed for them. In the first month, on the fourteenth day of the month at twilight, is the LORD's Passover. (Leviticus 23:4)

Here we see the "feast" of the weekly Sabbath is the "Lord" or "Head" of all the rest of the feasts. Sabbath comes first and foremost. Therefore, *the Sabbath is the threshold* that allows us entry into the rest of the Lord's feasts! It is the threshold to everything else that follows.

Consider the depth of this thought. The other seven feasts define intricate aspects of Yeshua's ministry, salvation, and coming Kingdom reign. But the Sabbath is the embodiment of them all. The Sabbath is to be revered every single week, *every day* of our lives. That is because the true Sabbath is Yeshua. He is our "daily bread." However, the other feasts are celebrated, as being fulfilled by Yeshua, at their "appointed times."

Since that revelation of Leviticus 23 is obviously true, how can we say all seven Feasts of the Lord have their direct and most embodied fulfillment in Yeshua, and then say this is somehow not true of the Sabbath *moed*? But...now we know the truth: The Sabbath is a feast! The Sabbath is Yeshua! He is the supreme Threshold of all the other Feasts of the Lord.

Now let's find out what Yeshua and the New Testament writers said about what we've just uncovered.

chapter fifty

THE FULFILLED WORD SPEAKS

Each of the laws of God was
foreshadowing things yet to come.

What does Yeshua Himself say about these matters? This consideration is important, because whatever He says is the end of the matter. He is the ultimate revelation of all Old Covenant shadows. The answer to the question is right there in the Scriptures; have a look:

> Come to me, all who labor and are heavy laden, and I will give you rest [Hebrew: *Shabath,* "Sabbath"]. (Matthew 11:28)

Yeshua made this declaration in direct response to the burdensome rituals and man-made traditions the rabbis and Pharisees had artificially concocted regarding the Sabbath. Following those rules had become excruciatingly tedious. Jesus' presence and ultimate sacrifice would provide freedom from that unholy load. In so doing, Jesus first made it clear that He, in fact, *is* the genuine Sabbath!

Ellicott's Commentary on the Bible:

The thought that was most prominent in [these words of Yeshua] at the time was that of the burdens grievous to be borne, the yoke of traditions and ordinances which the Pharisees and scribes had imposed on the consciences of men.[280]

Maclaren's Exposition of the Scriptures:

Jesus Christ, in this merciful invitation of His, speaks to all the men that have tried, and tried in vain, to satisfy their consciences and to obey the law of God, and says to them, "Cease your efforts, and no longer carry that burden of failure and of sin upon your shoulders. Come unto Me, and I will give you rest [Sabbath]."[281]

But that's not all. Just a few verses following that declaration of Matthew 11, we observe Yeshua asserting the following startling claim, one that had to have floored His original listeners:

For the Son of Man is Lord of the Sabbath. (Matthew 12:8)

Yeshua is our Sabbath because He is the Creator and "Lord of the Sabbath." He stands as the Head of all the Feasts of the Lord! It's really that simple.

Yeshua is the Creator of the universe, the One who stood there on that seventh day and declared everything to be "good" (John 1:1–3; Hebrews 1:1–3; Colossians 1:16–20; Revelation 4:11, 10:6). So as God, in human flesh, Yeshua alone gets to decide the true meaning of the Sabbath because He created it and He is our Sabbath rest...in the flesh. The law doesn't supersede Him. He supersedes and fulfills the law! One more time we see the bold truth staring at us: *It was always about Him.*

Then we also observe Yeshua asserting another life-giving Sabbath revelation in Mark 2:27:

The sabbath was made for man, and not man for the Sabbath.

We can translate the extent of what Yeshua is saying in Mark 2 as something like this: Humanity was not made just so Yeshua (our Sabbath) would *have* to go to Golgotha. Instead, His sacrifice, which brought us ultimate and eternal Sabbath, was made for us from the beginning!

Other Scriptures

Other New Testament Scriptures say the same thing, even more intricately. Consider the following:

> So then, there remains a Sabbath rest for the people of God, for whoever has entered God's rest [Yeshua our Sabbath] has also rested from his works as God did from his. Let us therefore strive to enter that rest, so that no one may fall by the same sort of disobedience. (Hebrews 4:9–11)

In other words, if we are "in" Yeshua, we are "in" the Sabbath, and are therefore keeping the Sabbath, in full, throughout our Threshold Covenant relationship.

MacLaren's Expositions (Hebrews 4:9):

> If you give to it what seems to be the correct interpretation—by referring it to Christ and Christ's heavenly condition. He that has entered into His rest—that is Jesus Christ.[282]

Matthew Henry's Concise Commentary (Hebrews 4:9):

> But those who do not believe [in Yeshua] shall never enter into this spiritual rest, either of grace here or glory hereafter. God has always declared man's rest to be in Him, and His love to be the only real happiness of the soul; and faith in his promises, through his Son, to be the only way of entering that rest.[283]

Jamieson-Fausset-Brown Bible Commentary (Hebrews 4:9):

> The law leads us to Christ, and there its office ceases, [the law] as that of Moses [representing the law] on the borders [another threshold picture!] of Canaan: it is Jesus, the antitype of Joshua, who leads us into the heavenly rest.[284]

Pulpit Commentary (Hebrews 4:10):

> God's rest [Sabbath] has been offered to man: man has not attained it [by law-keeping]: Jesus has; and in Jesus man may enter it [the true Sabbath].[285]

GotQuestions.org sums up Hebrews 4:9–11 like this:

> There is no other Sabbath rest besides Jesus. He alone satisfies the requirements of the Law, and He alone provides the sacrifice that atones for sin. He is God's plan for us to cease from the labor of our own works. We dare not reject this one-and-only Way of salvation (John 14:6) [we dare not trample on this threshold!].[286]

Now and Forever

The fourth chapter of Hebrews emphasizes that our genuine, fulfilled Sabbath is found only in our New Covenant relationship with our Creator/Elohim. Of course, we also know our Creator/Elohim is none other than Yeshua Himself (Colossians 1, Hebrews 1, John 1).

Not only that, but we are also assured that this New Covenant Sabbath is something we enjoy in Yeshua *now*…as well as in the ultimate "rest" we will bathe in during our eternal state of glory! The following resource eloquently explains this and indicates the direct connection to the Threshold Covenant in Yeshua.

An Exegetical Outline of Hebrews, "The Superiority of Christ and His Covenant (Hebrews 4:1–11):

> The audience [of Hebrews] is exhorted to "strive to enter that rest" (v. 11), as if they have not yet entered it but may in the future. On the other hand, the author says that we who "have believed enter that rest" (v. 3) and "whoever has entered God's rest has also rested from his works" (v. 10)
>
> [Hebrews refers to the] progressive or continuous action, "we who have believed are entering that rest," and to understand v.10 as referring to those who have died in faith and so have "entered God's rest" (cf. Rev 14:13).
>
> Thus **we have a continuum—we are entering God's rest by faith in the present** and **will enjoy it fully in the future** (similar to how we are presently being saved and yet will be saved in the future; cf. 1 Cor. 1:18 with Rom 5:9– 10).
>
> The author of Hebrews consistently places his readers on the doorstep of entering [at the threshold] their great reward (cf. 10:19–23, 35–39). Our earthly life is the process of crossing the eternal threshold into a "better country" (11:16).[287] (Emphasis added)

YESHUA OUR SABBATH

While the Old Covenant Law is supremely important, the completed biblical truth is that all the worship laws, all the Feasts of the Lord, and all the sacrifices in the Temple have found their fulfillment in *Yeshua Ha Mashiach*. In this way, the law of the Sabbath is also fulfilled through our blood covenant relationship in Yeshua.

> For since the law has but a shadow of the good things to come instead of the true form of these realities, it can never, by the same

sacrifices that are continually offered every year, make perfect those who draw near. (Hebrews 10:1)

Here's another passage that paints a beautiful picture of the fulfillment of our true Sabbath, in covenant relationship with Yeshua.

But when Christ had offered for all time a single sacrifice for sins, he sat down at the right hand of God. (Hebrews 10:12)

And [God] raised us up with Him and seated us with him in the heavenly places in Christ Jesus. (Ephesians 2:6)

The English phrase "sat down" or "seated," in the Greek text, comes from the word *kathizó*. The *NAS Exhaustive Concordance* defines *kathizó* to mean "rest" or "rested."[288]

Yeshua's messianic "work" was to restore creation through His blood-alliance sacrifice. His miraculous exploits during His three years of earthly ministry, His shed blood on Golgotha's tree, and His empty tomb became His "work" for humanity's salvation. Then, when He had completed that work—He *rested*.

This is a beautiful reflection of His original Creation event. Next, in the second creation event of His messianic "work," He *recreated us*! He did it by His own blood, and then…He rested (ceased). He embodied our Sabbath rest. This redemption process would only be offered "once, for all."

For Christ did not enter a sanctuary made with human hands that was only a copy of the true one; he entered heaven itself, now to appear for us in God's presence. Nor did he enter heaven to offer himself again and again, the way the high priest enters the Most Holy Place every year with blood that is not his own. Otherwise Christ would have had to suffer many times since the creation of the world. But he has appeared once for all at the culmination of the ages to do away with sin by the sacrifice of himself. (Hebrews 9:24–26)

The matter seems to be as plain as this: If we are in blood alliance with Yeshua, we are "keeping" the Sabbath "sacrifice." He is that Sabbath! In Him we are resting in the Father's household, having crossed the Threshold Covenant. We didn't step *on* the threshold in disrespect, but we stepped *over* the threshold, and willfully and respectfully entered through *the door* into a loving relationship with our Creator. That "door" is Yeshua (John 14:1–6).

Let us not then profane what God has done in *Yeshua Ha Mashiach*... our Perfect Sabbath, *forever*!

chapter fifty-one

THE OLD LAW OR THE NEW COVENANT?

Yeshua is the embodied Sabbath;
to reject Him is to miss Paradise...forever.

It's amazing that so many believers seem to have forgotten there was a strict penalty under the Old Covenant Law for *willfully* violating the Sabbath. Along these lines, it's also interesting that those who still hold to a legalistic keeping of the Sabbath law of Exodus 20 seem to forget that deliberately or flippantly ignoring the Sabbath law of old also carried the death penalty.[289]

So should all who now ignore the Old Covenant Sabbath law be put to death? How can one say we must keep the Sabbath exactly as prescribed in the Tanakh, but only the parts that don't include the death penalty? The New Covenant says if we attempt to keep the law under the Old Covenant as a way to "earn" a form of righteousness rather than live in Yeshua's fulfillment of that law under the New Covenant, then we are obligated to keep *every* nuance of that same Old Covenant law:

279

- I testify again to every man who accepts circumcision that he is obligated to keep the whole law. You are severed from Christ, you who would be justified by the law; you have fallen away from grace. (Galatians 5:3–4)
- But if you call yourself a Jew and rely on the law and boast in God and know his will and approve what is excellent, because you are instructed from the law.... While you preach against stealing, do you steal? You who say that one must not commit adultery, do you commit adultery? ...But now the righteousness of God has been manifested apart from the law, although the Law and the Prophets bear witness to it—the righteousness of God through faith in Jesus Christ for all who believe. (Romans 2:17–21; 3:21–22)
- For whoever keeps the whole law but fails in one point has become guilty of all of it. (James 2:10)

However, a much more ominous consideration is found in the next truth. Since the Sabbath law pointed to its total fulfillment as being only in Yeshua, then the penalty of "death" remains! *Think of that for a moment.*

Here is how. If one flat-out rejects Yeshua, then no redemption is left for that person. He or she has "trampled His blood underfoot" and refused the only means of obtaining the Threshold Covenant salvation. People who do this will never enter the Father's House. They are under the eternal penalty of death and separation from their Creator:

Jesus said to him, "I am the way, and the truth, and the life. No one comes to the Father except through me. (John 14:6)

Once again, consider how the New Covenant book of Hebrews clearly addresses this matter:

- How shall we escape if we neglect so great a salvation? (Hebrews 2:3).
- For it is impossible, in the case of those who have once been enlightened, who have tasted the heavenly gift, and have shared

in the Holy Spirit, and have tasted the goodness of the word of God and the powers of the age to come, and then have fallen away, [purposely ignored God's grace in Yeshua]to restore them again to repentance, [refusing to make the Threshold Covenant with Yeshua] since they are crucifying once again the Son of God to their own harm and holding him up to contempt. [They have trampled the covenant blood underfoot.] (Hebrews 6:4–6)
- How much worse punishment, do you think, will be deserved by the one who has trampled underfoot the Son of God, and has profaned the blood of the covenant by which he was sanctified, and has outraged the Spirit of grace? (Hebrews 10:29)

Even in Yeshua's ultimate fulfillment of the Sabbath law, there also exists the greater fulfillment of the consequences of ignoring the Sabbath rest He offers. After all, Yeshua is the embodied Sabbath! To reject Yeshua as Messiah and Lord is to miss Paradise *forever*. It is the sentence of eternal death. The New Testament makes it clear that going back to the law in an effort to earn righteousness is a foolish idea. After everything Yeshua has done to set us free, it's an abomination.

In the struggle to get back to certain Old Covenant forms of *authenticity of faith*, some have gone too far and tried to reinstitute protocols that were never meant to be exercised by post-Resurrection, Renewed Covenant believers. Some actually advocate living the way God's people did before the coming of *Yeshua Ha Mashiach*, observing the feasts in the old, unfulfilled ways and conducting life through a rabbi-decreed, kosher lens. There's been a lot of confusion over these matters, often placing any reference to the *authentic* Hebrew foundational understanding of the Scriptures under great scrutiny and suspicion.

However, it's no longer about the precise practices. The Renewed Covenant is all about the principles that governed those practices. Because of those principles and their ultimate fulfillment in Yeshua, the details of the ancient practices become unnecessary for our born-again faith walk with our Creator.

Are You Israel?

On the opposite side of the matter, there are some who still complain about their attention being constantly drawn to issues like the feasts and Sabbath requirements, ordinances they always assumed were intended for Israel alone. But the question I have for those confused by these issues is, "Are you Israel?"

Let me explain. If you have been grafted into the olive tree of "the completed Israel" of Romans 11 and are part of the "one new man" of Ephesians 2:15–22, then you are *spiritually* Israel; you've been invited to God's appointed times of meeting, as they have already been fulfilled in Yeshua!

- That he might create in himself one new man in place of the two, so making peace, and might reconcile us both to God in one body through the cross, thereby killing the hostility.... For through him we both [Jew and Gentile] have access in one Spirit to the Father. So then you are no longer strangers and aliens, but you are fellow citizens with the saints and members of the household of God, built on the foundation of the apostles and prophets, Christ Jesus himself being the cornerstone, in whom the whole structure, being joined together, grows into a holy temple in the Lord. In him you also are being built together [Jew and Gentile] into a dwelling place for God by the Spirit. (Ephesians 2:15–22)
- But it is not as though the word of God has failed. For not all who are descended from Israel [Jews alone] belong to Israel [spiritual Israel—the Bride of Yeshua!]. (Romans 9:6)
- Know then that it is those of faith who are the sons of Abraham. And the Scripture, foreseeing that God would justify the Gentiles by faith, preached the gospel beforehand to Abraham, saying, "In you shall all the nations be blessed." So then, those who are of faith are blessed along with Abraham, the man of faith. (Galatians 3:7–9)

- And if you [Jew and Gentile] are Christ's, then you are Abraham's offspring, heirs according to promise. There is neither Jew nor Greek, there is neither slave nor free, there is no male and female, for you are all [Jew and Gentile] one in Christ Jesus. (Galatians 3:28–29)

God Said It from the Beginning

Even under the sacrificial system of the Old Covenant, the "one new man concept" was God's heart from the beginning. For example, in the book of Numbers—straight from the Torah—we find that when God laid out specific rules for the daily, weekly, and "appointed-time" sacrifices, He also clearly spoke of the "one new man."

God made it clear that the sacrificial offerings *and* the Feasts of the Lord were not *just for the Jews*. They were for the Jews and the Gentiles. Both had to be willing, by faith, to submit to God's covenant of the sacrificial processes for the forgiveness of sins. And now we know why: They all pointed to Yeshua! He has always been the only "way" to salvation for Jews and Gentiles alike. Read it for yourself:

> Every native Israelite shall do these things in this way, in offering a food offering, with a pleasing aroma to the LORD. And if a stranger [a Gentile] is sojourning with you, or anyone [a Gentile] is living permanently among you, and he wishes to offer a food offering, with a pleasing aroma to the LORD, he [a Gentile] shall do as you do. For the assembly, there shall be one statute for you and for the stranger who sojourns with you, a statute forever throughout your generations. You and the sojourner shall be alike before the LORD. One law and one rule shall be for you and for the stranger [a Gentile] who sojourns with you. (Numbers 15:13–16)

Again, I will punctuate a truth many unnecessarily stumble over today. The Old Testament Sabbath law of Exodus 20 was pointing to Yeshua all along, including the penalty set for ignoring that law. Once again we see that the Law and sacrifices have always been about Yeshua. *Always*.

As Hebrews 10:1 reminds us, each of the genuine laws of God were foreshadowing the true things yet to come. And now we know there is nothing *truer* "yet to come" than Yeshua Himself!

So, now that we are in covenant with Yeshua, our Sabbath, exactly how do we go about keeping the Sabbath today—*in Him*?

chapter fifty-two

SABBATH KEEPING TODAY

It was a "mark" that identified the very day upon which "the sabbath day was nailed to the cross," and when the sun literally "went down" at noon!

In his letter to the Colossians, the Apostle Paul declares the following:

> And you, who were dead in your trespasses and the uncircumcision of your flesh, God made alive together with him, having forgiven us all our trespasses, by canceling the record of debt that stood against us with its legal demands. This he set aside, nailing it to the cross. He disarmed the rulers and authorities and put them to open shame, by triumphing over them in him [Yeshua].
>
> Therefore do not let anyone judge you by what you eat or drink, or with regard to a religious festival, a New Moon celebration or a Sabbath day. These are a shadow of the things that were to come; the reality, however, is found in Christ. (Colossians 2:13–17)

The context of this passage of Scripture is clear. The festivals and Sabbath days were merely *shadows of things to come* in Yeshua. This is exactly what I've been demonstrating through everything we've thus far uncovered.

William Barclay, who, for years before his death in 1978, was a professor of divinity and biblical criticism at the University of Glasgow, Scotland, wonderfully illuminates Paul's admonitions in Colossians 2:

> For those [in the early body of believers] who heard or read [Colossians 2] for the first time it would be crystal clear.... It is packed from beginning to end with allusions to the false teaching which was threatening to wreck the Colossian Church.... But every sentence and every phrase would go straight home to the minds and the hearts of the Colossians....
>
> They [the early Judaizers] observed yearly feasts and monthly new moons and weekly sabbaths. They drew out lists of days which specially belonged to God, on which certain things must be done and certain things must not be done. They identified religion with ritual.
>
> Paul's criticism of this stress on days is quite clear and logical. He says, "You have been rescued [in Yeshua] from all this tyranny of legal rules [the Old Covenant]. Why do you want to enslave yourself all over again? Why do you want to go back to...legalism and abandon freedom [in Yeshua]?" The spirit which makes Christianity a thing of regulations is by no means dead yet.[290]

Barclay was certainly correct. That same Chaldean spirit that wants even today's body of born-again believers to continue living in already-fulfilled rules and regulations is still with us! It has been with us from the very beginning of Yeshua's appearance on earth.

An Old Covenant Shocker

The Old Testament prophet Amos also told of the fulfillment of the Sabbath day in Yeshua. It would have been seen in cryptic form to his original audience. But take note of his exact words. No ancient Jewish prophet could have known the specifics of what practically everyone on the entire planet now knows concerning this matter.

Coffman's Commentary on the Bible:

> In what sense did God nail the sabbath to the cross of Christ? The words of course are highly figurative and symbolic. Many centuries before Christ, some tradesmen who resented keeping the sabbath day came to Amos and demanded to know:
>
>> When will *the new moon be gone*, that we may sell corn? and the sabbath that we may set forth wheat, making the ephah small and the shekel great, and falsifying the balances of deceit? (Amos 8:5).
>
> The prophet answered this question with words which to the prophet might have seemed to say that the sabbath would never be removed; but here is the word that God actually put into the mouth of Amos:
>
>> And it shall come to pass in that day, saith the Lord God, that I will cause the sun to go down at noon, and I will darken the earth in a clear day (Amos 8:9).
>
> These Scriptures teach that the sabbath day was to be abolished when God darkened the earth in a clear day and the sun went down at noon.
>
> This of course happened when Jesus was crucified; thus the sabbath day was nailed to His cross.[291]

Now look at Matthew 27. There we find the fulfillment of what Amos had been shown hundreds of years earlier. It was a "mark" that identified the very day upon which "the sabbath day was nailed to the cross," and when the sun literally "went down" at noon!

Now from the sixth hour [noon] there was darkness over all the land until the ninth hour [3 pm].... And behold, the curtain of the temple was torn in two, from top to bottom. And the earth shook, and the rocks were split. (Matthew 27:45, 51)

This is what the Apostle Paul was saying in Colossians. It's also what Dr. William Barclay, Dr. Coffman, and several other biblical scholars[292] point out concerning all the worship and Sabbath laws being completely fulfilled in Yeshua.[293]

Next, I'll outline what some of these biblical discoveries mean as we do our best to live out what Yeshua truly wants for us.

chapter fifty-three

PRACTICAL APPLICATION OF THE SABBATH

When the Sabbath walks with you and you are walking with Him, there is no need for the rule.

Let me lay out this matter as biblically accurate and realistically as I can. The Scriptures we examined in the last chapter and others like them make it clear that, for the born-again believer in Yeshua, Sabbath-keeping is a matter of spiritual freedom in the Holy Spirit. It is no longer a command from God to "strictly observe a specific day...or else!"

God's Word pointedly instructs us not to judge each other about keeping the Sabbath. It is, under the New Covenant, a matter each born-again believer needs to be fully convinced about: *Yeshua is our Sabbath*!

Sadly, most of today's believers have gotten the Sabbath mixed up with controversies concerning *which day* people should worship. Some say we should worship only on Saturdays and others say worship should only be on Sundays. Charlie down the road says Tuesday, but everybody thinks Charlie is a little bit crazy. So we just dismiss him. However, lest anyone should criticize Charlie, let it be known that people who are genuinely under the Threshold Covenant of the blood of Yeshua are free to gather to worship any day of the week.

> Where the Spirit of the Lord is, there is liberty. (2 Corinthians 3:17)

The Sabbath is no longer about a day, it's about the spirit in which we worship and the One we worship—*Yeshua Ha Mashiach*! If Charlie wants to get together with his group and worship Yeshua on Tuesday nights, that's wonderful. If his neighbor wants to gather with his group on Thursday to worship Yeshua, that's great, too. All of us must decide for ourselves, considering our overall lives, myriad family considerations, work requirements, and other obligations.

For example, my wife and I, living and daily ministering in Israel, set aside Friday evening through most of Saturday to observe our personal Sabbath and, often, to join in a time of worship. We frequently participate in and/or lead communal worship with congregations of Messianic Jewish believers throughout Israel.

Admittedly, it's fairly easy for us to choose this course, which just happens to line up with the Old Covenant commandments; however, we *choose* to set aside a Sabbath at that time. We don't do it then because of any desire to follow a strict, legalistic notion. Our decision to worship Friday–Saturday while we're living in Israel is simple: If we observed the Sabbath on Sunday or any other weekday, we would have very little ability to reach large numbers of believers, because Sunday and all the other weekdays are *workdays* in Israel!

Additionally, I would lose my ability to reach those who are still caught up in Orthodoxy, most of whom are still outside of salvation in Yeshua. Believe me, in Israel, that number is in the vast majority of the people we are trying to reach. Those folks wouldn't give me the time of day if they considered me a "Sabbath breaker" in the Orthodox Jewish sense. Therefore, for us, it would be nearly impossible to have any kind of meaningful and consistent worship gatherings or ministry opportunities in Israel on any other day.

Let me be clear: The groups of born-again believers I regularly meet with in Israel are *not* dogmatic about Friday evening worship, either. We have agreed to do it that way and at that time, because that's the period that works best in our situation.

In this matter, I am again accommodating the culture without compromising the preaching of the true Gospel through the Threshold Covenant (1 Corinthians 9:19–23). However, in the midst of this traditional Orthodox Jewish worship time, I *always* teach and preach that Yeshua has *fulfilled* all the feasts, the Temple sacrifices, and regulations, and that He has fulfilled the Sabbath law of the Old Covenant. It is my heart's desire to spread the message of this great, liberating, and eternal gift in Yeshua.

OTHER SABBATH DAYS

On the other hand, when I'm in Europe or in the United States, I gladly meet and worship with believers on Sundays, as members of the early Church often did.[294] Then again, in other places around the world where congregations are heavily persecuted for their faith in Yeshua and often have to meet secretly on whatever day of the week they can safely gather, I worship on those days with my brothers and sisters as well. I am *always* keeping the Sabbath—*regardless of the day* and what group I am with, because I am born again. In this matter, I am walking in the real Sabbath whenever, wherever, and with whomever I worship *Yeshua Ha Mashiach*.

A RESTORATIVE BREAK

The Sabbath is a *gift of rest*. It releases blessing into one's life. It excuses people from the demands of the weekly grind for one day and provides a break for restoration and renewal. It also gives believers an opportunity to worship Yeshua and reflect upon all He has done. How many times have you heard the pleading expression, "Stop the world, I want to get off!"? Well, the Sabbath is God's way of allowing us to do just that for one day each week.

Optimal human functioning requires a day of rest. Even though we don't need worldly affirmation of what God, our Creator, has told us all along, this physiological fact has been scientifically supported over and over. And, biblically speaking, when we take a day of intentional rest (Sabbath) and observe quiet time with Yeshua, great blessings certainly follow.[295]

Sabbath Rules

Are there any rules about what we should do on our chosen Sabbath? *No.* It is simply a God-ordained day of joy and relaxation, a time for appreciating the goodness of God and His blessings upon us through Yeshua. When the Sabbath walks with us and we are walking with Him, there is no need for the rule.

You might ask: "What if I miss a Sabbath rest day?" My answer is that the Sabbath rest is not meant to be a legalistic burden we must observe or else our Creator won't bless us. *No!* Missing Sabbath in any given week simply means we, sadly, miss out on the blessing of a precious gift of rest. We can always set aside another day that week, if at all possible. Life is sometimes very complex. Those complexities must be considered. However, whenever possible, an honest attempt should be made to *rest*—and rest in Yeshua!

To summarize: In Yeshua's fulfillment of the Sabbath, God has not appointed a specific time or day for worship. Nor has He appointed a certain day for rest and recuperation. He leaves that decision about when and where to us, but He *does care* that we do rest. The Sabbath, the feast days, and the Old Covenant worship laws are no longer about the *way to salvation* or about God's love for us. The laws are now all about the One whose very name is *Salvation—Yeshua Ha Mashiach*—and whose very presence is our Sabbath. Once we can get it through our heads that the true Sabbath is really about the pleasure of having *Him* in our lives, in our heart of worship, and in our rest, we'll be much happier and healthier. *That* is exactly what our Creator wants for us.

Part IX

Final Thresholds

All these, who were chosen as gatekeepers at the thresholds, were 212. They were enrolled by genealogies in their villages. David and Samuel the seer established them in their office of trust. So they and their sons were in charge of the gates of the house of the Lord, that is, the house of the tent, as guards. The gatekeepers were on the four sides, east, west, north, and south. And their kinsmen who were in their villages were obligated to come in every seven days, in turn, to be with these, for the four chief gatekeepers, who were Levites, were entrusted to be over the chambers and the treasures of the house of God.

1 Chronicles 9:22–26

[Jesus said to them,] "Enter by the narrow gate. For the gate is wide and the way is easy that leads to destruction, and those who enter by it are many. For the gate is narrow and the way is hard that leads to life, and those who find it are few."

Matthew 7:13–14

chapter 54

THE NEW JERUSALEM

As we think back over the adventurous study we've been through together, we see the culmination of all the elements of our investigation in these verses.

In the closing two chapters of Revelation (21–22), the Word of God concludes with a glimpse of the divine glory soon to come for those who belong to Yeshua through the Threshold Covenant relationship. It is the New Heaven and the New Earth, as well as the New Jerusalem—the *City of God*. We are also given a glorious revelation of the Temple of God that is present in the midst of it all!

The entire scenario is a beautiful picture that is also the final Sabbath rest for all of God's children. That eternally completed Sabbath was not only purchased by Yeshua on Golgotha's tree and through His empty tomb, but it is also our ultimate gift of rest and the divine Sabbath assurance that even now dwells within our souls through the work of His Holy Spirit. That Sabbath has nothing to do with laws, rituals, regulations, and burdensome rabbinical requirements. It's all about Yeshua—and it's all about us…the redeemed!

This final Threshold is what our entire spiritual journey has been all about. Entry over that threshold is only accomplished by following a biblically straight path. Neither the path *to* it nor the threshold that leads *through* it deviates from God's stated design and requirements. This is why it is so important that we have undertaken the hard work of exposing the Chaldean spirit—the demonic presence that often moves within the midst of our congregations of believers around the world.

One Genuine Threshold

While the arrogant and thoroughly pagan Roman Empire might have bragged that "all roads lead to Rome,"[296] I can assure you that none of the roads of this fallen earthly realm lead to the New Jerusalem, and, as we've seen, certainly not to the roads/thresholds of Rome or Babylon!

Yeshua put it this way in His very first publicly recorded sermon to the masses:

- Enter by the narrow gate. For the gate is wide and the way is easy that leads to destruction, and those who enter by it are many. For the gate is narrow and the way is hard that leads to life, and those who find it are few. (Matthew 7:13–14)
- Not everyone who says to me, "Lord, Lord," will enter the kingdom of heaven, but the one who does the will of my Father who is in heaven. On that day many will say to me, "Lord, Lord, did we not prophesy in your name, and cast out demons in your name, and do many mighty works in your name?" And then will I declare to them, "I never knew you; depart from me, you workers of lawlessness." (Matthew 7:21–23)

Now we understand why it's so critical to be sure we're on the right path: Here is where the genuine Threshold Covenant ultimately leads:

Then I saw a new heaven and a new earth, for the first heaven and the first earth had passed away, and the sea was no more. And I saw the holy city, New Jerusalem, coming down out of heaven from God, prepared as a bride adorned for her husband. And I heard a loud voice from the throne saying, "Behold, the dwelling place [tabernacle][297] of God is with man.

He will dwell [tabernacle] with them, and they will be his people, and God himself will be with them as their God. He will wipe away every tear from their eyes, and death shall be no more, neither shall there be mourning, nor crying, nor pain anymore, for the former things have passed away."

And he who was seated on the throne said, "Behold, I am making all things new." Also he said, "Write this down, for these words are trustworthy and true." And he said to me, "It is done! I am the Alpha and the Omega, the beginning and the end.

"To the thirsty I will give from the spring of the water of life without payment. The one who conquers will have this heritage, and I will be his God and he will be my son.

"But as for the cowardly, the faithless, the detestable, as for murderers, the sexually immoral, sorcerers, idolaters, and all liars, their portion will be in the lake that burns with fire and sulfur, which is the second death." (Revelation 21:1–8)

THE LAST FEAST

Those magnificent biblical truths even speak of the fulfillment of the Feast of Tabernacles…the last of the Feasts of the Lord outlined in Leviticus 23. The great promise of the ages in Yeshua is that we will forever tabernacle (dwell) with Him and continually drink from the "spring of the water of life," which represents the eternally abiding presence of *Yeshua Ha Mashiach* Himself![298]

Think of how often Yeshua told the world about these truths—especially, of all places, at the *Feast of Tabernacles* during the last few months of His life on earth.

Now the Jews'[299] Feast of Tabernacles was at hand:

> On the last day of the feast, the great day, Jesus stood up and cried out, "If anyone thirsts, let him come to me and drink. Whoever believes in me, as the Scripture has said, "Out of his heart will flow rivers of living water." (John 7:1–2, 37–38)

And the beautiful promises of Revelation 21 are not finished! We are shown much more:

> "Come, I will show you the Bride, the wife of the Lamb." And he carried me away in the Spirit to a great, high mountain, and showed me the holy city Jerusalem coming down out of heaven from God, having the glory of God, its radiance like a most rare jewel, like a jasper, clear as crystal.
>
> It had a great, high wall, with twelve gates, and at the gates twelve angels, and on the gates the names of the twelve tribes of the sons of Israel were inscribed—on the east three gates, on the north three gates, on the south three gates, and on the west three gates. And the wall of the city had twelve foundations, and on them were the twelve names of the twelve apostles of the Lamb. (Revelation 21:9–14)

John also sees the genuine Third Temple of God:

> And I saw no temple in the city, for its temple is the Lord God the Almighty and the Lamb. And the city has no need of sun or moon to shine on it, for the glory of God gives it light, and its lamp is the Lamb. By its light will the nations walk, and the kings of the earth will bring their glory into it, and its gates will never be shut

by day—and there will be no night there. They will bring into it the glory and the honor of the nations. (Revelation 21:22–26)

All of this imagery speaks of biblical *thresholds*! As we think back over the adventurous study we've been through, we see the culmination of all the elements of our investigation within these verses.

For example, we've already noticed the Feast of Tabernacles fulfilled in Paradise as we tabernacle with God forever. Then we are given the spiritual details of the New Jerusalem, the ultimate "household of God." Also note the language of "gates," "foundations," and "thresholds." In addition, there's the marriage language of the "bride and groom"—seen here as the Bride and the Lamb. And, that marriage partnership is actually called "the City of God"! This matrimonial language also evokes images of thresholds and celebrations, as well as "rehearsals."

Further, in these verses, John is caught up to a great, high "mountain" so he can be shown these things. Again, this hearkens back to Ezekiel's vision of the ultimate Temple of God, which that prophet was, like John, also shown from the top of a "high mountain" (Ezekiel 40:1–4).

Delusion, Diversion, and Deceit

In Revelation we even see the final destruction of the fake *Chaldean* thresholds we've been uncovering and exposing:

> But as for the cowardly, the faithless, the detestable, as for murderers, the sexually immoral, sorcerers, idolaters, and all liars, their portion will be in the lake that burns with fire and sulfur, which is the second death. (Revelation 21:8)

Think of how many of those Chaldean thresholds are related to the Easter *delusion* we revealed that has permeated the practices of God's own people and soiled the threshold of the pure Gospel message in these last days. Think also of the Temple *diversion* and the Sabbath *deceit*, as well as the dark threshold of the myriad rabbit trails the Chaldean spirit has continually pulled the Church through, employing each of those deceptions.

And those aren't the only deceptions. We must always be on guard. The deceiver is strong. He is vicious. He is relentless. And he is vile. He is also filled with rage, because he knows his time is drawing much closer to the end:

> But woe to you, O earth and sea, for the devil has come down to you in great wrath, because he knows that his time is short! (Revelation 12:12)

But never doubt, Yeshua has not left us alone to be at the mercy of the evil one and his minions:

- And they have overcome him by reason of the blood of the Lamb, and by reason of the word of their testimony; and they have not loved their life unto death. (Revelation 12:11, BEREAN LITERAL BIBLE)
- For he has said, "I will never leave you nor forsake you." (Hebrews 13:5)

chapter fifty-five

EVERYTHING IS CONNECTED

*Time was created for us, but it will one day be
changed into an immeasurable eternity as we
cross over the final threshold.*

What we've already seen is glorious. But in Revelation 21 we also view the beautiful picture of the "one new man" revealed in the promises of Ephesians 2. We witness it in the joining of the Old and New Covenants into the one new "city" or "household"— spiritual Israel.[300] It's all there, in the City of God, the New Jerusalem.

We see twelve gates named after each of the twelve tribes of Israel. We are also shown the twelve foundations, each foundation named after one of the twelve apostles. The twenty-four gates and foundations represent the joining of the Old Covenant with the New Covenant, as well as the "one new man" that always existed among God's people—Jews and Gentiles—even from the time of the Passover (Exodus 12:37–38).

That imagery also matches up with the twenty-four thrones (12 + 12) of chapters 4 and 5 of Revelation, most likely a mirrored picture of the Old and New Covenants representing the foundations of the new City of God. Even these pictures, according to a number of scholars, appear to mirror the "one new man" of Ephesians 2 and/or the *spiritual Israel* imagery attached to the 144,000 (12 x 12 x 1,000) that show up in Revelation 7 and 14.[301]

While we're on the topic of the one new man, don't forget we've previously uncovered how, on that very first Passover evening, a multitude of *Jews and Gentiles* came out of Egypt *together*, under the "blood of the Passover Lamb"! Then we saw that, even in the sacrificial covenants, *both Jews and Gentiles* were covered by the same blood sacrifices, but only if each was willing to follow God's divine paths in carrying them out properly—and together.

Also, in Revelation 21, we twice read about the redeemed of the "nations" dwelling in the New Jerusalem. Therefore, we again discover that the new city, the household of God, is made up of the blood alliance between the Jews and the Gentiles, dwelling in the midst of their Creator. There is no difference between them now, not in Paradise! All of those biblical truths, and more, are embedded right in the middle of Revelation 21.

REVELATION 22

Let's also remember Revelation 22; its first five verses attach directly to the theme of Revelation 21. Remember, the chapter and verse divisions in the books of the Bible came long after the books were written; John the Revelator did not organize his writings in Revelation in such a manner. Have a look at those five important verses, which also concern the New Jerusalem, the Holy City of God:

> Then the angel showed me the river of the water of life, bright as crystal, flowing from the throne of God and of the Lamb through the middle of the street of the city; also, on either side of the river, the tree of life with its twelve kinds of fruit, yielding its fruit each month.
>
> The leaves of the tree were for the healing of the nations. No longer will there be anything accursed, but the throne of God and of the Lamb will be in it, and his servants will worship him.

They will see his face, and his name will be on their foreheads. And night will be no more. They will need no light of lamp or sun, for the Lord God will be their light, and they will reign forever and ever. (Revelation 22:1–5)

There's a lot to think about in that short passage. For instance, notice that the last page of Revelation connects back to the first verses of Genesis.

Think of it: As noted in an earlier chapter, the first thing God (Yeshua) called forth was "light." That took place on the first day. Yeshua is the Light; He is the Light of Life and the Light of the World. We saw earlier that the theme of *light* ties also to Yeshua's Resurrection and the disciples finding the tomb empty—*on the first day* of the week!

Also, we discover the throne of God, in Revelation 4 and 5, is bathed in glorious light. Here, in Revelation 22, we see that light again, assuring us that because we are in *Threshold Covenant* through Yeshua's blood, we will always walk and live in His light, from this day forth. He will tabernacle with us, and we will tabernacle with Him. How amazing!

The "healing of the nations" speaks to the concept of *spiritual Israel* again, as well as to the "one new man" of Ephesians 2. Over and over, we see all of these themes, from Genesis to Revelation. And they all tie to the greater themes of the Threshold Covenant—our blood alliance in Yeshua…and the "one new man," Jews and Gentiles together, under that same blood alliance. Now we see the promise fulfilled; the two become "one" and rule and reign with our Creator and Savior forever. Yeshua, through the Apostle John, has given us a wonderful cluster of glimpses into the future, in order to assure us that He keeps His promises!

NEVER FORGET

So now, when we spend authentic *relationship time* communicating with God through prayer, worship, meditation upon His Word, and observing His appointed times as they are fulfilled in Yeshua (crossing over the threshold of temporal into the eternal realm), we're interacting in a different dimension altogether. While we may be present in the physical world, our interaction with the Father through His Holy Spirit is interdimensional. It's a dress rehearsal for when we're finally with Him, face-to-face, having crossed the final threshold into the New Jerusalem.

Yeshua is looking for a pleasing aroma of communication with us. Throughout the Old Testament, there are foreshadowings of what is to come in God's ultimate plan:

> Let my prayer be counted as incense before you. (Psalm 141:2)

That foreshadowing goes all the way up to the fulfillment of Yeshua's supreme blood alliance sacrifice and continues right up to the time we're living in now. The Old Testament—*the Tanakh*—was always about preparing us for something bigger. That something bigger is revealed in the New Covenant/Testament through Yeshua.

In this brief moment called "life," we're actually in an eternally significant stage of dress rehearsals. We're preparing ourselves to live in the other dimension—Paradise, the New Jerusalem, the Holy City of God. Every time we do the Father's will, we're practicing for life in that dimension!

> Your kingdom come, your will be done, on earth as it is in heaven. (Matthew 6:10)

It doesn't matter that our feet are on earth right now. Spiritually speaking, we're also in the other dimension. When we interact with God, it's the Spirit of Yeshua who lives inside of us that is communicating with the Father. If He dwells in the eternal dimension, it means we're also there through Him.[302]

> He has made us alive together with Christ—by grace you have been saved—and raised us up with him and seated us with him in the heavenly places in Christ Jesus. (Ephesians 2:5–6)

Yeshua came to earth as a man to dwell among us to show His glory and reveal Himself as God in the flesh so we could understand Him more perfectly through a tangible demonstration of His personhood. He lives outside of time. In fact, He created time! Time was created for us to give us the opportunity to choose the eternal Threshold Covenant with Him. However, "time" will one day be changed into an immeasurable eternity as we cross over the final threshold and into all the dimensions Yeshua has created for us. What a glorious day that will be!

Everything all along has always been part of the dress rehearsal for what is coming. It was permanently connected from the very beginning!

chapter fifty-six

THE TRUE ALIYAH

A number of Scripture passages indicate that God will return His people to Israel, but that's not about the individual redemption process.

One specific Hebrew word holds a great and treasured meaning for most Jewish people the world over. That word is *aliyah*. It means "go up."

That word is even used prior to a traditional Jewish wedding ceremony. During the ceremony itself, called an *aufruf,* the couple is *called up to the Torah* for a blessing. That wedding consecration is called an *aliyah*. When the dedication is completed, the entire congregation wishes the couple blessings and happiness by throwing soft candies at them.

The word *aliyah* has become most associated with the Jews from all over the world who are *returning* to their homeland—or, as it's often expressed, "going up to Jerusalem."

The Law of Return, passed by the Israeli parliament in 1950, gives all the dispersed Jews, as well as their children and grandchildren, the right to relocate to Israel. Upon their return, they can acquire Israeli citizenship on the basis of connecting to their Jewish identity.

As of 2022, Israel was home to approximately 46.2 percent of the world's Jewish population. While more than 7 million Jews are now living in the land of Israel, the number of Jews worldwide stands at approximately 15.3 million.[303]

Those who "make *aliyah*" have many reasons for journeying to Israel, whether it's because of persecution abroad, a deep love for the land itself, or perhaps a simple desire to broaden their Hebrew/Jewish adventure.

God allows certain things to happen in our fallen world in order to get His Word and offer of salvation in Yeshua widely dispersed among the Jewish people. What the Chaldean spirit may intend for confusion, distraction, or misunderstanding, God sometimes reverses and uses for good. In this case, He allows the earthly/political concept of *aliyah* to continue in order to demonstrate the genuine *spiritual aliyah*.

For example, when Jews leave Finland, Ethiopia, the United States, or any other nation and put their feet on the soil of Israel, they essentially enter a different dimension in terms of temporal geography and time zones. Does a dimension of this type have a *threshold*—a point of crossing over, a point of life-altering decision? In the spiritual realm, *yes*...it most certainly does.

Aliyah is a temporal type of a spiritual reality. Immigrants cross over borders and time zones to enter the physical land of Israel. But those who are born again in Yeshua cross over the dimensional threshold from temporal life into the eternal *New Jerusalem*.

Where is this other dimension? It's first within the heart and soul of the believer. It's just a veil that separates the temporal from the eternal. But between the physical and the eternal dimensions is a threshold that must be crossed in order to enter.

There's been a lot of confusion about the tradition of immigrants traveling to Israel as though there's something mystical about it. It's true a number of Scriptures indicate God will return His people to Israel, but that's not about the individual redemption process. Kissing the soil in Israel doesn't save anybody. What saves people, Jews or Gentiles, is Messiah Yeshua.

If I were to go to the United States and find a billionaire who was willing to finance *aliyah* for all the Jews in Brooklyn and have them flown here, would that save them? Would it guarantee their eternity in the Paradise of God? Of course, the answer is "no."

It's better for me to go to Brooklyn, preach the Gospel, and, through that biblical process of redemption, encourage the Jewish people to respond to the love of Yeshua in a born-again experience. When they repent for the ways they have dishonored their Creator, turn their backs on Orthodox traditions and the rudimentary ways of the Chaldean-influenced world, and follow *Yeshua Ha Mashiach*...that's the true *aliyah*. That's *aliyah* God's way—whether or not they ever set foot on the soil of Israel either to live here or merely visit. This is because "making [biblical] *aliyah*" is all about making it back to *spiritual Israel* forever and becoming a part of the "one new man."

I'm not saying Jews shouldn't return to Israel. I believe that nation should open its doors wide to any Jew who wants to return, or who is being persecuted anywhere in the world. It's wonderful if they come here to Israel. But if we don't preach the Gospel of *Yeshua Ha Mashiach* to those who return, then true *aliyah* has not served its purpose, and we've missed the mark. We've actually assisted those who are coming to Israel to *trample on* the threshold of God's grace unaware, leaving Yeshua completely out of the equation.

Man shall not live by bread alone, but by every word that comes from the mouth of God. (Matthew 4:4)

Those are the words of Jesus. The things of this world will never satisfy. We can fill our bellies with the best bread, fruits, and delicacies of Israel, but if we're not full of the Word of God, there will be an inner emptiness we find impossible to explain.

Jesus' words also constitute a *compound prophecy*. When we bring Jews back to Israel in response to the Scriptures that say they have to be regathered, we're to do more than feed the hungry and clothe the poor. We're to introduce them to spiritual Israel, the one that is eternal.

The day will come when physical Israel ceases to exist. Only the New Jerusalem will remain when the New Heaven and the New Earth are put in place. Only those who are covered with the sacrificial blood of Yeshua, the genuine Lamb of God, will enter over that final threshold.

That is the true and divine *aliyah*!

chapter fifty-seven

BLESSING ISRAEL

You can't bless Israel God's way unless you know who Israel really is.

Through the work of Messiah of Israel Ministries, we don't promote *aliyah* in terms of simply getting Jews to Israel in order to return them to the Land. When they come, we help them with whatever they need materially and logistically, of course. But, most importantly, we preach the Gospel of Yeshua. We answer their questions. We pray with them, worship with them, and disciple them. We show them the Threshold Covenant that is in *Yeshua Ha Mashiach*.

When I speak to Jews here in Israel who have just landed at the airport from many places around the world, I carefully search to find a way to preach the Gospel to them. I don't want them to make only a temporary *aliyah*. I want them to get their hearts set on doing *eternal aliyah* wherein they can cross the eternal threshold. But first they need to understand *God's threshold of grace*.

I believe every tourist, every person making *aliyah*, or every student coming to Israel to study needs more than a Jewish history lesson. They greatly need to be introduced to the genuine Messiah in Yeshua—the one they have always longed for. The one who came from Heaven and put on human flesh.

Furthermore, they need to be shown that He came here to Israel just as the prophets foretold! It was here where the Messiah laid down His life for them. It was here where He rose from the dead for the Jew *first*. He alone has fulfilled every one of the Feasts of the Lord that so many Jewish people love. They need to cross the *Grace Threshold* from unbelief and the Chaldean lies into understanding and belief to experience the fullest measure of what it means to be a completed Jew!

In my book, *Unmasking the Chaldean Spirit*, I explain in detail about all the travelers to Israel who are deceived, buying into the tourist traps, and seeking out false sites.[304] Satan doesn't want the biblically revealed sites discovered, because they would eventually become powerful witnesses to the Jewish people living there.

Most Jews recognize these tourist traps as false and often identify Christians as false because of their association with, and belief in, the inauthentic sites. They often mock Christian sightseers who run from one Roman Catholic location to another on a quest to see the real holy places. But Satan doesn't want the Jews identifying Christianity with biblical truth and historical reality. In that same way, he tries to prevent visitors or immigrants to Israel from discovering the Messiah by hearing the Gospel.

Who Are "God's People"?

Yes, God will regather His people, but who are His people? Are they only the Jewish people? No! They are *all* who enter over the genuine threshold of faith as the "one new man"—Jew or Gentile! Both came out of Egypt under that Passover Lamb and its blood poured onto the threshold of each house and splattered upon the doorposts and lentils. Both participated in the Feasts of the Lord. Both kept the sacrificial ordinances of the Lord. Both fought side by side as they made their way through the wilderness journey.

So when Jesus said, "I was sent only to the lost sheep of the house of Israel" (Matthew 15:24), He was talking about His mission to escort both Jews and Gentiles who accept Yeshua across the threshold of faith and eventually into the New Jerusalem.

Only when we understand the depths of His grace and the Threshold Covenant He offers can we understand what it means to trample *upon* it, to step *on* the threshold and profane it rather than step *over* it, enter the household of God, and honor it.

The only reason God drew people to Israel in 1948 at the time of the rebirth of the nation was to fulfill the master plan of salvation for the world. Israel had to be reborn, and people had to be there to constitute a nation. It was a foreshadowing of all of us being born again!

The two great prophecies of the Old Testament were the rebirth of Israel as a witness to the end-time generations of Jews and Gentiles and the rebirth of humanity itself—offered only through the prophesied Messiah, in *Yeshua Ha Mashiach*, the Lamb slain before the foundation of the world.

The prophecy of the coming of Yeshua was fulfilled first in the first century AD. The return of Israel came next—after almost 1,900 years of the Gospel being preached around the world. The world has never been the same since these two monumental events. And both were prophesied—thousands of years before they occurred—in only one book in all the world—the Word of God, from Genesis to Revelation.

Now we are living in the first generation to see an influx of Jewish people flocking back to Israel. Think of it! If only 10 percent of the funds designated to assist Jewish people in making *aliyah* were actually used to proclaim the Chaldean-free Gospel of Yeshua, I can't imagine how many salvations would actually take place in Israel! Instead, Satan is having a party. He's using the diluted and misinterpreted Word of God against God's people.

A huge percentage of the Jews who come to Israel are not religious at all. Many are secular Jews. However, a number become "religious" when they get here through the secular process of *aliyah*. Why is that?

Why do I see an Ethiopian bus driver wearing a *yarmulke* (a skullcap signifying devotion)? He wasn't wearing a *yarmulke* in Ethiopia. Why do I see a Jew from France wearing a beard in Israel? His face was probably shaven in France. It's because when Jews from around the world make *aliyah*, members of the Israeli Orthodox rabbinic movement contact them immediately and convince them to become Orthodox.

Is this what God really wants from His people—*yarmulkes* and beards? This, too, is all about the Chaldean spirit trying to distract folks from finding the genuine threshold. Satan will escort people to the threshold of the borders and citizen privileges of Israel through *aliyah*, but he certainly won't get anybody to the final threshold of the New Jerusalem.

Satan doesn't care if Jewish people enjoy the pleasures of this world by living in Israel and thinking that somehow they are now religious even "saved." Satan knows they're not saved and are still separated from God by their sin, because Satan has kept them from the Threshold Covenant— the alliance that's only available through the blood of Yeshua. Satan will deceive "even the very elect" if that were truly possible.

> For false christs and false prophets will arise and perform great signs and wonders, so as to lead astray, if possible, even the elect. (Matthew 24:24)

When people help Jews make *aliyah*, they think they're blessing Israel, but if they're not involved in building the New Jerusalem and are only blessing the temporal Israel, they could actually be grieving the Holy Spirit without even knowing it.

> And even they [the Jewish people of the last days], if they do not continue in their unbelief, will be grafted in, for God has the power to graft them in again. (Romans 11:23)

The Hebrew word translated in Romans 11 as "again" should have been translated "back"; God has the power to graft them "back." There is a concept in the Bible about the Jews returning to Israel, but it's focused on *spiritual* Israel, so it's for both *Jews and Gentiles*. God has provided a way for them to be grafted back through Yeshua. So, when someone helps a Jew return to Israel, it needs to be through the truth of Romans 11:22–24. That is the *real* "back"!

> **Note then the kindness and the severity of God:** severity toward those who have fallen, but God's kindness to you, provided you continue in his kindness. Otherwise you too will be cut off. And even they, if they do not continue in their unbelief, will be grafted in, for **God has the power to graft them in again.** For if you were cut from what is by nature a wild olive tree, and grafted, contrary to nature, into a cultivated olive tree, **how much more will these, the natural branches, be grafted back into their own olive tree.** (Romans 11:22–24, emphasis added)

That is something I've been trying to explain for years. But it's a difficult idea for people to grasp, because of all the rabbit-trail rabbinic teachings, the Chaldean spirit attacks, and the Roman Christian traditions that are thousands of years old and are embedded in the beliefs and practices of congregations of believers all over the world. It's an all-out spiritual war, just as the Word of God prophesied.

How Do We Bless Israel?

> I will bless those who bless you and curse those who curse you; and all the families of the earth will be blessed through you. (Genesis 12:3, BSB)

We can't bless Israel God's way unless we know who it really is. What is God's definition of "blessing?" Am I blessing Israel by going to a neighborhood and handing out food to everyone there? Is that blessing Israel? Temporarily, *yes*. But is that the ultimate blessing God is talking about? No.

God's talking about *salvation*, plain and simple! "Blessing Israel" means spreading the truth of the Gospel message of *Yeshua Ha Mashiach* to Jews and Gentiles alike. All believers are ambassadors to Israel. Our job description is found in Matthew 28:19–20:

> Go therefore and make disciples of all nations, baptizing them in the name of the Father and of the Son and of the Holy Spirit, teaching them to observe all that I have commanded you. (Matthew 28:19–20)

That's how we bless Israel!

chapter fifty-eight

THE JOURNEY

He wants you to be with Him in the New Jerusalem,
the Holy City of God. He has amazing and eternal plans for you!

Thank you so much for taking this biblical excursion with me. It has been my honor to lead you along this sometimes difficult path. It's also been a great pleasure to my soul that you have allowed me to share some of the most important and personal revelations I've learned in my own continual search for God's truth.

It is my deepest prayer that you'll now begin to see the concepts of the Threshold Covenant on practically every page of the Bible. I am convinced you'll be thrilled as you begin to see those revelations with ever-increasing frequency. Recognizing them and understanding their context and importance will transform your personal study of God's Word. In fact, I'm still discovering images, and even out-and-out declarations, of this great biblical truth as I continue to uncover the unsearchable riches of the Word of God.

But beware, my friend. If you have taken your step over the blood-bought Threshold Covenant, you already know Satan is prowling around like a roaring lion seeing if he can trip you up, sideline you, or even devour your joy, freedom, and faith walk with Yeshua. At least now you know a little bit more about why he's stalking you so closely.

The truth is Satan detests you. You represent the eternal Kingdom that will soon overwhelm and destroy his temporary kingdom. He fears you. He wants to cripple your anointing. He wants to drag you into one of his Chaldean traps. But this is our journey! This is our wilderness wandering! I urge you to faithfully complete it. Do not fear the giants looming before you.

Satan desires to drag you into temptations, lies, addictions, filth, and many other paths that can lead you away from following God's Word and into human traditions and perversions of that Word. Each is nothing more than a false threshold. They mark decision points in your life…and once you cross over them, Satan might well be able to derail your anointed Kingdom work. Don't let him do it!

Remember these promises and blessings, and many more like them:

- Every spirit that does not confess Jesus is not from God. This is the spirit of the antichrist, which you heard was coming and now is in the world already. Little children, you are from God and have overcome them, for he who is in you is greater than he who is in the world. (1 John 4:3–4)
- But you are not in darkness, brothers, for that day to surprise you like a thief. For you are all children of light, children of the day. We are not of the night or of the darkness. So then let us not sleep, as others do, but let us keep awake and be sober. For those who sleep, sleep at night, and those who get drunk, are drunk at night. But since we belong to the day, let us be sober, having put on the breastplate of faith and love, and for a helmet the hope of salvation. For God has not destined us for wrath, but to obtain salvation through our Lord Jesus Christ, who died for us so that whether we are awake or asleep we might live with him. Therefore encourage one another and build one another up, just as you are doing. (1 Thessalonians 5:4–11)

- For though we walk in the flesh, we are not waging war according to the flesh. For the weapons of our warfare are not of the flesh but have divine power to destroy strongholds. We destroy arguments and every lofty opinion raised against the knowledge of God, and take every thought captive to obey Christ. (2 Corinthians 10:3–5)

If you haven't yet stepped over the genuine Threshold Covenant of *Yeshua Ha Mashiach*, if you haven't come into a biblical blood alliance with Him, I pray that after reading this book and hearing the Lord speak to your heart by His Holy Spirit, *now* might be that time. He wants you to be with Him in the New Jerusalem, the Holy City of God! He has amazing and eternal plans for you—plans you cannot even conceive at this point in your life's journey.

So, fight the fight, finish the race, and keep the faith—until you cross the threshold that is the ultimate and eternal finish line. It is the dimensional divide between this fallen earth and the Paradise that is soon to come…forever.

Come into the household of God, into *the Father's House*, into the loving presence of the Creator of your soul.

And on that day, you'll hear Him say, "Well done, my good and faithful servant…now, enter in to your rest!"

About the Author

Messianic Rabbi Zev Porat was born and raised in Israel in a deeply devout Jewish Orthodox family and tradition. His journey from Orthodoxy to faith in *Yeshua Ha Mashiach* is a lengthy saga of profound supernatural interventions and amazing revelations from Heaven's throne, as expanded upon within the pages of this book.

The Lord of Glory continues to greatly enlarge Zev's ministry reach around the world. He continues to appear on numerous Christian television and radio programs throughout the United States and Europe. He preaches and teaches in pulpits and conferences. He sends out a weekly video and newsletter update. Zev ministers to house groups, discipling new believers all over Israel. He and his team are often found in the streets, sidewalks, and important places of congregating people—including the Kotel area in downtown Jerusalem's Old City. His ministry team also touches the lives of Holocaust survivors and their families. All to the glory of Yeshua.

Zev, and his wife Lian, currently reside in Tel Aviv, Israel. To discover more about Zev's life and vibrant global ministry, visit his website at:

www.messiahofisraelministries.com.

USE THE QR-CODE BELOW TO ACCESS MANY SPECIAL DEALS AND PROMOTIONS ON BOOKS AND FILMS FEATURING DISCOVERY, PROPHECY, AND THE SUPERNATURAL!

NOTES

1. Exodus 12:22. The word "threshold" is the correct rendering of the Hebrew. See the following three commentaries entries at https://biblehub.com/commentaries/exodus/12-22.htm.
Barnes' Notes on the Bible: "Bason—The word means "threshold" in some other passages and in Egyptian, and is taken here in that sense by some versions. If that rendering be correct, it would imply that the lamb was slain on the threshold."
Ellicott's Bible Commentary: In the bason.—"The word translated 'bason' has another meaning also, 'threshold;' and this meaning was preferred in the present place both by the LXX [Septuagint]. and by Jerome."
Pulpit Commentary: "The Septuagint and Vulgate render—'that is on the threshold.' *Saph*— the [Hebrew] word translated 'basin' has the double meaning. None of you shall go out."
Hebrew. 5592. "caph," Biblehub.com, https://biblehub.com/hebrew/5592.htm.
Strong's Exhaustive Concordance: "From Hebrew *caphaph*, in its original sense of containing; a vestibule (as a limit); also a dish (for holding blood or wine)—bason, door (post), gate, threshold."
2. *Yeshua*: Hebrew word for Jesus.
3. "At the Foot of the Mountain"
Coffman's Bible Commentary: "'And builded an altar under the mount....' The ratification of the covenant took place not on Mount Sinai, but at the foot of it. That is where the blood was sprinkled."
Bridgeway Bible Commentary: "In ancient times covenants were usually

sealed by blood, and at Sinai too God and his people were joined in a blood ritual.... To emphasize the closeness of this covenant relation with God, the representatives of Israel went up into the mountain, where they saw the glory of God and ate the meal of the peace offering in fellowship together."

4. Greek. 3438. *moné*: "Most often translated in the Greek as: lodging, dwelling-place, room, abode." https://biblehub.com/greek/3438.htm.
The word "room" is also a common translation of *moné* in a number of modern translations. https://biblehub.com/john/14-2.htm.
This Greek word is used only in one other place in the entire New Testament: John 14:23. And in this verse, *moné* is most often translated as "home" or "abode." The thought is "a home, or living place, that has plenty of room for everyone—including actual rooms or "places."
"Jesus answered him, 'If anyone loves me, he will keep my word, and my Father will love him, and we will come to him and make our home with him.'" (John 14:23).

5. The word *Yeshu* is widely known, even among Orthodox Jews of today, to be a long-held traditional acronym for the Hebrew expression *yemach shem vezichro*, which means, "May his name and memory be obliterated."
Carl Gallups and Zev Porat. *The Rabbi, the Secret Message, and the Identity of Messiah* (Crane, MO: Defender, 2017), 56.

6. This is the short account of that weeklong period of miraculous intervention in our lives as told in longer form in my 2017 book, *The Rabbi, the Secret Message and the Identity of Messiah* referenced in the preceding note.

7. *Aliyah* is the immigration of Jews from around the world to the prophetically restored nation of Israel. It is traditionally described as "the act of going up" towards the holy city of Jerusalem.

8. "The 'Fertile Crescent,' a term coined by University of Chicago Egyptologist James Henry Breasted, refers to a crescent-shaped region in Western Asia. Formed by the Tigris and Euphrates rivers and the Mediterranean Sea, this region gave rise to some of the world's earliest civilizations. The Fertile Crescent, often referred to as 'the cradle of civilization,' is the crescent-shaped region in Western Asia and North Africa that spans the modern-day countries of Iraq, Turkey, Syria, Lebanon, Israel, Palestine and, for some scholars, Egypt."

9. University of Chicago. "The Fertile Crescent, explained," UChicago News, accessed 7/3/23, https://news.uchicago.edu/explainer/fertile-crescent-explained.
Hebrew. Covenant, 1285. "Berith," Biblehub.com.
Strongs Exhaustive Concordance: "From barah (in the sense of cutting (like bara'); a compact (because made by passing between pieces of flesh)—covenant. See Hebrew *barah*. See Hebrew *bara'*. https://biblehub.com/hebrew/1285.htm."

10. In Syria and in Egypt (even as late as the 1890s), when a guest worthy of special honor is welcomed to a home, the blood of a slaughtered or "sacrificed" animal is shed on the threshold of that home as a means of adopting the newcomer into the family, or of making a covenant union with the guest. And every such primitive covenant in blood includes an appeal to the protecting deity to ratify it as between the two parties and himself.
See: H. Clay Trumbull. *The Threshold Covenant or the Beginning of Religious Rites*, (I. *A Blood Welcome at the Door*) (New York: Scribner's, 1896), https://www.gutenberg.org/files/49216/49216-h/49216-h.htm.

11. Jacob Weingreen. *A Practical Grammar for Classical Hebrew*, 2nd ed., (Oxford: Oxford University Press, 1959), 304.

12. Jared Parker. "Cutting Covenants," (third paragraph), accessed 1/23/23, https://rsc.byu.edu/gospel-jesus-christ-old-testament/cutting-covenants#_edn4.

13. E. J. Bickerman. "Cutting A Covenant," In: *Studies in Jewish and Christian History* (2 vols), accessed 2/2/23, https://brill.com/display/book/9789047420729/Bej.9789004152946.i-1242_002.xml.

14. See an image of an ancient threshold groover at the following link, from the ruins of Pompeii during the time of the Roman Empire, the time during which Jesus lived out His ministry life: https://www.pompeiiinpictures.com/pompeiiinpictures/R6/6%2013%2007_files/image048.jpg.
Threshold "groover." Hebrew, 5592. "caph," Biblehub.com, https://biblehub.com/hebrew/5592.htm.
Strong's Exhaustive Concordance: "From Hebrew *caphaph*, in its original sense of containing; a vestibule (as a limit); also a dish (for holding blood or wine)—bason, door (post), gate, threshold."

15. "This ritual constituted the formal ratification of the Mosaic Covenant

by which Yahweh adopted Israel as His 'son' (cf. Genesis 15). The parallel with the inauguration of the New Covenant is striking (cf. Matthew 26:28; 1 Corinthians 11:25). In all such ceremonies the oath of obedience [Exodus 24:7] implied the participants' willingness to suffer the fate of the sacrificed animals if the covenant stipulations were violated by those who took the oath.'"
See: *Dr. Constable's Expository Notes on Exodus 24:4:* https://www.studylight.org/commentary/exodus/24-4.html.

16. See James B. Pritchard, ed., *Ancient Near Eastern Texts Relating to the Old Testament,* 3rd ed. with supplement (Princeton, NJ: Princeton, 1969), xix. Pritchard has conveniently compiled English translations of many extrabiblical texts related to the Old Testament into one volume.

17. What was circumcision in the Bible about? From *Reasons to Believe*: "It is important to keep in mind that the practice of circumcision, first and foremost, signified the covenantal relationship between Yahweh (the God of Israel) and Abraham and his descendants. God instituted the practice as a reminder to Israel that they owed their very existence to Yahweh. God promised Abraham a son well after Sarah was of childbearing age. And that son, Isaac, gave rise to the nation of Israel. In other words, because circumcision is a religious ritual with covenantal significance, this practice does not require a medical or biological rationale. Neither does the practice necessarily mean that the foreskin is a flawed design.... Still, it is remarkable that the timing and details of the process prescribed by Yahweh reflect sound medical practices. And the recognition that circumcision confers medical benefits indicates that God's plan for signifying his covenant with Abraham and his descendants was, indeed, sound and reflected divine wisdom."
See: Rana, Fazale. "Why Would God Command Circumcision?" Reasons.org, 2/10/21, https://reasons.org/explore/blogs/the-cells-design/why-would-god-command-circumcision.
Also see: Mayo Clinic. "Circumcision (male)," https://www.mayoclinic.org/tests-procedures/circumcision/about/pac-20393550.

18. Trumbull, *The Threshold Covenant* (full reference at endnote 9): "Originally the covenant sacrifice at the threshold was with the one God of life. But as monotheism degenerated into polytheism, the idea came to prevail

of different deities in different portions of the door, or of different deities in different districts of country or in different offices of life.... It was much the same in the Old World as in the New. In ancient and in modern times, and in widely different portions of the world, there are indications that the threshold of the home was the primitive altar; and that the side-posts and lintel of the doorway above the threshold bore symbols or inscriptions in proof of the sacredness of the entrance to the family home, and in token of an accomplished covenant with its guardian God, or gods."

19. See the image on p. 24 for the location of the lintels and doorposts.

20. Trumbull, *The Threshold Covenant*" ("A Blood Welcome at the Door"): "The primitive altar of the family would seem to have been the threshold, or doorsill, or entranceway, of the home dwelling-place. This is indicated by surviving customs, in the East and elsewhere among primitive peoples, and by the earliest historic records of the human race. It is obvious that houses preceded temples, and that the housefather was the earliest priest. Sacrifices for the family were, therefore, within or at the entrance of the family domicile. "While the guest is still outside, the host takes a lamb, or a goat, and, tying its feet together, lays it upon the threshold of his door. Resting his left knee upon the bound victim, the host holds its head by his left hand, while with his right he cuts its throat. He retains his position until all the blood has flowed from the body upon the threshold. Then the victim is removed, and the guest steps over the blood, across the threshold; and in this act he becomes, as it were, a member of the family by the Threshold Covenant."

21. According to Moses' prescription laid out in Exodus 12, it is, however, a biblical consideration of importance that the Israelites most likely had no idea why Moses' detailed requirements were made for the sacrificial lamb to be secured on the tenth day of Nissan and then slaughtered on the fourteenth day...precisely. Nor did they know how the application of the blood, according to those prescriptions, also made the sign of Yeshua's Crucifixion cross, or that He would actually become the ultimate fulfillment of the Passover Lamb they would use on this night. Neither would they have understood the picture of the Passover as the beginning of all the Feasts of the Lord, as that would only be later revealed at Mt. Sinai, and how all the events of that Passover experience

(the Red Sea crossing, the desert wandering, the entry into the Promised Land, etc.) would one day directly relate to the most important elements of the entire Gospel message carried out in the person of Yeshua. The threshold blood covenant they *would* understand, but the depth of what they were actually setting in motion that particular night, at Moses' instructions, concerning the salvation that would be offered to the entire globe through Yeshua's cross almost two thousand years into their future was still only a far-off shadow.

22. *Cambridge Bible for Schools and Colleges:* "The blood of the slain lamb to be applied to the doorposts and lintel of the house in which it is eaten,—as it were, to consecrate the house, and protect its inmates against destruction. This rite is probably a survival of an earlier, perhaps pre-Yahwistic stage, of usage. The Bedawin of the present day, when a new house is dedicated, sprinkle its doors and front with the blood of a goat slaughtered at the ceremony. See p. 411; and Lees, *The Witness of the Wilderness* (1909), p. 180. See https://biblehub.com/commentaries/exodus/12-7.htm.

Exodus 12:21–23, New English Translation: "Exodus 12:22… The Greek and the Vulgate translate סַף (saf, 'basin') as 'threshold.' W. C. Kaiser reports how early traditions grew up about the killing of the lamb on the threshold" ("Exodus," EBC 2:376). See https://www.biblegateway.com/passage/?search=Exodus%2012%3A21-23&version=NET&interface=amp.

23. See *Witness in the Wilderness: W. C. Kaiser*, here: https://babel.hathitrust.org/cgi/pt?id=njp.32101073671123&view=1up&seq=200.

H. Clay Trumbull. *The Threshold Covenant or the Beginning of Religious Rites*, (v. Hebrew Passover or Cross-over, Sacrifice 1. New Meaning in an Old Rite…") (New York: Scribner's, 1896), https://www.gutenberg.org/files/49216/49216-h/49216-h.htm.

H. Clay Trumbull biography: "Henry Clay Trumbull (June 8, 1830–December 8, 1903) was an American clergyman and author. He became a world-famous editor, author, and pioneer of the Sunday school movement. After his military service, Trumbull became New England secretary for the American Sunday-school Union. In 1875, he and his family moved to Philadelphia where he became editor of the *Sunday School Times*. He held this position until his death in 1903. Among his associates was evangelist Dwight L. Moody. Trumbull was the Lyman Beecher Lecturer at Yale Divinity School in 1888. He was also the author of thirty-eight books. Trumbull was known for his commitment to 'personal evangelism' which entailed telling friends and acquaintances about spiritual salvation through Christ's vicarious atonement. In this way, he was an early practitioner of modern-day Evangelical Christianity." See https://en.wikipedia.org/wiki/Henry_Clay_Trumbull.

24. Deuteronomy 31:30–32:1–43. This great poem of victory was delivered just prior to Moses' death on Mount Nebo. It "praises the faithfulness and power of the Lord, decries the faithlessness and wickedness of Israel, and predicts the consequent divine punishment; it adds, however, that in the end the Lord will relent and will vindicate his people." https://www.britannica.com/search?query=Song+of+Moses.

25. Trumbull, *The Threshold Covenant*, "A Blood Welcome at the Door": "To step over or across the blood, or its substitute, on the doorsill, is to accept or ratify the proffered covenant; but to trample upon the symbol of the covenant is to show contempt for the host who proffers it, and no greater indignity than this is known in the realm of primitive social intercourse." The following excerpt is from 119 Ministries at https://www.119ministries.com. See https://3182d453b68388416980-71bc4c8fd3e50b4ee0e248e517d3026f.ssl.cf2.rackcdn.com/uploaded/t/0e8148026_1544483025_the-threshold-covenant-transcript.pdf.

"In Eastern culture, the way a person would show hatred toward someone who wants to be in covenant is by refusing to step over the threshold. Instead, the person showing hatred towards the covenant would trample and stomp on the threshold of a person's home. This was considered worse than cursing at your neighbor. Now with that in mind, please consider this verse prayerfully and carefully."

26. See Ezekiel 28:11–19. God called Satan a "guardian cherub" and placed him in the Garden of Eden as its caretaker. Instead, Satan profaned it and took it for his own.

Smith's Bible Commentary (Ezekiel 28:14): "Moreover the word of the LORD came unto me, saying, Son of man, take up a lamentation upon the king of Tyrus, and say unto him, Thus saith the Lord GOD (Ezekiel 28:11-12); Now, at this point there is a switch and we go behind the scenes and God is now addressing Himself unto Satan. And this is probably one of the most graphic descriptions of Satan that exists in the Bible." https://www.studylight.org/commentary/ezekiel/28-14.htm.

27. The chapters that follow about the Chaldean spirit are largely influenced by the material presented in *Unmasking the Chaldean Spirit* (Crane, MO: Defender, 2023) 73–89.

28. For examples, see 1 Timothy 4:1, Revelation 9:20, 16:14, 18:2.

29. *Jewish Encyclopedia*. "Demonology" (Demons in the Bible). Accessed 12/2/20. http://www.jewishencyclopedia.com/articles/5085-demonology.

36. *The Theosophal Glossary*: "Chaldeans, or Kasdim. At first a tribe, then a caste of learned Kabbalists. They were the savants, the magians of Babylonia, astrologers and diviners." H. P. Blavatsky, *The Theosophal Glossary*. https://library.indstate.edu/about/units/rbsc/cordell/PDFs/blavatsky_h_1892x_theosophical.pdf. (p. 75).

30. Ibid., *Theosophal Glossary*. Also see R. Campbell Thompson, *The Devils and Evil Spirits of Babylonia: Being Babylonian [Chaldean] and Assyrian Incantations against the Demons, Ghouls, Vampires, Hobgoblins, Ghosts, and Kindred Evil Spirits, Which Attack Mankind*, Vol. 1 "Evil Spirits." (London: Luzac, 1903). https://publicdomainreview.org/collection/spells-against-the-evil-spirits-of-babylonia-1903.

31. It is from the Greek word *ecclesia*, used throughout the New Testament, that we get the English word "church." *Ecclesia* simply, and emphatically, means "the called-out ones." It does not have anything directly to do with a building with a steeple on it, for example. Nor does it have anything to do with Christian denominations. The "called-out ones" are the "one new man" spoken of in Ephesians 2. The called-out ones are the "new temple" of the last days. They are Jew and Gentile who are born again under the blood of Yeshua—those who have truly made the divine blood alliance with our Creator through the Threshold Covenant principles.

See *Strong's Concordance*: NT:1577: "Ekklesia (ek-klay-see'-ah); from a compound of NT:1537 and a derivative of NT:2564; a calling out, i.e. (concretely) a popular meeting, especially a religious congregation (Jewish synagogue, or Christian community of members on earth or saints in heaven or both).''

(*Biblesoft's New Exhaustive Strong's Numbers and Concordance with Expanded Greek-Hebrew Dictionary.* © 1994, 2003, 2006 Biblesoft, Inc. and International Bible Translators, Inc.)

32. This reminds us of King Saul, Israel's first king, who sought to speak with the deceased prophet Samuel. Saul visited the witch of Endor to have Samuel "summoned up" from the dead. See 1 Samuel 28.

Matthew Poole's Commentary (1 Samuel 28): "Samuel said to Saul; as the devil appeared in Samuel's shape and garb, so also he speaketh in his person, that he might insnare Saul, and encourage others to seek to him in this wicked way." https://biblehub.com/commentaries/1_samuel/28-15.htm.

Gill's Exposition of the Entire Bible (1 Samuel 28): "And Samuel said to Saul, why hast thou disquieted me to bring me up? ...This makes it a clear case that this was not the true Samuel...he was brought up by Saul, by means of a witch, and through the help of the devil." https://biblehub.com/commentaries/1_samuel/28-15.htm.

Jamieson-Fausset-Brown Bible Commentary (1 Samuel 28): "The story has led to much discussion whether there was a real appearance of Samuel or not. On the one hand, the woman's profession, which was forbidden by the divine law, the refusal of God to answer Saul by any divinely constituted means, the well-known age, figure, and dress of Samuel, which she could easily represent herself, or by an accomplice—his apparition being evidently at some distance, being muffled, and not actually seen by Saul, whose attitude of prostrate homage, moreover, must have prevented him distinguishing the person though he had been near, and the voice seemingly issuing out of the ground, and coming along to Saul—and the vagueness of the information, imparted much which might have been reached by natural conjecture as to the probable result of the approaching conflict—the woman's representation—all of this has led many to think that this was a mere deception." https://biblehub.com/commentaries/1_samuel/28-15.htm.

Amazing Facts Ministry (https://www.amazingfacts.org/about-us/our-story): "The spirit that appeared to him could not have been from heaven, because

God had specifically forbidden all such forms of communication with the dead. If the spirit wasn't Samuel, it could only have been a demon."
See: *The Truth About Death*. "How did Saul speak to Samuel at Endor?" Amazing Facts Ministry, accessed 6/1/23. https://www.truthaboutdeath.com/q-and-a/id/1607/t/how-did-saul-speak-to-samuel-at-endor-.

33. For an excellent scholarly resource and in-depth biblical study on the Garden's location as being within the area of Jerusalem, see: Gallups, Carl. *Gods of Ground Zero: The Truth of Eden's Iniquity*, (Crane, MO: Defender Publishing, 2018). (I served as a research assistant to the author of this book).

34. Babylonia is sometimes called "Shinar" or the "land of Babylon," but usually it is called the "land of the Chaldeans." Its inhabitants are a few times referred to as "Babylonians," but typically as Chaldeans.
The name "Shinar" occurs eight times in the Hebrew Bible, in which it refers to Babylonia. "Shinar" was the Hebrew name of a land that included both Babylon and Erech—i.e., both northern and southern Babylonia. See Emil G. Hirsch, George A. Barton., "Shinar," *Jewish Encyclopedia*, accessed 12/27/20, http://www.jewishencyclopedia.com/articles/13582-shinar.

35. Genesis 2:10–14 lists four rivers in association with the Garden of Eden: Pishon, Gihon, Hiddekel (the Tigris), and Phirat (the Euphrates). These lands lie north of Elam, immediately to the east of ancient Babylon, which does lie within the region being described. See Speiser, E. A. (1994). "The Rivers of Paradise." In Tsumura, D. T.; Hess, R. S. (eds.). I *Studied Inscriptions from Before the Flood*. Eisenbrauns. https:// www.google.com/books/edition/I_Studied_Inscriptions_from_Before_the_F/ g5MGVP6gAPkC?hl=en&gbpv=1&bsq=Speiser,+%22The+Rivers+of+Paradis e%22+Cush&pg=PA38&printsec=frontcover.

36. See Gallups, *Gods of Ground Zero*.

37. *Jamieson-Fausset-Brown Bible Commentary:* "Land of Shinar—The fertile valley watered by the Euphrates and Tigris was chosen as the center of their union and the seat of their power."
Pulpit Commentary: Babylonia (cf. Genesis 10:10). "The derivation of the term is unknown, though it probably meant the land of the two rivers. Its absence from ancient monuments (Rawlinson) suggests that it was the Jewish name

for Chaldaea." See Genesis 11:2, "Commentaries," Biblehub. com, https://biblehub.com/commentaries/genesis/11-2.htm.

38. Driscoll, Mark. "What Is the Spirit of Babylon?" Realfaith.com. Accessed 12/ 22/20. https://realfaith.com/daily-devotions/what-is-the-spirit-of-babylon.

39. *Pulpit Commentary:* "Like Jeremiah and Ezekiel, Isaiah knows the people as Chaldeans (Kasdim), the capital as Babylon." Isaiah 23:13. Biblehub.com. https://biblehub.com/commentaries/isaiah/23-13.htm.

Barnes' Notes on the Bible: "Behold the land of the Chaldeans—This is a very important verse, as it expresses the source from where these calamities were coming upon Tyre; and as it states some historical facts of great interest respecting the rise of Babylon. Isaiah 23:13. Biblehub.com. https://biblehub.com/commentaries/isaiah/23-13.htm.

40. "Chaldean. כַּשְׂדִּי adj. 1. Chaldean. 2. astrologer. [From כַּשְׂדִּים =) Chaldeans), which is related to Akka. mat Chaldu, dissimilated from mat Kashdu (= landof the Chaldeans).... According to others Akka. Kashdu and Heb. כַּשְׂדִּי lit.mean "conquerors," and are connected with Akka. kashādu (= to conquer).] כִּישּׁוּף m.n. PBH magic, sorcery, witchcraft. [Verbal n. of כָּשַׁף. See כשׁף.].See *Klein Dictionary*, כִּשּׁוּלְךָ. "Chaldean," Sefaria, accessed 12/22/20, https://www.Sefaria.org/Klein_Dictionary%2C_%D7%9B%D6%B7%D6%BC%D7%A9 %D6%B0%D7%82%D7%93%D6%B4%D6%BC%D7%99?lang=bi.

41. On "The Great City" of Revelation 11:8:

Jamieson-Fausset-Brown Bible Commentary: "The difficulty is, how can Jerusalem be called 'the great city,' that is, Babylon? By her becoming the world's capital of idolatrous apostasy, such as Babylon originally was, and then Rome has been; just as she is here called also "'Sodom and Egypt.'"

Meyer's New Testament Commentary: "It has been inferred [2892] that not the actual Jerusalem is to be regarded as the scene, but the allegorically so-called great city, Papal Rome, or rather the Romish Papacy, which actually extends over the whole earth."

Barnes' Notes on the Bible: "So far as the language is concerned, it might apply either to Jerusalem or to Rome—for both were eminently characterized by such acts of oppression toward the true children of God as to make it proper to I compare their cruelties with those which were inflicted on the Israelites by the Egyptians.... While, therefore, it must be admitted that the language is such as could be literally applied only to Jerusalem, it is still true that it is such language as might be figuratively applied to any other city strongly resembling that, and that in this sense it would characterize Rome above all other cities of the world."

42. For all three commentary entries, see: https://biblehub.com/commentaries/revelation/11-8.htm.

Robert Morris, pastor of the largest congregation in the Dallas-Fort Worth metroplex, one of the largest churches in the United States, attests: "The name Chaldean means 'wanderer.' The root of the word means 'to lay waste or to destroy.' The historical Chaldeans conquered lands, robbed people of their money and goods, and stole the next generation—the young future leaders—brainwashing their minds and morals. The metaphoric Chaldeans of Paul's day—and today—were demons with the same destructive aims and strategies. They want to take control of territories that aren't theirs."

See Morris, Robert. *Truly Free: Breaking the Snares That So Easily Entangle (Beware the Chaldeans)*, (Nashville: W Publishing, Imprint of Thomas Nelson, 2015) 50. https://www.google.com/books/edition/Truly_Free/8Re.MBQAAQBAJ?hl=en&gbpv=1&dq=Chaldeans:+as+it+were+demons.+The+r oot+word+means+to+lay+waste+or+to+destroy.+And+the+actual+word+means+wanderers.&pg=PA50&printsec=frontcover.

43. In an in-depth article on this topic, theologian, pastor, and major media biblical pundit Mark Driscoll reveals the following:

"God creates a Kingdom that is called His bride. Satan counterfeits with a kingdom that is called Babylon, the 'mother of prostitutes' (Revelation 17:5). The spirit of Babylon is at work in every nation and generation. For this reason, the last book of the Bible, Revelation, is closely connected to Daniel, as they both have prophecy about the end of human history and beginning of eternity with the Second Coming of Jesus Christ. Long after the nation of Babylon had ceased to exist, Revelation reveals that the demonic spirit of Babylon remains at work in the world.

"What Is the Spirit of Babylon?" Realfaith.com. Accessed 12/22/20. https://realfaith.com/daily-devotions/what-is-the-spirit-of-babylon.

"Mark Driscoll is the pastor of Trinity Church in Scottsdale, Arizona. He holds a master's degree in exegetical theology from Western Seminary in Portland, Oregon. Driscoll has debated Deepak Chopra on one of his multiple appearances on ABC's *Nightline*; discussed marriage with Barbara Walters on *The View*; bantered with the hosts at *Fox and Friends*; cohosted *Loveline with Dr. Drew*; and argued for the truth of God's Word on separate occasions with Piers Morgan and D. L. Hughley on CNN." See https://realfaith.com/about.

44. Regarding the cross of Yeshua being called a "tree," see Galatians 3:13, Acts 5:30, 10:39, 13:29, 1 Peter 2:24.

45. The Greek altars to "the unknown God(s)" were "discovered" by demonic divination. The ancient Greeks were looking for the "portals" or "thresholds" where they might contact the proper "god" and make a blood sacrifice to that "god" (a threshold sacrifice), especially in times of "emergency" intervention requests made to those "gods."

For examples, see the following entries found at https://biblehub.com/commentaries/acts/17-23.htm.

Meyer's NT Commentary: "It is related that Epimenides put an end to a plague in Athens by causing black and white sheep, which he had let loose on the Areopagus, to be sacrificed on the spots where they lay down…to the god concerned (yet not known by name), namely, who was the author of the plague; and that therefore one may find at Athens altars without the designation of a god by name. From this particular instance the general view may be derived, that on important occasions, when the reference to a god known by name was wanting, as in public calamities of which no definite goal could be assigned as the author, in order to honour or propitiate the god concerned by [a blood] sacrifice."

Barnes' Notes on the Bible: "There was a remarkable altar raised in Athens in a time of pestilence, in honor of the unknown god which had granted them deliverance. Diogenes Laertius says that Epimenides restrained the pestilence in the following manner: 'Taking white and black sheep, he led

them to the Areopagus, and there permitted them to go where they would, commanding those who followed them to sacrifice to the god to whom these things pertained or who had the power of averting the plague, whoever he might be [wherever these individual sheep might stop, the sacrifice was to be made! See *Ellicott's Commentary*.], without adding the name and thus to allay the pestilence. From which it has arisen that at this day, through the villages of the Athenians, altars are found without any name' (Diog. Laert., book i, section 10). This took place about six hundred years before Christ, and it is not improbable that one or more of those altars remained until the time of Paul."
Ellicott's Commentary for English Readers: "A story connected with Epimenides of Crete, who, as a prophet of great fame, was invited to Athens at a time when the city was suffering from pestilence, is sometimes referred to as affording a probable explanation of its origin. Diogenes Laertius (Epimen. c. 3) relates that he turned sheep loose into the city, and then had them sacrificed, where they stopped, to the god thus pointed out, i.e., to the one whose image or altar was nearest to the spot, and that 'altars without a name' were thus to be seen in many parts of Athens; and it has been supposed that this may have been one of these altars, erected where there was no image near enough to warrant a sacrifice to any known deity, and as Epimenides is stated to have offered sacrifices on the Areopagus, that such an altar may have been standing within view as St. Paul spoke."
46. Ibid. "The Greek altars to 'the unknown God(s)' were 'discovered' by what actually was demonic divination."
47. *Meyer's NT Commentary.*
48. The Lamb slain Before the beginning of the world. See Revelation 13:8 and 1 Peter 1:20.
49. A *mezuzah* is a piece of parchment called a *klaf*, contained in a decorative case and inscribed with specific Hebrew verses from the Torah. These verses consist of the Jewish prayer *Shema Yisrael*, beginning with the phrase: "Hear, O Israel, the Lord our God, the Lord is One." Wikipedia contributors, "Mezuzah," Wikipedia, The Free Encyclopedia, https://en.wikipedia.org/w/index.php?t itle=Mezuzah&oldid=1058221921 (accessed 12/2/22).
50. Deuteronomy 6:9. *Keil and Delitzsch Biblical Commentary on the*

Old Testament, Biblehub.com, https://biblehub.com/commentaries/deuteronomy/6-9.htm.

51. Deuteronomy 6:9. *Jamieson-Fausset-Brown Bible Commentary*, Biblehub.com, https://biblehub.com/commentaries/deuteronomy/6-9.htm.

52. See H. Clay Trumbull. *The Threshold Covenant or the Beginning of Religious Rites*, (2. Reverence for the Threshold Altar.) (New York: Scribner's, 1896), https://www.gutenberg.org/files/49216/49216-h/49216-h.htm. "Threshold" and "foundation" are used interchangeably in primitive life. The sacredness of the threshold stone of a building pivots on its position as a foundation stone, a beginning stone, a boundary stone. Hence the foundation stone of any house or other structure was sacred as the threshold of that building.

53. Those sixteen out of more than four dozen translations that use "inward parts" are: KJV, American Standard Version, English Revised Version, JPS Tanakh 1917, Webster's Bible Translation, World English Bible, Young's Literal Translation, Literal Standard Version, King James 2000 Bible, Geneva Bible of 1587, Bishops' Bible of 1568, Coverdale Bible of 1535, Darby Bible Translation, A Faithful Version, American King James Version. See https://biblehub.com/jeremiah/31-33.htm.

54. Jeremiah 31:33. "Inward Parts." Hebrew 7130. *Qereb*. The inner parts of the body—or the entrails. See scriptural examples that follow. "You shall also take the fat from the ram and the fat tail and the fat that covers the entrails, [Heb. *qereb*: inner parts] and the long lobe of the liver and the two kidneys with the fat that is on them, and the right thigh [for it is a ram of ordination]", (Exodus 29:22). See fifteen other examples of *qereb* as "entrails" from Exodus through Leviticus here: https://biblehub.com/hebrew/hakkerev_7130.htm.

55. See Jeremiah 31:33. (Parallel Versions), Biblehub.com, https://biblehub.com/jeremiah/31-33.htm.

56. Ibid. "Inward Parts." Hebrew 7130. *Qereb*.

57. Exodus 12:9. *Keil and Delitzsch Biblical Commentary on the Old Testament*, Biblehub.com, https://biblehub.com/commentaries/exodus/12-9.htm.

58. BC News. "COVID-19's Toll on Mental Health; During the first

9 months of the pandemic, Americans reported rates of depression and anxiety six times higher than in 2019, Boston College researchers find," Boston College, 4/24/23, https://www.bc.edu/bc-web/bcnews/campus-community/faculty/anxiety-and-stress-spike-during-pandemic.html#:~:text=Confirming%20anecdotal%20evidence%20that%20the,report%20in%20the%20journal%20Translational.

59. Veronica Tucci and Nidal Moukaddam. "We Are the Hollow Men: The worldwide epidemic of mental illness, psychiatric and behavioral emergencies, and its impact on patients and providers," *J Emerg Trauma Shock*. Jan–Mar 2017; 10(1): 4–6. doi: 10.4103/0974-2700.199517, https://www.ncbi.nlm.nih.gov/pmc/articles/PMC5316796.

Also see Klaus W. Lange. "Coronavirus Disease 2019 (COVID-19) and Global Mental Health," *Glob Health J*. 2021 Mar; 5(1): 31–36. Published online2/13/21. doi: 10.1016/j.glohj.2021.02.004, https://www.ncbi.nlm.nih.gov/pmc/articles/PMC7881705.

60. Ibid.

61. George P. Landow. (December 2001). "The Light of the World." Victorian Web. Archived from the original on 9/14/20. Retrieved 9/3/16. https://victorianweb.org/painting/whh/replete/light.html.

62. Ibid.

63. Dr. Lehman Strauss. "Bible Prophecy (A Principle of Prophetic Interpretation; Isaiah's Prophecies; Micah's Prophecies)," Bible.org. Accessed 11/4/17. https://bible.org/article/bible-prophecy.

Note: A compound prophecy, or a compound reference, is one that either contains several layers of meaning and context or one that begins as a reference to one thing or person, but then shifts to a symbolic reference to something or someone else. See several examples of this well-known biblical phenomenon in the above-listed reference material by Dr. Strauss.

64. Dr. Joseph R. Nally Jr. has a doctorate of divinity from the North American Reformed Seminary and a master of divinity from Reformed Theological Seminary. He engaged in advanced studies in church history in Switzerland (on John Calvin), Germany (on Martin Luther), and the Czech

Republic (on Jan Hus). He holds undergraduate degrees from Georgia College (BBA) and Georgia Military College (ABA).

65. See more here: https://thirdmill.org/mission/teamBio.asp/id/15.
 Dr. Joseph R. Nally Jr. "Question: I noticed that in another answer you called the new covenant the renewed covenant. Can you please explain?" thirdmill.org, accessed 2/12/23, https://thirdmill.org/answers/answer.asp/file/40555.

66. *Keil and Delitzsch Biblical Commentary on the Old Testament:* "The suffix in אֵלַי (to me) refers to the speaker. This is Jehovah, according to Zechariah 12:1, the creator of the heaven and the earth. דקרו את־אשר, not 'Him whom they pierced,' but simply 'whom they pierced.' ...Thus the transition from the first person (אֵלַי) to the third (עָלָיו) points to the fact that the person slain, although essentially one with Jehovah, is personally distinct from the Supreme God." See https://biblehub.com/commentaries/zechariah/12-10.htm.
Jamieson-Fausset-Brown Bible Commentary: "The change of person is due to Jehovah-Messiah speaking in His own person first, then the prophet speaking of Him.... And the ancient Jews interpreted it of Messiah." See https://biblehub.com/commentaries/zechariah/12-10.htm.

67. *Clarke's Commentary:* Take not what is not thy own in any case. Let all ancient divisions, and the usages connected with them, be held sacred. Bring in no new dogmas, nor rites, nor ceremonies, into religion, or the worship of God, that are not clearly laid down in the sacred writings. "Stand in the way; and see, and ask for the old paths, which is the good way, and walk therein; and ye shall find rest for your souls;" Jeremiah 6:16. See https://www.studylight.org/commentary/proverbs/22-28.html.
Smith's Bible Commentary: The landmark is the guidelines, and in a spiritual sense, unfortunately, we are living in the day when many men have sought to remove the spiritual type of landmarks or the foundational truths of the Word of God. And what confusion has ensued when men start playing around with the foundational truths of Christianity. Questioning the authority of the Word of God. Questioning the deity of Jesus Christ. And men starting to remove these landmarks. Confusion results. See https://www.studylight.org/commentary/proverbs/22-28.html.

Keil and Delitzsch Biblical Commentary on the Old Testament: Regarding the inviolability of boundaries established by the law, vid., at Proverbs 15:25. עולם גבול denotes "the boundary mark set up from ancient times, the removal of which were a double transgression, because it is rendered sacred by its antiquity." See https://biblehub.com/commentaries/proverbs/22-28.htm.
68. "Spiritual Israel." For examples, see Ephesians 2:11–22, Romans 11 (all), Galatians 3:28–29.
Cambridge Bible for Schools and Colleges (on Galatians 3): "The Apostle has established the assertion of Galatians 3:7 that [all] believers are the true children of Abraham and heirs of the promise. 'Union with Christ constitutes the true spiritual descent from Abraham, and secures the inheritance of all the Messianic blessings by promise, as against inheritance by law'."
69. Threshold of Trembling
Calvin's Commentary on the Bible: "The word סף, saph, means a threshold almost everywhere in Scripture. But some think that it means here a cup, and then they translate רעל, rol, drunkenness, or fury. But as this word also means breaking, it is not unsuitable to say that Jerusalem is here called a threshold at which people stumble, so that he who comes against this threshold either breaks a bone or receives some other injury. The meaning then is, that access to Jerusalem would be closed up, so that enemies would not overcome it, though they reached the walls and the gates, for they would stumble, as it is said, at the threshold." See https://www.studylight.org/commentary/zechariah/12-2.html.
Cambridge Bible for Schools and Colleges: (Cup of trembling) "Rather, bowl of reeling. The word is used of the bowl or bason in which the blood of the Paschal lamb was caught, Exodus 12:22, of the bowls used in the Temple service, 1 Kings 7:50, and more generally, 2 Samuel 17:28. [In other words, involving the entire Threshold Covenant of Passover!]" (Parentheses in the original) See https://biblehub.com/commentaries/zechariah/12-2.htm.
Strong's Exhaustive Concordance: "Bason, bowl, cup, door post, gate, post, threshold. From caphaph, in its original sense of containing; a vestibule (as a limit); also a dish (for holding blood or wine)—bason, bowl, cup, door (post), gate, post, threshold." See https://biblehub.com/hebrew/5592.htm.

70. Zechariah 12:2. *Pulpit Commentary*, Biblehub.com, https://biblehub.com/commentaries/zechariah/12-2.htm.

71. Zechariah 12:2. *Jamieson-Fausset-Brown Bible Commentary*, Biblehub.com, https://biblehub.com/commentaries/zechariah/12-2.htm.

72. *Keil and Delitzsch Biblical Commentary on the Old Testament:* "The 'cup of reeling,' i.e., a goblet filled with intoxicating drink, is a figure very frequently employed to denote the divine judgment, which intoxicates the nations, so that they are unable to stand any longer, and therefore fall to the ground and perish (see at Isaiah 51:17)." See https://biblehub.com/commentaries/zechariah/12-2.htm.

73. Diane Roblin-Lee. *The Porn Factor*, byDesign Media, Paris, Ontario, Canada, 2017, p. 15.

74. The Cedarmont Kids website: https://cedarmont.com.

75. Action Choruses, *The Cedarmont Kids*, © Copyright 1956 by Zondervan Music Publishers, accessed 2/12/23, https://mojim.com/usy162913x11x7.htm.

76. Britannica. "Veneration of objects," Britannica.com, accessed 2/21/23, https://www.britannica.com/topic/Roman-religion/Veneration-of-objects.

77. Janus. "Guardian of the Threshold," accessed 2/21/23, https://www.credoreference.com/content/entry/mcgods/janus/0.embed.

78. *Varro apud Augustine De Civitate Dei* VII 9 and 3; *Servius Aen.* I 449; *Paulus ex Festus s. v. Chaos* p. 45 L. See: https://en.wikipedia.org/wiki/Janus.

79. The only versions I have been able to find that seem to nail the proper translation as "leap on" the threshold are the King James Version, American King James Version, Smith's Literal Translation, Geneva Bible of 1587, and the Webster's Bible Translation. The following translations also use "leap on," but they add the word "temple" to the text—when that word is not even in the original Hebrew text. Those versions are the New American Standard Bible, NASB 1995, and the NASB 1977.https://biblehub.com/parallel/zephaniah/1-9.htm.

80. *Pulpit Commentary* on Zephaniah 1:9: "The LXX. [Septuagint], followed by Jerome, renders, 'who fill the house of the Lord their God.' This is plainly

erroneous, as there is no question here about the temple at Jerusalem." See https://biblehub.com/commentaries/zephaniah/1-9.htm.

81. Milcom. *Strong's Exhaustive Concordance*: "From melek for Molek; the national idol of the Ammonites." See https://biblehub.com/hebrew/4445.htm.

82. See *Barnes' Notes on the Bible*: "The kindred and equally horrible worship of 'Molech, the abomination of the children of Ammon' 1 Kings 11:7, was brought in by Solomon in his decay, and endured until his high place was defiled by Josiah 2 Kings 23:13–14. It is probable then that this was 'their king,' of whom Zephaniah speaks, whom Amos and after him Jeremiah, called 'their king;' but speaking of Ammon. Him, the king of Ammon, Judah adopted as 'their king.' They owned God as their king in words; Molech." See https://biblehub.com/commentaries/zephaniah/1-5.htm.

Zephaniah 1:1. *Jamieson-Fausset-Brown Bible Commentary*, Biblehub.com, https://biblehub.com/commentaries/zephaniah/1-1.htm.

83. Zephaniah 1:7. *Pulpit Commentary*, Biblehub.com, https://biblehub.com/commentaries/zephaniah/1-7.htm.

84. Zephaniah 1:7. *Jamieson-Fausset-Brown Bible Commentary*, Biblehub.com, https://biblehub.com/commentaries/zephaniah/1-7.htm.

85. Zephaniah 1:7. *Gill's Exposition of the Entire Bible*, Biblehub.com, https://biblehub.com/commentaries/zephaniah/1-7.htm.

86. Johnson, Allen, Ray. "The New Prophets of Baal," creationsong.org, 1/15/20, https://creationsong.org/the-new-prophets-of-baal. Also see "Hosea," biblestudytools.com, https://www.biblestudytools.com/commentaries/matthew-henry-complete/hosea/13.html.

87. Dr. White, Andrew, MD. "Abortion and the Ancient Practice of Child Sacrifice [Molech]," biblicalarcheology.org, 1/5/12, https://biblearchaeology.org/research/contemporary-issues/2243-abortion-and-the-ancient-practice-of-child-sacrifice.

88. Zephaniah 1:9. *Jamieson-Fausset-Brown Bible Commentary*, Biblehub.com, https://biblehub.com/commentaries/zephaniah/1-9.htm.

89. Zephaniah 1:9. *Barnes' Notes on the Bible*, Biblehub.com, https://biblehub.com/commentaries/zephaniah/1-9.htm.

90. Zephaniah 1:9. *Henry's Complete Commentary on the Bible*, Studylight.org, https://www.studylight.org/commentary/zephaniah/1-9.html.
91. "As a biblical connection, ancient texts from the region connect Dagon as the father of Baal, another false god highlighted throughout later Old Testament history." Mooney, Britt. "Who Was Dagon in the Bible, and What Happened to This Idol?" Biblestudytools.com, 2/3/23, https://www.biblestudytools.com/bible-study/topical-studies/who-was-dagon-in-the-bible-and-what-happened-to-this-idol.html.
92. *Matthew Poole's Commentary:* "*Dag* in Hebrew signifies a fish. And hence their opinion seems most probable, that this idol of Dagon had in its upper parts a human shape, and in its lower parts the form of a fish." See: https://biblehub.com/commentaries/1_samuel/5-4.htm.
93. Dr. James Burton Coffman (May 24, 1905–June 30, 2006) was a respected Christian minister and scholar who is best known for his extensive commentary on the entire Bible, which spans thirty-seven volumes and is highly regarded for its accessibility and depth of analysis. Born in Texas in 1905, Coffman attended Abilene Christian College and the University of Southern California, where he earned his master's degree. *Coffman's Bible Commentary* was the result of many years of study and research, and it quickly became a valuable resource for Christians around the world. His commentary was known for its clear and straightforward writing style, as well as its attention to historical and cultural context. See: https://www.studylight.org/commentaries/eng/bcc.html.
94. The following powerfully illustrates the point of this book and chapter: *Coffman's Commentary on the Bible (Matthew 11:12):* "Admitted to be one of the difficult passages of the New Testament, this verse in all probability was accurately understood and expounded by John McGarvey who wrote: Jesus here pictures the kingdom of heaven as a besieged city. The city is shut up, but the enemies which surround it storm its walls and try to force an entrance.… The gates of Christ's kingdom were not opened until the day of Pentecost (Acts 2); but men, hearing it was about to be opened, sought to enter it prematurely, not by the gates which God would open, …but by such breaches as they themselves sought to make in its walls.

"Instances of such violence are: (1) Some tried to make him king by force (John 6:15). (2) the mother of James and John sought to obtain secular appointments for her sons in the kingdom (Matthew 20:21). (3) Some supposed the kingdom would appear immediately (Luke 19:11). (4) The apostles quarreled over who should be the greatest (Luke 22:24–30). (5) The apostles themselves seemed anxious for it to be done "at this time" (Acts 1:6). Furthermore, they envisioned a restoration of rule to Israel! John McGarvey further wrote: 'The people were full of preconceived ideas with regard to the kingdom, and each one sought to hasten and enjoy its pleasures as one who impatiently seizes upon a bud and seeks with his fingers to force it to bloom. The context shows that even John the Baptist was then seeking to force the kingdom.' This view does not rule out the possibility discussed above that there was an element of genuine doubt in John's mind. It is also of interest to note that some of the Ante-Nicenes referred this 'violence' to the zeal men should have in striving after the kingdom, thus construing the words in a favorable sense; but, without doubt, McGarvey's exegesis of this passage appears more safe and perceptive of the Savior's true meaning." See: Matthew 11. (*Coffman's Commentary*) Verse 12, https://www.studylight.org/commentaries/eng/bcc/matthew-11.html.

95. *Dr. Thomas L. Constable's Expository Notes:* "Probably Jesus meant that the religious leaders of His day were trying to bring in the Kingdom in their own carnal way (a false threshold) while refusing to accept God's way (the true threshold covenant) that John and Jesus announced. (Note: Toussaint, *Behold the...*, pp. 151–52; Walvoord, p. 82.)

See: Matthew 11. (*Dr. Thomas Constable's Bible Commentary*, verses 12–13), https://www.studylight.org/commentaries/eng/dcc/matthew-11.html.

96. For a historically balanced and heavily referenced article, based on numerous scholarly resources, see the following Wikipedia entry: "Constantine the Great," accessed 5/5/22, https://en.wikipedia.org/wiki/Constantine_the_Great.

97. 2 Timothy 3:5. *Ellicott's Commentary for English Readers*, Biblehub.com, Https://biblehub.com/commentaries/2_timothy/3-5.htm.

98. 2 Timothy 3:5. *MacLaren's Expositions*, Biblehub.com, Https://biblehub.com/commentaries/2_timothy/3-5.htm.

99. The Hebrew word translated "feasts" doesn't refer to a smorgasbord like one would find at a fancy hotel; the Hebrew word is *moed* (Strong's 4150), and it means "appointed time, place, or meeting."

100. While the earliest Jewish believers in Yeshua would have certainly honored the Sabbath in their own homes, and perhaps among other Jewish believers, no place in the New Testament indicates the early Jewish believers continued to meet with and worship with the synagogue congregations on the Sabbath. In fact, most were eventually ostracized and put out of those synagogues. Instead, they eventually separated from the synagogue services and centered their meetings and worship exclusively around the person of Yeshua.
Compare these, in order: Mark 16:9 (the first day of the week); John 20:19 (the first day of the week); John 20:26 (the first day of the week); Acts 20:7 (the first day of the week); 1 Corinthians 16:2 (the first day of the week). Then see the following commentary entries:

Expositor's Greek Commentary on 1 Corinthians 16:2: "The earliest mention of this Christian day, going to show that the First Day, not the Sabbath, was already the sacred day of the [early congregations] (cf. Acts 20:7.)"

Ellicott's Commentary on the Bible for 1 Corinthians 16:2: "Already the day of the week on which Christ had risen had become noted as a suitable day for distinctively Christian work and Christian worship."

Ellicott's Commentary on the Bible for Acts 20:7: "Upon the first day of the week....This and the counsel given in 1 Corinthians 16:2, are distinct proofs that the [earliest congregations] had already begun to observe the weekly festival of the Resurrection in place of, or, where the disciples were Jews, in addition to, the weekly Sabbath."

Expositor's Greek New Testament Bible Commentary for Acts 20:7: "We must remember that 1 Cor. had been previously written, and that the reference in 1 Corinthians 16:2 to 'the first day of the week' for the collection of alms naturally connects itself with the statement here in proof that this day had been marked out by the Christian [congregations] as a special day for public worship, and for 'the breaking of the bread.'"

101. About Mark Nanos: "A Jewish historian with a research focus on the Apostle Paul," PhD, University of St. Andrews, Scotland, 2000, PhD, Honorary, University of Lund, Sweden, 2019, 1996 National Jewish Book Award for Christian-Jewish Relations, Society of Biblical Literature (cofounder, "Paul within Judaism" section), *Studiorum Novi Testamenti Societas*. See https://marknanos.com/about/.
Also see: Nanos, Mark D., *The Mystery of Romans: The Jewish Context of Paul's Letter*, (Minneapolis: Fortress Publishing, 1996).
Also see: Elliott, Neil. "The Mystery of Romans: The Jewish Context of Paul's Letter: A Review Article in *The Journal of Beliefs and Values* 18.1, on the book *The Mystery of the Romans*, by Mark Nanos," (1997), pp. 103–107. The College of St. Catherine, St. Paul, MN, https://marknanos.com/wp-content/uploads/2019/11/Mystery-Neil-Elliott-Rev-Mystery-JBV.pdf.
102. Cameron, Averil. "The Reign of Constantine, A.D. 306–337: From Part I-Narrative,," accessed 2/15/23, Cambridge University Press,3/28/08, https://www.cambridge.org/core/books/abs/cambridge-ancient-history/reign-of-constantine-ad-306337/B346E9BB78105974652BCF2626045530.
103. Ibid. For a historically balanced and heavily referenced article using numerous scholarly resources, see the following Wikipedia entry: "Constantine the Great."
104. PBS. "The Roman Empire in the First Century: Augustus," accessed 2/2/23, https://www.pbs.org/empires/romans/empire/augustus_religion.html. "Roman religion had many gods and spirits and Augustus was keen to join their number as a god himself. This was not unusual: turning political leaders into gods was an old tradition around the Mediterranean. There was also precedent in Roman history—Aeneas and Romulus, who had helped found Rome, were already worshipped as gods."
105. Mardi Gras is tied directly to Easter and the Constantinian decree of AD 325. See: Mardi Gras Traditions. "When is Mardi Gras?" mardigrastraditions.com, accessed 5/3/23, https://mardigrastraditions.com/when-is-mardi-gras.
106. Urlin, Ethel L. "Festivals, Holy Days, and Saints' Days: A Study in Origins and Survivals in Church Ceremonies & Secular Customs," (London, 1915, by Simpkin, Marshall, Hamilton, Kent) 73–74. Accessed

3/1/23, https://ia601605.us.archive.org/15/items/festivalsholyday00urli/festivalsholyday00urli.pdf.

"There is a reflection of ancient solar or fire-worship in some well-known Easter ceremonies. For instance, at Jerusalem, at Easter, the belief is, that in obtaining fresh fire from the Holy Sepulchre, which is supposed to be kindled by a miracle, luck is ensured for the coming year. Every year on Easter Saturday a new fire is miraculously kindled at the Holy Sepulchre at Jerusalem. It descends from heaven and ignites a candle which the patriarch holds in his hand, while with eyes closed he wrestles all night in prayer in the Chapel of the Angel. Worshippers meanwhile wait anxiously in the body of the church, and great are the transports of joy when at one of the windows of the chapel, all dark a minute before, suddenly appears a hand holding a lighted taper. The crowd eagerly press forward to ignite their tapers at the holy flame."

Ethel Lucy Urlin was a British historical author who wrote from the late 1800s to the early 1900s. Her three known books were: *A Short History of Marriage: Marriage Rites, Customs, and Folklore in Many Countries and All Ages*; *Festivals, Holy Days, & Saints' Day*; *Dancing, Ancient and Modern* (Published in London and New York City).

107. Bibleinfo.com writers, "What Is Ash Wednesday?", accessed 2/12/23, https://www.bibleinfo.com/en/questions/ash-wednesday-bible.

108. "Eostre: A learned borrowing from Old English Ēostre, the Northumbrian variant of West Saxon Ēastre (a word referring to "the rising dawn" to indicate the season of Spring) and ēastre ("Easter"), from Proto-West Germanic *$austr$ā, from Proto-Germanic *$Austr$ǭ....Eostre: A West Germanic goddess of the spring season. (paganism) A pagan festival celebrated either in March or April to welcome the Spring, also called Ostara or Easter."

See: Pete Jennings (1998), *The Norse Tradition: A Beginner's Guide*, Headway, p. 40. Also see: Wikipedia. "Eostre." Accessed 2/15/23, https://en.wiktionary.org/wiki/Eostre.

109. For the naysayers who would claim there is no real or lasting evidence for the Venerable Bede's claims about Eostre, see the following:

"Frankish historian Einhard also writes in his Vita Karoli Magni (early 9th c. AD) that after Charlemagne defeated and converted the continental Saxons to

Christianity, he gave Germanic names to the Latin months of the year, which included the Easter-month Ostarmanoth. The Old English Ēostre is therefore a distant cognate of numerous other dawn goddesses attested among Indo-European-speaking peoples, including Uṣás, Ēṓs, and Aurōra. In the words of the *Encyclopedia of Indo-European Culture*, 'a Proto-Indo-European goddess of the dawn is supported both by the evidence of cognate names and the similarity of mythic representation of the dawn goddess among various Indo-European groups.'... All of this evidence permits us to posit a Proto-Indo-European *haéusōs 'goddess of dawn' who was characterized as a 'reluctant' bringer of light for which she is punished. In three of the Indo-European stocks, Baltic, Greek and Indo-Iranian, the existence of a Proto-Indo-European 'goddess of the dawn' is given additional linguistic support in that she is designated the 'daughter of heaven'."

110. See Sermon, Richard (2008). "From Easter to Ostara: The Reinvention of a Pagan Goddess?" *Time and Mind*. 1 (3): 331–343.

Also see Wikipedia https://en.wikipedia.org/wiki/%C4%92ostre.

"In 2011 Philip A. Shaw wrote that the subject has seen 'a lengthy history of arguments for and against Bede's goddess ostre, with some scholars taking fairly extreme positions on either side' and that some theories against the goddess have gained popular cultural prominence. Shaw noted that 'much of this debate, however, was conducted in ignorance of a key piece of evidence, as it was not discovered until 1958. This evidence is furnished by over 150 Romano-Germanic votive inscriptions to deities named the matronae Austriahenae, found near Morken-Harff and datable to around 150–250 AD.' Most of these inscriptions are in an incomplete state, yet most are complete enough for reasonable clarity of the inscriptions. As early as 1966 scholars have linked these names etymologically with ostre and an element found in Germanic personal names."

See: Shaw, Philip A. *Pagan Goddesses in the Early Germanic World: Eostre, Hreda and the Cult of Matrons*. (Bristol Classical Press, 2011) 52.

Landau, Brent. "Why Easter Is Called Easter, and Other Facts About the Holiday: A Bible scholar explains the holiday's name and date", usnews.com, April 12, 2017,https://www.usnews.com/news/national-news/articles/2017-04-12/why-easter-is-called-easter-and-other-little-known-facts-about-the-holiday. Brent Landau is a lecturer in religious studies at the University of Texas at Austin.

111. Denova, Rebecca. "Constantine's Conversion to Christianity," WorldHistory.org, *World History Encyclopedia*, 5/10/21,https://www.worldhistory.org/article/1737/constantines-conversion-to-christianity.

112. The roots of the *Eostre*/Easter pagan origins are infinitely more than just "popularly considered"; they are profusely recorded and documented in unquestionable scholarly sources, as noted in the previous chapter and, as documented in even greater detail over the next several chapters. The words "popularly considered" are what I call "mushy words." They tell the truth, but at the same time, they attempt to soften the blow of the truth they've told.

113. It appears the reference to "incongruity" is speaking of the Nicene Council, called by Constantine in AD 325 for this very purpose. That "unity" is what was eventually "called for" in the churches. This indeed is a monumental admission by the RCC.

One of the main events of that meeting was to impose the singular service of worship, then known as Easter, upon all the churches, rather than practicing what some of the churches in the Roman Empire were still doing—celebrating the biblical Feast of Passover as the Crucifixion, and not "Easter." Here, again, is that attesting portion of the letter Constantine wrote to all the churches right after the AD 325 Nicene Council:

"At the council we also considered the issue of our holiest day, Easter, and it was determined by common consent that everyone, everywhere should celebrate it on one and the same day. For what can be more appropriate, or what more solemn, than that this feast from which we have received the hope of immortality, should be kept by all without variation, using the same order and a clear arrangement?"

See: Fourth-Century Christianity. "Emperor Constantine to All Churches Concerning the Date of Easter," accessed 2/23/23, https://www.fourthcentury.com/urkunde-26.

114. *The New Catholic Encyclopedia* (1967 edition, rev.), Vol. 5, "Easter and Its Cycle," 2003 edition, pp. 10–13, accessed 3/1/23, https://cvdvn.files.wordpress.com/2018/05/new-catholic-encyclopedia-vol-5.pdf.

115. *Catholic Encyclopedia*. "Easter," *New Advent Encyclopedia*, accessed 3/29/23, https://www.newadvent.org/cathen/05224d.htm.

116. Fourth-Century Christianity. "Emperor Constantine to All Churches Concerning the Date of Easter," accessed 2/23/23, https://www.fourthcentury.com/urkunde-26/. Ancient source used: Socrates, *Church History* 1.9. Modern edition used: W. Bright, *Socrates' Ecclesiastical History*, 2nd ed., (Oxford: Clarendon Press, 1893).
Other ancient sources: Eusebius, *Life of Constantine* 3.17–18; Theodoret, *Church History* 1.9, *Anonymous Church History* 2.37.10.

117. Terullian (AD 155 AD—c. AD 220) was a prolific early Christian writer from Carthage in the Roman province of Africa. He was the first Christian to produce an extensive corpus of Latin Christian literature.
See: https://en.wikipedia.org/wiki/Tertullian (All referenced with renowned scholarly works.)
We still have copies of Tertullian's original works. In them, he confirms that the term "Easter" was in use in the Roman Empire long before the time of Constantine. See https://www.tertullian.org/fathers2/NPNF2-02/Npnf2-02-10.htm#P1694_729385.

118. Travers, Penny. "Origin of Easter: From Pagan Festivals and Christianity to Bunnies and Chocolate Eggs," 4/14/17, https://www.abc.net.au/news/2017-04-15/the-origins-of-easter-from-pagan-roots-to-chocolate-eggs/8440134; https://www.abc.net.au/news/2017-04-15/the-origins-of-easter-from-pagan-roots-to-chocolate-eggs/8440134.

119. *Encyclopædia Britannica* 11th Edition (Easter): 412 (in twenty-nine slim volumes). Cambridge University Press (1910–11). Accessed 3/1/23, https://deriv.nls.uk/dcn23/1883/4019/188340192.23.pdf.
Note from author: The original encyclopedia entry quoted in this chapter is written in Old English. I have translated it into the modern rendering—word for word—for readability's sake.

120. Urlin, *Festivals, Holy Days, and Saints' Days*, A Study in Origins and

Survivals in Church Ceremonies & Secular Customs," p. 73. Accessed 3/1/23, https://ia601605.us.archive.org/15/items/festivalsholyday00urli/festivalsholyday00urli.pdf.

121. Got Questions: "Who was Ishtar, and is there any connection between Ishtar and Easter?" accessed 1/28/23, https://www.gotquestions.org/Ishtar-Easter.html.

Interestingly, Got Questions does admit that Ishtar was an ancient goddess of fertility and sex: "Ishtar was an ancient Mesopotamian goddess of war, fertility, and sex.... She is featured in the Epic of Gilgamesh, and the 'Ishtar Gate' was part of Nebuchadnezzar's Babylon."

122. Bolinger, Hope. "What Is the Difference Between Easter and Ishtar?" Crosswalk.com, 1/13/21, https://www.crosswalk.com/special-coverage/easter/what-is-the-difference-between-easter-and-ishtar.html.

123. Alexander Hislop's biography: "Alexander Hislop (1807–1865) was a Free Church of Scotland minister known for his criticisms of the Roman Catholic Church. Alexander's brother Stephen Hislop (lived 1817–1863) became well known in his time as a missionary to India and a naturalist. Alexander was for a time parish schoolmaster of Wick, Caithness. He was for a time editor of the *Scottish Guardian* newspaper. As a probationer he joined the Free Church of Scotland at the Disruption of 1843. He was ordained in 1844 at the East Free Church, Arbroath, where he became senior minister in 1864. He wrote several [eleven] books, his most famous being *The Two Babylons: Papal Worship Proved to Be the Worship of Nimrod and His Wife.*" See https://darkbooks.org/articles/Alexander-Hislop.html.

124. See reprints of Hislop's original book here: https://www.amazon.com/Two-Babylons-annotated-Alexander-Hislop-ebook/dp/B006GRSMMO/ref=sr_1_1.

125. Queen of Heaven – Ishtar – Astarte – Asherah – Ashtoreth – Baal – Molech – Direct relationships (Phoenicians).

Ashtoreth, Asherah, Astarte, and Ishtar are all manifestations of the same goddess who was worshipped in different regions, where people were divided by language and geography. Ashtoreth (a Hebrew name) was the supreme female deity of the Phoenicians, associated with Baal, the supreme god."

Brooklyn Museum. "Ashtoreth," accessed 5/1/23, https://www.brooklynmuseum.org/eascfa/dinner_party/heritage_floor/ashtoreth.

"The phrase queen of heaven appears in two passages of the Bible, both in the book of Jeremiah. The first passage deals with the things the Israelites were doing that provoked the Lord to anger. Entire families were involved in idolatry. The children gathered wood, and the men used it to build altars to worship false gods. The women were engaged in kneading dough and baking cakes of bread for the 'Queen of Heaven' (Jeremiah 7:18). This title referred to Ishtar, an Assyrian and Babylonian goddess also called Ashtoreth and Astarte by various other groups. She was thought to be the wife of the false god Baal, also known as Molech. The motivation of women to worship Ashtoreth stemmed from her reputation as a fertility goddess, and, as the bearing of children was greatly desired among women of that era, worship of this 'queen of heaven' was rampant among pagan civilizations."

Got Questions. "Who is the Queen of Heaven?" accessed 2/21/23. https://www.gotquestions.org/Queen-of-Heaven.html.

126. Hislop, Alexander. *The Two Babylons* (1858), See Hislop's original quotes here: https://www.cbcg.org/twobaby/sect32.html. Accessed 2/27/23. Also see reprints of Hislop's original book here: https://www.amazon.com/Two-Babylons-annotated-Alexander-Hislop-ebook/dp/B006GRSMMO/ref=sr_1_1.

127. Bhagat, Dhruti. "The Origins and Practices of Holidays: Beltane and The Last Day of Ridván," Boston Public Library, 4/30/19, https://www.bpl.org/blogs/post/the-origins-and-practices-of-holidays-beltane-and-the-last-day-of-ridvan.

"Beltane is a Pagan holiday, and one of the eight Sabbats. It falls about halfway between the spring equinox (Ostara) [Eostre: See the following referenced article] and the coming summer solstice, Litha. The holiday celebrates spring at its peak, and the coming summer. Beltane also sometimes goes by the name May Day. This holiday is associated very strongly with fertility for pagans."

Also see: Bhagat, Dhruti. "The Origins and Practices of Holidays: Ostara, Holi, and Purim." Boston Public Library, March 18, 2019.

"Ostara is a wiccan holiday and one of their eight Sabbats. Ostara celebrates the

spring equinox. The word Ostara comes from the Anglo-Saxon goddess name, Eostre. Eostre represented spring and new beginnings." https://www.bpl.org/blogs/post/the-origins-and-practices-of-holidays-ostara-holi-and-purim.
128. Bible Dictionaries: *Watson's Biblical & Theological Dictionary* (Baal), accessed 3/2/2323, https://www.studylight.org/dictionaries/eng/wtd/b/baal.html.
"It is remarkable that we do not find the name Baal so much in popular use east of Babylonia; but it was general west of Babylonia, and to the very extremity of western Europe, including the British isles. The worship of Bel, Belus, Belenus, or Belinus, was general throughout the British islands; and certain of its rites and observances are still maintained among us, notwithstanding the establishment of Christianity during so many ages."
129. Bonwick, James. "Irish Druids and Old Irish Religions (Beltane)," 1894, accessed 3/2/23, https://www.libraryireland.com/Druids/Beltane.php.
"Baal or Bel is associated with the fires. Beltane was the Lucky Fire through which cattle were passed for purification.... As Scotland, especially the western part, was largely peopled from Ireland, it would not be surprising to recognize Baal or fire-worship there. A Breton priest was once called *Belec*, which means a servant of Baal. Outside Paris, Baal fires were lighted on St. John's Eve.... As a boy, I have rushed, with my playmates, through the smoke of these bonfires, without a suspicion that we were repeating the homage paid to Baal in the Valley of Hinnom."
James Bonwick: "One of Australia's most prolific writers was James Bonwick (1817–1906), teacher, historian, and archivist.... He has attracted considerable attention from bibliographers. Dr. George Mackaness compiled a list which appeared in the *Journal of the Royal Australian Historical Society*, E. E. Pescott's James Bonwick...with a bibliography of his writings published in 1939 and Sir John Ferguson's list appeared in the fifth volume of his *Bibliography of Australia* (Sydney, 1963), pp. 365–80. See http://latrobejournal.slv.vic.gov.au/latrobejournal/issue/latrobe-11/t1-g-t3.html.
130. "The name 'Britain' comes from the Phoenician word *Baratanac*, meaning 'land of tin.'" See Mortada, Rami. Ambassador. "Embassy of Lebanon in the United Kingdom," 3/18/23, http://london.mfa.gov.lb/britain/

english/embassy-of-lebanon-in-united---kingdom/welcome-letter.
See also https://all-geo.org/metageologist/2013/03/cornwall-tin-pasties-and-the-world.

"The Phoenicians, a now vanished pre-Roman civilisation in North Africa, traded directly with Cornwall. The name 'Britain' comes from the Phoenician name "Baratanac," meaning "Land of Tin." The Greek historian Herodotus, who is the source for much of the little we know about the ancient world, describes how tin comes from the Cassiterides, "lands of tin" that sat beyond Gaul (France).... when Julius Caesar [of the Roman Empire] invaded Britain, but modern historians have suggested Cornwall's tin deposits were a motive." Also see Dr. Green, Caitlin, R. "Some Possible Phoenician/Punic Names in Britain and Ireland," accessed 3/23/23, https://www.caitlingreen.org/2016/12/punic-names-britain.html.

131. *The English Bible Dictionary.* "Baal, God of Phoenicians and Canaanits," (From the Coptic Orthodox Church Heritage site) [Egyptian Christian Orthodox] accessed 3/3/23, https://st-takla.org/bible/dictionary/en/b/baal-god.html.

"The supreme male divinity of the Phoenician and Canaanitish nations, as Ashtoreth [Ishtar] was their supreme female divinity.... There can be no doubt of the very high antiquity of the worship of Baal.... We find this worship also in Phoenician colonies. The religion of the ancient British islands much resembled this ancient worship of Baal, and may have been derived from it."

132. Morris Jastrow, Jr., George A. Barton. Ashtoreth: "The name given in the Old Testament to the old Semitic mother-goddess, called in Phenicia, Ashtarte; in Babylonia, Ishtar; and in Arabia, Athtar....

"The Goddess in Phoenicia. Ashtarte was the chief goddess of the Sidonians, among whom she was worshiped as an independent divinity, and also under the name 'Ashtarte of the name of Baal,' as a counterpart of Baal. https://www.jewishencyclopedia.com/articles/2005-ashtoreth."

133. Department of Ancient Near Eastern Art: The Metropolitan Museum of Art. 10/04, "The Phoenicians (1500–300 B.C.)", accessed 3/1/23, https://www.metmuseum.org/toah/hd/phoe/hd_phoe.htm.

"Sea traders from Phoenicia and Carthage (a Phoenician colony traditionally founded in 814 B.C.) even ventured beyond the Strait of Gibraltar as far as Britain in search of tin."

134. Sammes, Aylett. "The antiquities of ancient Britain derived from the Phœenicians, wherein the original trade of this island is discovered, the names of places, offices, dignities, as likewise the idolatry, language and customs of the people," by Aylett Sammes (Date of writing unknown; est. 1636–1679) In the University of Michigan Library. *A Description of the Renowned Island of Britain in General.* (Chapter I. "A Description of Ancient Britain")

"BRITAIN, the most Renowned Island of the whole World, was called by the Ancient Greeks ⟨in non-Latin alphabet⟩ , afterwards it took the name of BRITANNIA, but more truly, BRETANICA, from the Adjacent Islands called, BARAT-ANAC, or BRATANAC by the Phoenicians, from the abundance of Tynn, and * Lead-Mines, found in them.

"It was always esteemed a very considerable part of the World, even in the height of the Roman Empire.... Skilfullest Marriners, the Phoenicians; who carefully, and studiously concealed this Treasure from the World, being exceeding jealous, least the source and head of their Trade being discovered.... Let us consider, that upon the first discovery of them [Briton Isles] by the Phoenicians, they were to the then known World, just as the West Indies were at first to Europe." https://quod.lib.umich.edu/e/eebo/A61366.0001.001/1:5?rgn=div1;view=fulltext.

135. Ancient Roman History at UNRV.com. "Tin in the Roman Empire," Accessed 2/24/23, https://www.unrv.com/economy/tin.php.

"Some of the earliest references to tin come from Phoenician traders dating to 1500 BC. Phoenician colonies (later Carthaginian) that developed in what is now southern Spain traded avidly with local residents. Of course, we now know that these islands represent the farthest reach of the ancient world, the British Isles.... By the invasions of Caesar in the mid first century BC, the British source of tin was certainly known to the Romans. His invasions, though with several other motives, may have been partially inspired by the thought of controlling the valuable mines of Britannia."

About: United Nations of Roma Victrix (UNRV) – referenced by *National Geographic, The New York Times, Britannica, Smithsonian Magazine*, BBC,

Carnegie Melon University, *World History Encyclopedia*, and others.

136. In reference to Baal's connection to Astarte and Ishtar, see the following from the *World History Encyclopedia*:
"[Baal] became a central deity of the Canaanite pantheon which would inform, first, Canaanite beliefs and, later, Phoenician religion. The Phoenician city of Baalbek (in modern-day Lebanon) was his cult center where he [Baal] was worshipped with his consort Astarte, goddess of love, sexuality, and war (associated with the goddess Inanna/Ishtar, among others)."
See: Mark, Joshua. "Baal", worldhistory.org, 11/5/21, https://www.worldhistory.org/baal.
About the *World History Encyclopedia*: "Every submission to the encyclopedia is carefully reviewed by our editorial team, making sure only the highest quality content is published to our site. Our publication follows academic standards, but it is written in an easy-to-read manner with students and the general public in mind. As a result, our publication is recommended by many educational institutions including: Oxford University, Common Sense Education, School Library Journal, MERLOT, University of Wisconsin-Madison. We were the proud winners of the .eu Web Award for education in 2016, and we have organizational and media partners in Europe, North America, and South America. World History Encyclopedia has also received grants from cultural and research organizations in the United Kingdom and the United States of America. We are a non-profit organization dedicated to transparency." https://www.worldhistory.org/static/about.

137. Scott, John C (2018). "The Phoenicians and the Formation of the Western World." *Comparative Civilizations Review*. Accessed 3/3/23 (78). Also see: Editors, *Britannica*. "Phoenicia: Historical rRgion, Asia," accessed 3/3/23, https://www.britannica.com/place/Phoenicia.

138. Killebrew, Ann E. "Canaanites," *Oxford Bibliographies*, accessed 3/23/23, https://www.oxfordbibliographies.com/display/document/obo-9780195393361/obo-9780195393361-0216.xml.
"Though who is a Canaanite remains ambiguous, most recent scholarship understands Canaanites not as an ethnic designation but employs it to refer to the 2nd millennium BCE inhabitants of diverse identities residing in a

region that contemporary Akkadian, Egyptian, and Ugaritic texts and later Phoenician/Punic and Hebrew accounts refer to as Canaan.... Later ancient writers and many scholars today consider the northern coastal Canaanites to be the precursors or ancestors of the 1st millennium Phoenicians."

139. Lipiński, Edward. *Dieux et déesses de l'univers phénicien et punique* [*Gods and Goddesses of the Phoenician and Punic Universe*]. *Orientalia Lovaniensia analecta* (in French). Vol. 64. (Leuven, Belgium: Leuven University Press. 1995) pp. 128–154.

"Under the Roman Empire, the cult of ʿAštōrt [Ishtar] had spread till the foot of Hadrian's Wall in Britannia, where she was invoked using her Phoenician name and associated to the "Tyrian Hēraklēs," that is to Melqart, thus being a continuation of the close connection between Melqart and ʿAštōrt [Ishtar], and attesting of the Phoenician origin of this cult."

140. Waddell, L. A. *The Phoenician Origins of Scots & Anglo-Saxons; Discovered by Phoenician-Sumerian Inscriptions In Britain, By Pre-Roman Briton Coins & a Mass of New History*, (London, Williams and Norgate, Ltd.– 1924) Read the entire book here: (Preface) p. v.

https://electricscotland.com/history/The_Phoenician_Origin_of_Britons.pdf.

From Waddell's book on the Phoenician origins and cultural influences of the ancient Britons (Preface, p. v):

"That long-lost origin and early history of our ancestors, the Britons, Scots and Anglo-Saxons, in the " Prehistoric " and Pre-Roman periods, back to about 3000 B.C., are now recovered to a great extent in the present work, by means of newly discovered historical evidence. And so far from these ancestral Britons....disclosed by the newly found historical facts to have been from the very first grounding of their galley keels upon Old Albion's shores, over a millennium and a half of years before the Christian era, a highly civilized and literate race, pioneers of Civilization, and a branch of the famous Phoenicians." Lieutenant Colonel Laurence Austine Waddell: CB, CIE, FLS, LLD, MCh, IMS RAI, FRAS. Scottish Explorer and archeologist. Fellow of Royal Anthropological Institute, Ppofessor of chemistry and pathology, Linnean &; Folk-Lore Societies, Hon. correspondent. Indian Archaeological Survey, professor of Tibetan, London University, and Indian Army surgeon.

141. Rawlinson, George. "History of Phoenicia," (chapter IX, "Ships, Navigation, and Commerce"), (London: Longmans, Green, and Co., 1889). Rawlinson was Camden professor of ancient history in the University of Oxford, canon of Canterbury, and corresponding member of the Royal Academy of Turin.
"The Phoenicians with their extensive commercial dealings, both in the West and in the East, became interested in diffusing it, British tin probably drove all other out of use, and obtained the monopoly of the markets wherever Phoenician influence prevailed." See https://www.gutenberg.org/files/2331/2331-h/2331-h.htm.
142. "Ashtoreth, Asherah, Astarte, and Ishtar are all manifestations of the same goddess who was worshipped in different regions, where people were divided by language and geography. Ashtoreth (a Hebrew name) was the supreme female deity of the Phoenicians, associated with Baal, the supreme god." Brooklyn Museum. "Ashtoreth," accessed 5/1/23, https://www.brooklynmuseum.org/eascfa/dinner_party/heritage_floor/ashtoreth.
143. Ibid. In reference to Baal's connection to Astarte and Ishtar, see the following from WorldHistory.org.
144. Levant: the historical region of Syria ("Greater Syria"), which includes present-day Israel, Jordan, Lebanon, Palestine, Syria, and most of Turkey southwest of the middle Euphrates. Its most significant characteristic is that it is the land bridge between Africa and Eurasia. Steiner & Killebrew, p. 9, archived 11/1/22 at the Wayback Machine. Accessed 3/12/23, https://web.archive.org/web/20221101142956/https://books.google.com/books?id=5H4fAgAAQBAJ&pg=PT32.
145. Killebrew, "Canaanites," *Oxford Bibliographies*, accessed 3/23/23. Though who is a Canaanite remains ambiguous, most recent scholarship understands Canaanites not as an ethnic designation but as a reference to the second-millennium BCE inhabitants of diverse identities residing in a region that contemporary Akkadian, Egyptian, and Ugaritic texts, and later Phoenician/Punic and Hebrew accounts, refer to as Canaan.... Later ancient writers and many scholars today consider the northern coastal Canaanites to be the precursors or ancestors of the first-millennium Phoenicians.

146. The people commonly referred to as Phoenicians were actually a Canaanite people. Canaanites are a larger group of ancient Semitic-speaking peoples that emerged in the Levant several thousand years before the Christ event. The seafaring Phoenicians did not refer to themselves by that name, but rather are thought to have referred to themselves as *Kena'ani*, meaning "Canaanites." See Scott, John C (2018). "The Phoenicians and the Formation of the Western World." *Comparative Civilizations Review*. Accessed 3/3/23 (78).
Also see Editors, *Britannica*. "Phoenicia: Historical Region, Asia," accessed 3/3/23, https://www.britannica.com/place/Phoenicia.
147. Ancient Roman History at UNRV.com. "Tin in the Roman Empire," accessed 2/24/23, https://www.unrv.com/economy/tin.php.
148. *Watson's Biblical & Theological Dictionary* ("Baal"), accessed 3/2/22.
"In Ireland, Beltein is celebrated on the twenty-first of June.... There, as they make fires on the tops of hills, every member of the family is made to pass though the fire; as they reckon this ceremony necessary to ensure good fortune through the succeeding year. This resembles the rites used by the Romans in the Palilia." [Here is the documented ancient Roman connection!]
149. Hislop, Alexander. *The Two Babylons*, accessed 2/27/23.
150. Online Etymology Dictionary. "Paschal (adj.)", accessed 3/1/23, https://www.etymonline.com/word/paschal.
"[The] Easter egg is attested by 1825, earlier pace egg (1610s). Easter bunny is attested by 1904 in children's lessons; Easter rabbit is by 1888; the paganish customs of Easter seem to have grown popular c. 1900; before that they were limited to German immigrants.
"If the children have no garden, they make nests in the wood-shed, barn, or house. They gather colored flowers for the rabbit to eat, that it may lay colored eggs. If there be a garden, the eggs are hidden singly in the green grass, box-wood, or elsewhere. On Easter Sunday morning they whistle for the rabbit, and the children imagine that they see him jump the fence. After church, on Easter Sunday morning, they hunt the eggs, and in the afternoon the boys go out in the meadows and crack eggs or play with them like marbles. Or sometimes children are invited to a neighbor's to hunt eggs." [Phebe Earle Gibbons, "Pennsylvania Dutch," Philadelphia, 1882]

151. Also see: Sifferlin, Alexandra. "What's the Origin of the Easter Bunny?" Time.com, 2/21/20, https://time.com/3767518/easter-bunny-origins-history. "The seasonal chocolate eggs and the bunny who delivers them are nowhere to be found in scripture. The exact origins of the Easter bunny are clouded in mystery. One theory is that the symbol of the rabbit stems from pagan tradition, specifically the festival of Eostre—a goddess of fertility whose animal symbol was a bunny. Rabbits, known for their energetic breeding, have traditionally symbolized fertility. Eggs are also representative of new life, and it's believed that decorating eggs for Easter dates back to the 13th century. Hundreds of years ago, churches had their congregations abstain from eggs during Lent, allowing them to be consumed again on Easter.
Urlin, Ethel L. "Festivals, Holy Days, and Saints' Days...."..
152. "Inanna-Ishtar," Encyclopedia.com, accessed 5/20/23, https://www.encyclopedia.com/social-sciences/encyclopedias-almanacs-transcripts-and-maps/inanna-ishtar.
About Encyclopedia.com: "As the Internet's premier collection of online encyclopedias, Encyclopedia.com provides you reference entries from credible, published sources like Oxford University Press and Columbia Encyclopedia." https://www.encyclopedia.com/about.
153   Also see Daniels, Morg. "Ancient Mesopotamian Transgender and Non-Binary Identities," *Academus Education*, 6/30/21, https://www.academuseducation.co.uk/post/ancient-mesopotamian-transgender-and-non-binary-identities. (This is a decidedly, in writing, pro-gay and pro-transgender site that is also aware of the academic resources attesting to this fact.) "The most highly venerated deity in Ancient Mesopotamia was Inanna, who was also known as Ishtar after the two were merged. She was known as the Queen of Heaven and was the goddess of sex, war and justice. She also was believed to have the ability to change a person's gender."
Gilad, Elan. "Do Passover Eggs and Easter Eggs Have a Shared Origin? The original use of eggs on both holidays is obscure, but use eggs they both do. Why?", *Haaretz*, 4/4/21, https://www.haaretz.com/israel-news/2021-04-04/ty-article/are-passover-eggs-and-easter-eggs-related/0000017f-dbe8-d3a5-af7f-fbeeaaac0000.

154. Ibid.

155. Dallas Baptist University. "Ancient Christian Martyrdom: A Brief Overview," accessed 3/1/23, https://www3.dbu.edu/mitchell/anceint_christian_martyrdom.htm#:~:text=By%20200%2C%20the%20faith%20had,million%20killed%20for%20the%20faith.

"In the first few centuries, Christianity grew quickly. By AD100, it had become mostly Gentile and had begun to break from its Jewish origins. By 200, the faith had permeated most regions of the Roman Empire, though Christians were mostly in the larger urban areas (Gaul, Lyons, Carthage, Rome). By 325, an estimated 7 million were Christians with as many as 2 million killed for the faith."

156. The only exception might be the Gospel of Luke and the book of Acts—both in the New Testament. Both are written by the same Luke and prevailing thought is that Luke was a Gentile.

However, see the following excellent research, and others like it, indicating that Luke was indeed Jewish. I also hold to this view: Dr. Thomas S. McCall. "What Luke a Gentile?", Zola Levitt Ministries.com, https://www.levitt.com/essays/luke.

157. Denova, Rebecca. "The Separation of Christianity from Judaism (Jewish-Christian Relations in the Earliest Communities)," *World History Encyclopedia*, 6/21/21, https://www.worldhistory.org/article/1785/the-separation-of-christianity-from-judaism.

158. Messianic Bible. "Constantine and the Foundations of Anti-Semitism," messianicbible.com, accessed 2/24/23, https://free.messianicbible.com/feature/constantine-foundations-of-anti-semitism.

159. Denova, Rebecca. "Constantine's Conversion to Christianity," WorldHistory.org, *World History Encyclopedia*, 5/10/21, https://www.worldhistory.org/article/1737/constantines-conversion-to-christianity.

160. Ibid.

161. Ibid.

162. Veldt, S. Mark, "Christian Attitudes toward the Jews in the Earliest Centuries A.D." (2007). Dissertations. 925. https://scholarworks.wmich.edu/dissertations/925.

163. Denova, Rebecca. "Constantine's Conversion to Christianity."
164. Fourth Century Christianity. "Emperor Constantine to all Churches Concerning the Date of Easter," Wisconsin Lutheran College, accessed 2/23/23. Ancient source used: Socrates, *Church History* 1.9. Other ancient sources: Eusebius, *Life of Constantine* 3.17–18; Theodoret, *Church History* 1.9; Anonymous *Church History* 2.37.10. Modern edition used: W. Bright, *Socrates' Ecclesiastical History, 2nd edition* (Oxford: Clarendon Press, 1893).https://www.fourthcentury.com/urkunde-26.
165. Acts 6:7 is one passage that affirms this.
166. Denova, Rebecca. "The Separation of Christianity from Judaism...."
167. Messianic Bible. "Constantine and the Foundations of Anti-Semitism," messianicbible.com, accessed 2/24/23, https://free.messianicbible.com/feature/constantine-foundations-of-anti-semitism.
168. Biblestudy.org. "Israel's Wilderness Wars Timeline," biblestudy.org, accessed 3/4/23, https://www.biblestudy.org/maps/first-wilderness-wars.html.
169. Gerard S. Sloyan, Professor Emeritus of Religion Temple University,"Christian Persecution of Jews over the Centuries," accessed 2/24/23, https://www.ushmm.org/research/about-the-mandel-center/initiatives/ethics-religion-holocaust/articles-and-resources/christian-persecution-of-jews-over-the-centuries/christian-persecution-of-jews-over-the-centuries.
170. The "woman" is Israel, then the "one new man" of Ephesians 2—the congregation of true believers in Yeshua, both Jew and Gentile: *Jamieson-Fausset-Brown Bible Commentary:* "This episode (Re 12:1–15:8) describes in detail the persecution of Israel and the elect Church by the beast, which had been summarily noticed, Re 11:7–10, and the triumph of the faithful, and torment of the unfaithful. …The Church, Israel first, and then the Gentile Church; clothed with Christ [Jew and Gentile together as the one new man in Yeshua]."
Cambridge Bible for Schools and Colleges: "More certain is the reference, or at least similarity of imagery, to Genesis 37:9, where "the eleven stars," … represent Jacob's eleven sons, bowing down to Joseph, the twelfth. Here, the ideal Israel appears in the glory of all the patriarchs: Abraham, Isaac and Jacob,

and their wives, are hers, and of the Twelve Tribes none is wanting. The whole description, in fact, is interpreted in Romans 9:5. See especially Micah 4:10; Micah 5:3: where it is her [Israel's] travail from which He is to be born Who is born in Bethlehem."

Expositor's Greek Testament: "Probably represented to the prophet the true Israel or Zion of God (Wernle, 276–288) in which his Christ had been born (cf. John 16:21, with John 14:30, also En. xc. 37). The prophet views the national history of Israel as a long preparation for the anguish and woe out of which the messiah was to come."

For all three commentaries, see https://biblehub.com/commentaries/revelation/12-1.htm.

171. Fourth-Century Christianity. "Emperor Constantine to All Churches…".
172. Hebrew and "Christian" calendar dating problems for Easter and Passover.
1. Rosovsky, Lorne. "It's about Time," Chabad.org, accessed 4/4/23, https://www.chabad.org/library/article_cdo/aid/407511/jewish/Its-About-Time.htm.
2. Yale Library. "About the Hebrew Calendar," accessed 4/3/23, https://web.library.yale.edu/cataloging/hebraica/about-hebrew-calendar.
3. Royal Museums Greenwich. "When Is Easter? Working Out When Easter Falls Requires an Astronomical Calculation," accessed 3/23/23, https://www.rmg.co.uk/stories/topics/when-easter.
4. Myer, Robinson. "The Ancient Math That Sets the Date of Easter and Passover: Why Don't the Two Holidays always Coincide? It Is, to Some Degree, the Moon's Fault." *The Atlantic*, 4/19/19, https://www.theatlantic.com/science/archive/2019/04/why-dont-easter-and-passover-always-line/587572.
173. Hebrew and Christian calendar dating problems for Easter and Passover. Myer, Robinson. "The Ancient Math…"
174. Greek. #1577. "Ecclesia," biblehub.com, https://biblehub.com/greek/1577.htm. "An assembly, congregation, church; the Church, the whole body of Christian believers."
175. Find more about Pastor Carl Gallups at www.carlgallups.com.

I asked Pastor Gallups to write this section with me because the two of us have been together in voluntary cooperative ministry for many years. In those years, we've tediously uncovered the truths you are about to read, and we've presented those truths in national and international television and radio broadcasts, teaching/preaching/conference settings, and in articles posted on various Internet sites. The two of us even went to the Temple Institute offices on the Temple Mount in downtown Old City Jerusalem and talked to some officials there who spoke directly to the chief rabbi of the Institute on our behalf. After their feedback, we were able to glean a lot of insight on what's really going on with the "construction" of a "new temple" on the Temple Mount. (This information is recounted in detail in Carl's 2020 book, *Masquerade* [Crane, MO: Defender Publishing]).

In this section of this book you're now reading, Carl's treasure trove of research material and insight have been combined with my lifelong understanding and additional research of the contextual nuances of the Hebrew language and biblical prophecies of the Temple, as well as the ancient and modern cultures of the Hebrew people as a whole. We pray you will find this section helpful to your understanding of the importance of Yahweh's Threshold Covenant.

176. For an example, take a look at what *The Jewish Chronicle* (the world's oldest Jewish newspaper, established in 1841) said about this very topic in November 2008:

"In this period following the Ninth of Av, many [Israeli Jews] express their hope for binyan Beit Hamikdash, rebuilding of the Temple. Some may feel ambivalent about this. Animal sacrifices are alien to our religious sensibilities today. Rabbi Abraham Isaac Kook, a great 20th century authority, opined that in the rebuilt third Temple there will only be vegetarian offerings. A very different religio-political reality would be required for the temple to be rebuilt now, given the presence of Muslim holy sites on the Temple Mount. Ultimately, the meaning of the Temple is universal: "For my house shall be called a house of prayer for all peoples" (Isaiah 56:7). See https://www.thejc.com/judaism/jewish-words/beit-hamikdash-1.5786.

177. See *Times of Israel*, January 2023. Gross, Judah Ari. "Ben Gvir faces dilemma as activists ask to hold Passover sacrifice on Temple Mount: Each year, fringe group tries to slaughter a lamb in line with its interpretation of a biblical edict, and is always denied. But now it's asking a different kind of police

minister." *Times of Israel*, 1/3/23, https://www.timesofisrael.com/ben-gvir-faces-dilemma-as-activists-ask-to-hold-passover-sacrifice-on-temple-mount. "Most Israeli security officials believe that permitting the Passover sacrifice on the Temple Mount would prompt fierce protests by Muslims, in Jerusalem, the West Bank and in neighboring Arab countries, who would see it as a major change to the status quo on the holy site. As a result, these requests have always been denied, though activists have been permitted to perform the ritual slaughter of a lamb within the Old City, but outside the Temple Mount."

178. For a detailed study, see Gallups' book, *Masquerade*, pp.49–61. In that book, Carl profusely documents (with mainstream media articles, Israeli government documents, and several published surveys taken among the Israeli people, as well as a lengthy testimony from me regarding the information I have in this matter from government and rabbinic officials) that the vast majority of Israelis, even Orthodox Jews, do not want a rebuilt Temple on the Temple Mount.

The idea that all the Jews want this to happen is a giant money-making scheme. I know what I'm talking about. I live here. I was born and raised here. I know the people. I know a good number of the "power people" here. I have talked in confidence with many about this issue.

Carl's book lays out the practically indisputable evidence of this claim. In that book, Carl and I relate our trip to the Temple Institute on the Temple Mount, where we spoke with important representatives there. We were even able to get in touch with the chief rabbi of the Institute through his representatives. You may be shocked to hear of our meeting and what was actually said regarding the rebuilding of the Temple on the Temple Mount.

179. As a pertinent side note, there are some who believe a Third Temple doesn't have to be built in the vicinity of the Wailing Wall [Hebrew: *kotel*]. They claim this area was never the original location of the Temple in the first place. They believe the original Temple site was *below* that area, in the City of David portion of Old Jerusalem. Regardless of where it might be built, that's not the topic we are exploring here. We are researching the question of the larger matter: Does the Bible, anywhere, *insist* that a Third Temple must be built in the last days?

180. Strauss, "Bible Prophecy"
181. Mooney, Brit. "Is the Third Temple in Jerusalem Literal or Symbolic?" Crosswalk.com, 5/17/21, https://www.crosswalk.com/special-coverage/end-times/what-is-the-third-temple.html.
"The short answer is that nowhere [in God's entire Word] do we see a physical Third Temple being built on this Earth.... So why would we make a physical Third Temple necessary?"
182. *Hieron*, Greek. #2411. Strong's: "A temple, either the whole building, or specifically the outer courts, open to worshippers." https://biblehub.com/greek/2411.htm.
183. Several translations therefore use the phrase "at the temple" or "in the temple courtyard" to make this proper distinction. (Examples: NIV, Berean Standard Bible, God's Word® Translation, Majority Standard Bible.) https://biblehub.com/luke/19-47.htm.
Thayer's Greek Lexicon: Strong's NT 1722: "ἐν, a preposition taking the dative after it; Hebrew בְּ; Latin in with abl.; English in, on, at, with, by, among." https://biblehub.com/greek/1722.htm.
184. "The Holy of Holies in the Second Temple was an empty chamber, without the Ark of the Covenant. When the Roman General Pompey conquered Jerusalem around 63 B.C., he demanded the privilege of entering the Holy of Holies. When he did, he came out saying that he could not understand what all the interest was about the sanctuary, when it was only an empty room."
Dr. Thomas S. McCall. "Where Is the Ark of the Covenant?," Zola Levitt Ministries, January 1997, https://www.levitt.com/essays/ark.
185. Sometimes *naos* is used symbolically of the entire Temple, but the context of that usage must specifically be understood by the listener, because, as stated previously, *naos* and *hieron* are not precise synonyms. See, for example, John 2:19–21:
"Jesus answered them, 'Destroy this **temple**, and I will raise it again in three days.' The Jews replied, 'It has taken forty-six years to build this **temple**, and you are going to raise it in three days?' But the **temple** he had spoken of was his body." (NIV; emphasis added)

The word *naos* is used in each of these instances of "temple." *Naos* specifically means the "Holy of Holies" of the *hieron*. Yet, because the *naos* is the exact place where the presence of God is represented in the *hieron*, then the *naos* becomes understood for the entire structure that encompasses it. But the context has to be very specific, as it was when Jesus spoke the words recorded in John 2.

186. *Naos*, Greek. #3485.

Thayer's Greek Lexicon: "Used of the temple at Jerusalem, but only of the sacred edifice (or sanctuary) itself, consisting of the Holy place and the Holy of holies. "Metaphorically, of a company of Christians, a Christian church, as dwelt in by the Spirit of God: 1 Corinthians 3:16; 2 Corinthians 6:16; Ephesians 2:21; for the same reason, of the bodies of Christians, 1 Corinthians 6:19. of the body of Christ, John 2:21, and according to the Evangelist's interpretation in 19 also." https://biblehub.com/greek/3485.htm.

"Naos is used most frequently in the metaphorical sense throughout the New Testament—denoting either the church or the Christian individually, or to speak of the literal body of Jesus Christ Himself." See every use of the word *naos* here: https://biblehub.com/greek/strongs_3485.htm.

187. My good friend and US ministry partner Carl Gallups gave me an illustration of these word usages that might help make the differences crystal clear. Say, for example, Carl asked me to meet him at his church. Let's also say that when I drove into the parking lot, I saw him go into the sanctuary portion of the larger church complex. Then, I went inside the sanctuary to meet with him. If, later on, I was telling someone else about my meeting with Carl, I could tell them that I met with Carl at his "church." Or, I could also have said that I met with Carl "in the sanctuary of his church." Both statements would be true, but the last one would be the most accurate because the sanctuary is a specific place or room *within* the entire complex of the larger church edifice. It's the same in the Greek language with *hieron* and *naos*. The *naos* is a specific room (behind the curtain and in the Holy of Holies) within the entire complex of the *hieron*.

188. The Word of God itself does not actually make this claim. But it is a natural and biblically plausible conclusion. As already noted, Paul only speaks of the actual Temple on the Temple Mount once, and that instance is only used

to make a point about the rituals that were taking place there in his earthly lifetime (1 Corinthians 9:13). Yet, when he speaks of his being "caught up to paradise," he says he saw some things that he wasn't permitted to tell the church (2 Corinthians 12:1–4). It stands to reason Paul would have known of the coming destruction of the Temple in Jerusalem. After all, he did see the man of lawlessness, the demonic outpouring of the last days, the Rapture event, and the return of the Lord with the saints. This would also explain why he so heavily insisted upon teaching the early Church that the true *naos* temple of God was the individual Christian (collectively, the *ecclesia*). It appears that Paul obviously had been shown the destruction of the Temple, which occurred only three years after his martyrdom.

189. Seven more examples follow. I give them because I want to emphasize that this is serious scholarship supported by vast numbers of renowned commentators

1. *Clarke's Commentary:* "So that sitting in the temple of God-having the highest place and authority in the Christian Church, he acts as God taking upon himself God's titles and attributes, and arrogating to himself the authority that belongs to the Most High." https://www.studylight.org/commentary/2-thessalonians/2-4.html.

2. *Gill's Exposition of the Scriptures:* "So that he as God sitteth in the temple of God"; not in the temple of Jerusalem, which was to be destroyed and never to be rebuilt more, and was destroyed before this man of sin was revealed; but in the church of God, so called, 1 Corinthians 3:16." https://biblehub.com/commentaries/2_thessalonians/2-4.htm.

3. *Barnes' Notes on the Bible:* "Sitteth in the temple of God—That is, in the Christian church. It is by no means necessary to understand this of the temple at Jerusalem, which was standing at the time this Epistle was written, because: (1) The phrase "the temple of God" is several times used with reference to the Christian church, 1 Corinthians 3:16, 1 Corinthians 3:17; 2 Corinthians 6:16; Ephesians 2:21; Revelation 3:12; and, (2) The temple was the proper symbol of the church, and an apostle trained amidst the Hebrew institutions would naturally speak of the church as the temple of God. https://www.studylight.org/commentary/2-thessalonians/2-4.html.

4. *Henry's Complete Commentary on the Bible:* "As God was in the temple of old, and worshipped there, and is in and with his church now, so the antichrist here mentioned is some usurper of God's authority in the Christian church." https://www.studylight.org/commentary/2-thessalonians/2-4.html.

5. *Whedon's Bible Commentary:* "Temple of God. Not the Jewish temple, which is never called so in the New Testament, but unquestionably the Christian Church. See 2 Corinthians 6:16; Ephesians 2:21. This seating himself in supremacy in the Church is a vivid picture of the inauguration of each new pope." https://www.studylight.org/commentaries/eng/whe/2-thessalonians-2.html.

6. *Ellicott's Commentary for English Readers:* "The temple of God.—Though the image is drawn from the Jewish temple, we may say with some confidence that Paul did not expect the Antichrist as a prose fact to take his seat in that edifice…. It seems, therefore, most probable that the great Apostasy will not become avowedly atheistic, but will be an apostasy (so to speak) within the Church, and that the Man of Sin, who heads that Apostasy, will make special claim upon the Christian Church. https://biblehub.com/commentaries/2_thessalonians/2-4.htm.

7. *Cambridge Bible for Schools and Colleges:* "Within the temple of God—not in Jerusalem alone," says Chrysostom, "but in every church." https://biblehub.com/commentaries/2_thessalonians/2-4.htm.

190. 2 Thessalonians 2:4. *Alford's Greek Testament Critical Exegetical Commentary*, Studylight.org, https://www.studylight.org/commentaries/eng/hac/2-thessalonians-2.htm.

191. 2 Thessalonians 2:4. *Coffman's Commentary on the Bible*, studylight.org, https://www.studylight.org/commentary/2-thessalonians/2-4.html.

192. 2 Thessalonians 2:4. *Pulpit Commentary*, Biblehub.com, https://biblehub.com/commentaries/2_thessalonians/2-4.htm.

193. In 2 Peter, the Apostle Peter calls the writings of Paul "scripture." Peter and John were copastors, along with James, of the first church in Jerusalem (Acts 2). It is highly unlikely Peter would be familiar with Paul's "scriptures" and would be using them himself, *but not John*—especially by the time Revelation was written.

"As he does in all his letters when [Paul] speaks in them of these matters. There are some things in them that are hard to understand, which the ignorant and unstable twist to their own destruction, as they do the other Scriptures" (2 Peter 3:16)."

194. Revelation 11:1, *Pulpit Commentary*, Biblehub.com, https://biblehub.com/commentaries/revelation/11-1.htm.

195. Revelation 11:1, *Jamieson-Fausset-Brown Bible Commentary*, Biblehub.com, https://biblehub.com/commentaries/revelation/11-1.htm.

196. Revelation 11:1, *Barnes' Notes on the Bible*, Biblehub.com, https://biblehub.com/commentaries/revelation/11-1.htm.

197. Mooney, Brit. "Is the Third Temple in Jerusalem Literal or Symbolic?" Crosswalk.com, 5/17/21, https://www.crosswalk.com/special-coverage/end-times/what-is-the-third-temple.html.

198. Hebrew. 1965. "hekal", biblehub.com, https://biblehub.com/hebrew/1965.htm.
"A palace, temple—the building itself. Not a dedicated part of it, as in *miqdash*, but the entire structure of the temple or palace."

199. Hebrew. 4720. "miqdash", biblehub.com, https://biblehub.com/hebrew/4720.htm. "A sacred place, holy place, a sanctuary portion of the temple wherein God dwells and/or meets with His people."

More notes and study:

Because the Temple edifice (*heykal*) actually housed the *miqdash* (the Holy of Holies—the presence of God), it was sometimes also called the *Beit Hamikdash*, meaning "the House of the Holy of Holies" or "the Holy House." *Beit Hamikdash* refers only to the Temple in Israel, and not just any temple (pagan or otherwise), but only in the sense that it is the literal, brick-and-mortar structure that encapsulates the *miqdash* (Holy of Holies) of Yahweh. See also https://www.chabad.org/library/article_cdo/aid/144586/jewish/The-Holy-Temple.htm and https://www.thejc.com/judaism/jewish-words/beit-hamikdash-1.5786.

200. Inner Sanctuary: Debir/Devir, Masculine Noun, (Strong's 1687). (Synonym of the Hebrew *miqdash* and the Greek *naos*.
See https://biblehub.com/hebrew/1687.htm. (Also see 1 Kings 6:5 for one

example of its use, meaning "the inner sanctuary. The place where God spoke.") "Within the Tabernacle, at the very core, behind a thick curtain, was the holiest of holy places, the 'inner sanctuary.' This centre sanctuary was sometimes called the Holy of holies [*l-qodesh ha-qodashim*], (or "Most Holy place"), but occasionally it was referred to as the Devir.

"The Devir/debir shared the root letters dalet-bet-resh (DBR) with the Hebrew word, dabar/davar (Strong's 1697), meaning "WORD." In other words, the Inner Sanctuary could also be described as the Holy Word Space. It was the space where the Word of God lived; it was the space where the Presence of YHWH spoke…a place of oracle." https://hebrewwordlessons.com/2022/07/24/devir-the-inner-sanctuary-place-of-the-word.

Note: Think of the definition of the *devir*! This invokes the imagery of John 1:1–3, 12: "In the beginning was the Word, and the Word was with God and the Word was God…and the Word became flesh and dwelt among us."

201. Gregg, Steve. "Making Sense of Ezekiel's Temple Vision," 6/1/2012, https://www.equip.org/articles/making-sense-ezekiels-temple-vision. Christian Research Institute: "While God spoke to Israel through various prophets in the past, the revelation that has come through Christ is more comprehensive because He is no mere prophet, but 'the brightness of [God's] glory and the express image of His person.' The New Testament is not a mere appendix added to the writings of the Old Testament prophets. It is a revelation of the new order in Jesus Christ, in whom all previous revelation finds its fulfillment, and through whom all previous revelation must be understood.

202. Greek. #1577. "Ecclesia."

203. Also in Mark 13:14.

204. Strauss, "Bible Prophecy…".

205. Britannica. "Antiochus IV Epiphanes," accessed 3/9/23, https://www.britannica.com/biography/Antiochus-IV-Epiphanes.

206. Ibid.

207. For further study and evidence of this truth, see the commentaries on Matthew 24 at this link: https://biblehub.com/commentaries/matthew/24-15.htm.

208. Britannica. "Siege of Jerusalem: Jewish-Roman war [70 CE]," accessed 3/9/23, https://www.britannica.com/event/Siege-of-Jerusalem-70.

209. For further study of the various interpretations of Jesus' prophecies of the "abomination that causes desolation" and the very real struggle the classic commentaries had with the precise interpretation of Jesus' words, read through the commentaries on Matthew 24 at this location: https://biblehub.com/commentaries/matthew/24-15.htm.

210. Other translations that include the word "temple" are Holman Christian Standard Bible, New International Version, Berean Standard Bible, Brenton Septuagint Translation, Douay-Rheims Bible, Good News Translation, Majority Standard Bible, Coverdale Bible of 1535, Douay-Rheims Bible (Catholic), and the Catholic Public Domain Version. See https://biblehub.com/parallel/daniel/9-27.htm.

211. Daniel 9:27. Various Bible translations. See https://biblehub.com/parallel/daniel/9-27.htm.

212. See all 109 of the uses of the word here: https://biblehub.com/hebrew/strongs_3671.htm.

213. Daniel 9:27. *Cambridge Bible for Schools and Colleges*, Biblehub.com, https://biblehub.com/commentaries/daniel/9-27.htm.

214. Daniel 9:27. *Benson Commentary*, Biblehub.com, https://biblehub.com/commentaries/daniel/9-27.htm.

215. Daniel 9:27. *Coffman's Commentary on the Bible*, Studylight.org, https://www.studylight.org/commentaries/eng/bcc/daniel-9.html.

216. Ibid.

217. Gregg, "Making Sense of Ezekiel's Temple Vision.

218. "The prophecies given in the Old Covenant and the ones given under the New Covenant cannot contradict each other regarding how the last days will ultimately culminate."

Ellicott's Commentary for English Readers: "The Apostles do not rest solely on direct revelation made to their own consciences, but rather dwell on the significance of historical facts (e.g., Romans 1:4; 2 Peter 1:17), or, still more frequently and strongly, on the interpretation of Old Testament Scriptures (e.g., Hebrews 1:8; Hebrews 2:12-13; 2 Peter 1:19). If, therefore, we can find material in the Old Testament which, taken in conjunction with our Lord's own words, could have supplied Paul—or rather, the [universal] consent of the early Church—with the doctrine of the Last Things as we find it stated in the apostolic writings, we shall be justified in using those Old Testament materials in the explanation of the New [and vice versa]." https://biblehub.com/commentaries/2_thessalonians/2-3.htm.

219. Dr. Walter Martin: "Founder of the Christian Research Institute: https://www.equip.org/about/our-history. Dr. Martin held four earned degrees including a Master of Arts in Philosophy from New York University, where he was a student alongside television evangelist D. James Kennedy. He subsequently earned a Ph.D. in 1976 from California Coast University. As the author of the influential "The Kingdom of the Cults" (1965), he has been dubbed by the conservative Christian columnist Michael J. McManus the "godfather of the anti-cult movement." See: Michael J. McManus, "Eulogy for the Godfather of the Anti-cult Movement," *The Free Lance-Star*, Fredericksburg, VA, 8/26/89.

220. Gregg, "Making Sense of Ezekiel's Temple Vision."

221. "And the devil who had deceived them was thrown into the lake of fire and sulfur where the beast and the false prophet were, and they will be tormented day and night forever and ever" (Revelation 20:10).

222. Hebrew. #8548. "tamid," Biblehub.com https://biblehub.com/hebrew/8548.htm. "The Tamid sacrifice is known among the Jews as the Daily Sacrifices as in the lambs brought daily to the Temple on the Temple Mount."

223. *Keil and Delitzsch Biblical Commentary on the Old Testament* (Daniel 11:36): These words before us [Daniel 11:31-36] are expressly referred to Antichrist, and 2 Thessalonians 2:4. https://www.studylight.org/commentaries/eng/kdo/daniel-11.html.

224. Hebrew. #8548. "tamid."

225. Daniel 12 is ultimately about the "time of the end"—the very last days before the return of Yeshua, during the time of the rebuilt *naos* of God, the new "temple," the Church. See the following:

Ellicott's Commentary for English Readers: "A time of trouble.—This is the tribulation spoken of in Matthew 24:21–22, which follows, as it does in the

Book of Daniel, the wars, rumors of wars, and uprisings of sundry nations. (See Matthew 24:6–7.)" https://biblehub.com/commentaries/daniel/12-1.htm. *Jamieson-Fausset-Brown Bible Commentary:* "Compare Da 12:4, 13; as Da 12:6, 7 refer to Da 7:25, that is, to the time of Antichrist.... The political resurrection of the Jews under the Maccabees is the starting-point of transition to the literal resurrection about to follow the destruction of Antichrist by Christ's coming in glory. The language passes here from the nearer to the more remote event, to which alone it is fully applicable." https://biblehub.com/commentaries/daniel/12-1.htm.

Pulpit Commentary: "To the time of the end. The end is not the end of the persecution of the days of Antiochus—that is already past; we have now reached the consummation of all things.... This is to be looked upon as a description of the last time, when circumstance shall remove the seal from the book." https://biblehub.com/commentaries/daniel/12-4.htm.

226. As noted earlier, we must still fully recognize the *compound* nature of the prophecies of Daniel, understanding that they were most likely, first, allusions to the coming Antiochus in 168 BC, then to the AD 70 destruction of Jerusalem, and then to the ultimate fulfilment in the days of Antichrist and his attack on the *naos* of God. Again, almost all the classical scholars saw this same pattern in Daniel's prophecies of the "abomination that causes desolation."

227. Daniel 11:36. *Keil and Delitzsch Biblical Commentary on the Old Testament,* Studylight.org, https://www.studylight.org/commentaries/eng/kdo/daniel-11.html.

228. Daniel 11:36. *Jamieson-Fausset-Brown Bible Commentary,* Biblehub.com, https://biblehub.com/commentaries/daniel/11-36.htm.

229. Daniel 11:36. *Benson Commentary,* Biblehub.com, https://biblehub.com/commentaries/daniel/11-36.htm.

230. Daniel 11:36. *Ellicott's Commentary for English Readers,* Biblehub.com, https://biblehub.com/commentaries/daniel/11-36.htm.

231. Daniel 12:1. *Jamieson-Fausset-Brown Bible Commentary,* Biblehub.com, https://biblehub.com/commentaries/daniel/12-1.htm.

232. Romans 12:1. *Meyer's Commentary,* Biblehub.com, https://biblehub.com/commentaries/romans/12-1.htm.

233. Greek. 40. "hagios," Biblehub.com, https://biblehub.com/greek/40.htm. *Strong's Exhaustive Concordance*: "sacred (physically, pure, morally blameless or religious, ceremonially, consecrated)—(most) holy (one, thing), saint. A place, object, or person."

234. Greek. 5117. "Topos," Biblehub.com, https://biblehub.com/greek/5117.htm. *Strong's Exhaustive Concordance*: "A place, a spot, or a location…properly, any portion of space marked off, as it were, from surrounding, space; used of a. an inhabited place, as a city, village, district: Luke 4:37; Luke 10:1; Acts 12:12; Acts 16:3; Acts 27:2, 8; 1 Corinthians 1:2; 2 Corinthians 2:14; 1 Thessalonians 1:8; Revelation 18:17."

235. "Let the reader understand…."
1. *Ellicott's Commentary for English Readers:* "There appears, however, to be no sufficient reason why [the words, "Let the reader understand"] should not be received as part of the discourse itself, bidding one who read the words of Daniel to ponder over their meaning till he learnt to recognize their fulfilment in the events that should pass before his eyes." https://biblehub.com/commentaries/matthew/24-15.htm.
2. *Pulpit Commentary:* "It seems more natural to take the clause as uttered by Christ himself with a silent reference to the words of the angel to Daniel, 'Know therefore and understand' (Daniel 9:25; comp. 12:10). The Lord would point emphatically to the prophecy of Daniel, and his own interpretation thereof. He seems also to imply that the application is not at once obvious, and needs spiritual insight to discern it." https://biblehub.com/commentaries/matthew/24-15.htm.

236. Ibid. Daniel 12 is ultimately about the "time of the end" the very last days before the return of Yeshua, during the time of the rebuilt *naos* of God—the new "temple"…the church. See the following three commentary explanations.

237. Dr. Menn, Jonathan. "Ezekiel's Vision of a New Temple: Ezekiel 40–48," Thirdmill.org, accessed 3/21/23 [a brief summary of Appendix 3 in the book titled *Biblical Eschatology* (2nd ed., Wipf and Stock, 2018)], https://thirdmill.org/magazine/article.asp/link/jon_menn%5Ejon_menn.BEA3.html/at/Ezekiel's%20Vision%20of%20a%20New%20Temple.

238. Hebrew. 1004. *bayith*, Biblehub.com, https://biblehub.com/hebrew/1004.htm.

239. Ibid.
240. Ezekiel 44:3. *Ellicott's Commentary*, Biblehub.com, https://biblehub.com/commentaries/ezekiel/44-3.htm.
241. Ezekiel 44:3. *Barnes' Notes on the Bible*, Biblehub.com, https://biblehub.com/commentaries/ezekiel/44-3.htm.
242. Ezekiel 44:3. *Jamieson-Fausset-Brown Bible Commentary*, Biblehub.com, https://biblehub.com/commentaries/ezekiel/44-3.htm.
243. *The Pulpit Commentary, Vincent's Word Studies, Gill's Exposition of the Bible, Jamieson-Fausset-Brown Bible Commentary*, and the *Expositor's Greek Testament* each note how this passage in Revelation is directly connected to Ezekiel's temple vision. See https://biblehub.com/commentaries/revelation/21-10.htm.
244. Got Questions. "What is the significance of Ezekiel's temple?" Gotquestions.org, accessed 3/15/23, https://www.gotquestions.org/Ezekiel-temple.html.
245. The larger commentary portion from the *Jamieson-Fausset-Brown Bible Commentary* on the topic of Ezekiel's temple is as follows:
"The arrangements as to the land and the temple are, in many particulars, different from those subsisting before the captivity. There are things in it so improbable physically as to preclude a purely literal interpretation.
"The general truth seems to hold good that, as Israel served the nations for his rejection of Messiah, so shall they serve him in the person of Messiah, when he shall acknowledge Messiah (Isa 60:12; Zec 14:17–19; compare Ps 72:11).
"The ideal temple exhibits, under Old Testament forms (used as being those then familiar to the men whom Ezekiel, a priest himself, and one who delighted in sacrificial images, addresses), not the precise literal outline, but the essential character of the worship of Messiah as it shall be when He shall exercise sway in Jerusalem among His own people, the Jews, and thence to the ends of the earth.
"The very fact that the whole is a vision (Eze 40:2), not an oral face-to-face communication such as that granted to Moses (Nu 12:6–8), implies that the directions are not to be understood so precisely literally as those given to the Jewish lawgiver. The description involves things which, taken literally, almost involve natural impossibilities....

"A temple with sacrifices now would be a denial of the all-sufficiency of the sacrifice of Christ...."

"As in the beginning God promised to be a 'sanctuary' (Eze 11:16) to the captives at the Chebar, so now at the close is promised a complete restoration and realization of the theocratic worship and polity under Messiah in its noblest ideal (compare Jeremiah 31:38–40).

"In Revelation 21:22 'no temple' is seen, as in the perfection of the new dispensation the accidents of place and form are no longer needed to realize to Christians what Ezekiel imparts to Jewish minds by the imagery familiar to them. In Ezekiel's temple holiness stretches over the entire temple, so that in this there is no longer a distinction between the different parts, as in the old temple." See https://biblehub.com/commentaries/ezekiel/40-1.htm.

246. Ezekiel 40:1. *Jamieson-Fausset-Brown Bible Commentary*, Biblehub.com, https://biblehub.com/commentaries/ezekiel/40-1.htm.

247. Jonathan Menn (JD, Cornell Law School; MDiv, Trinity Evangelical Divinity School) was a board-certified civil trial lawyer for many years. After receiving his MDiv, summa cum laude, from Trinity Evangelical Divinity School in 2007, he served as East Africa director of Equipping Pastors International for six years. He is now the director of Equipping Church Leaders-East Africa (ECLEA). He travels regularly to East Africa, where he teaches pastors and church leaders. His extensive written teaching materials on biblical subjects and details of his teaching trips to Burundi, Kenya, Rwanda, Tanzania, and Uganda are available at www.eclea.net, https://www.amazon.com/stores/author/B00FEGSCOQ/about.

248. Dr. Menn, Jonathan. "Ezekiel's Vision of a New Temple: Ezekiel 40–48," Thirdmill.org, accessed 3/21/23 a brief summary of Appendix 3 in the book titled *Biblical Eschatology* (2nd ed., Wipf and Stock, 2018)], https://thirdmill.org/magazine/article.asp/link/jon_menn%5Ejon_menn.BEA3.html/at/Ezekiel's%20Vision%20of%20a%20New%20Temple.

249. Revelation 21:22. *Ellicott's Commentary for English Readers*, Biblehub.com, https://biblehub.com/commentaries/revelation/21-22.htm.

250. Revelation 21:22. *Coffman's Commentary*, Studylight.org, https://www.studylight.org/commentaries/eng/bcc/revelation-21.html.

251. 2 Samuel 7:13. *Barnes' Notes on the Bible*, Biblehub.com, https://biblehub.com/commentaries/2_samuel/7-13.htm.

252. 2 Samuel 7:13. *Pulpit Commentary*, Biblehub.com, https://biblehub.com/commentaries/2_samuel/7-13.htm.

253. Blue Letter Bible. "Quotations from the Old Testament in the New Testament," blueletterbible.org, https://www.blueletterbible.org/study/pnt/pnt08.cfm.
The top four NT books that quote Old Testament passages: Revelation – 249, Matthew – 98, Hebrews – 86, Romans – 74. See the number of OT quotes in every NT book at the link.

254. Gregg, "Making Sense of Ezekiel's Temple Vision." This article first appeared in the "Practical Hermeneutics" column of the *Christian Research Journal*, volume 35, number 03 (2012).

255. Dr. Peter Pett, BA, BD, (Hons-London), DD, is a retired Baptist minister and college lecturer. He holds a BD (good honours) from King's College London and was trained at what is now the London School of Theology (formerly London Bible College). His current commentaries on the entire Bible excludes 1 and 2 Chronicles, Esther, Job, and Psalms 67–150 because the material for these has not yet been written. https://www.studylight.org/commentaries/eng/pet.html.

256. Ezekiel 45. *Pett's Commentary on the Bible*, Studylight.org, https://www.studylight.org/commentaries/eng/pet/ezekiel-45.html.

257. "Being built together into a dwelling place…"
HELPS Word-studies "(Cognate: 3619 oikodomē—properly, a building (edifice) serving as a home; (figuratively) constructive criticism and instruction that builds a person up to be the suitable dwelling place of God, i.e. where the Lord is 'at home.' See https://biblehub.com/interlinear/ephesians/2-21.htm.

258. The Greek word used in Ephesians 2 for "house, or household" is Strong's #3609: *oikeios*. See https://www.bibletools.org/index.cfm/fuseaction/Lexicon.show/ID/G3609/oikeios.htm. However, the Hebrew equivalent would be *bayith*, "house" or "household." See https://biblehub.com/hebrew/1004.htm.

259. The Christian Research Institute was founded by Dr. Walter Martin,

PhD. Dr. Martin was the author of the renowned and globally bestselling book *Kingdom of the Cults*.
260. Gregg, "Making Sense of Ezekiel's Temple Vision.".
261. Genesis 2:2–3. "Rested." (Hebrew 7673. Shabath). "To cease, desist, stop, rest." https://biblehub.com/hebrew/7673.htm.
262. O'Hair, J. C. "Part 7: From Adam to Moses," Berean Bible Society, accessed 4/2/23, https://www.bereanbiblesociety.org/from-adam-to-moses.
263. Colossians 2:16. *Coffman's Commentary on the Bible*, Studylight.org, https://www.studylight.org/commentaries/eng/bcc/colossians-2.html.
264. Mark 2:27. *Pulpit Commentary*, Biblehub.com, https://biblehub.com/commentaries/mark/2-27.htm.
265. Merriam Webster Dictionary. "Convocation," accessed 3/23/23. An assembly of persons called together to a meeting. https://www.merriam-webster.com/dictionary/convocation.
266. Hebrew. 4744. "Miqra," Biblehub.com, https://biblehub.com/hebrew/4744.htm.
Strong's Exhaustive Concordance: "Miqra, Assembly, calling, convocation, reading.From qara'; something called out, i.e. also a rehearsal."
267. Hebrew. 71212. "Qara," Biblehub.com https://biblehub.com/hebrew/7121.htm.
Strong's Exhaustive Concordance: "To preach, proclaim, or make famous—or be famous."
268. Hebrew. 4186. "moshab," Biblehub.com, https://biblehub.com/hebrew/4186.htm.
NAS Exhaustive Concordance: "inhabited places, where they lived, dwellings, habitations, a dwelling place."
269. Leviticus 23:3. *Keil and Delitzsch Biblical Commentary on the Old Testament*, Biblehub.com, https://biblehub.com/commentaries/leviticus/23-3.htm.
270. Leviticus 23:3. *Jamieson-Fausset-Brown Bible Commentary*, Biblehub.com, https://biblehub.com/commentaries/leviticus/23-3.htm.
271. Leviticus 23:3. *Pulpit Commentary*, Biblehub.com, https://biblehub.com/commentaries/leviticus/23-3.htm.

272. Jewish Virtual Library. "Worship," accessed 4/2/23, https://www.jewishvirtuallibrary.org/worship.

273. Editors of Britannica. "Synagogue: Judaism," accessed 3/3/23 https://www.britannica.com/topic/synagogue.

274. The Editors of Encyclopaedia Britannica. "Temple of Jerusalem: Judaism," accessed 4/6/23, https://www.britannica.com/topic/Temple-of-Jerusalem.

275. For an amazing and highly revelational affirmation of this fact, I urge you to read Carl Gallups' book, *The Yeshua Protocol* (Crane, MO: Defender, 2022).

276. Hebrews. 4150. "Moed," Biblehub.com. https://biblehub.com/hebrew/4150.htm. Translated as a: "feast, fixed time or season, a festal gathering."

277. John 5:1 calls this unknown feast the "Feast of the Jews." Remember, this was written by John, an Orthodox messianic Jew. So, he could not have been speaking of one of the Feasts of the Lord. He never would have called one of those events a "Feast of the Jews." This had to have been one of the "Feasts" that was, through history, "added" as festival days (such as Purim or the Feast of Dedication; see John 10:1) by the Jewish people themselves.

While Hanukkah (also called the "Festival of Lights" or the "Feast of Dedication," which celebrates the purification of the Temple by Judas Maccabaeus in 164/167 BC) was mentioned in John 10:22, Purim (which celebrates the deliverance of the Jews in the time of Esther) was established by Esther's uncle, Mordecai.

These are not included in the seven appointed "Feasts of the Lord." They could legitimately be called the "Feasts of the *Jews*."

1. *Ellicott's Commentary for English Readers:* "The only feast which falls in this interval is the Feast of Purim, and it is with this that the best modern opinion identifies the feast of our text." https://biblehub.com/commentaries/john/5-1.htm.

2. *Meyer's New Testament Commentary:* "This is no other than the feast of Purim." https://biblehub.com/commentaries/john/5-1.htm.

3. *Cambridge Bible for Schools and Colleges:* "The only feast which fits in satisfactorily is Purim. We saw from John 4:35 that the two days in Samaria

were either in December or January. The next certain date Isaiah 6:4, the eve of the Passover, i.e. April. Purim, which was celebrated in March (14th and 15th Adar), falls just in the right place in the interval. This feast commemorated the deliverance of the Jews from Haman, and took its name from the lots which he caused to be cast (Esther 3:7; Esther 9:24; Esther 9:26; Esther 9:28). https://biblehub.com/commentaries/john/5-1.htm.

278. Hebrews. 4150. "Moed," Biblehub.com. https://biblehub.com/hebrew/4150.htm. Translated as a: "feast, fixed time or season, festal gathering."

279. Biblestudy.org. "Meaning of Numbers in the Bible: The Number 8," accessed 3/4/23, https://www.biblestudy.org/bibleref/meaning-of-numbers-in-bible/8.html.

"The number 8 represents a new beginning, meaning a new order or creation, and man's true 'born again' event when he is resurrected from the dead into eternal life…. His resurrection occurred three complete days after he was buried, which was at the end of the weekly Sabbath day that fell on Nisan 17. Nisan 17 was day 8, counting inclusively, from the time Christ was selected as man's sacrificial Lamb…. Jesus showed himself alive 8 times after his resurrection from the dead. His first appearance alive was to Mary Magdalene (Mark 16:9–11). He then showed himself to two disciples traveling to Emmaus (Luke 24). Next, he appeared to all the disciples except Thomas (John 20:19–24) then a week later to all them when Thomas was present (John 20:26–29). According to the apostle Paul, Christ also was seen by 500 believers at one time (1Corinthians 15:4–7). Jesus also met his disciples at the appointed place in Galilee (Matthew 28:16–17) and on Galilee's shores (John 21:1– 24). His final meeting was on the Mount of Olives, where he gave his followers instructions before ascending to heaven (Acts 1)."

280. Matthew 11:28. *Ellicott's Commentary on the Bible*, Biblehub.com, https://biblehub.com/commentaries/matthew/11-28.htm.

281. Matthew 11:28. *Maclaren's Exposition of the Scriptures*, Biblehub.com, https://biblehub.com/commentaries/matthew/11-28.htm.

282. Hebrews 4:9. *Maclaren's Exposition of the Scriptures*, Biblehub.com. https://biblehub.com/commentaries/hebrews/4-9.htm.

283. Hebrews 4:9. *Matthew Henry's Concise Commentary*, Biblehub.com. https://biblehub.com/commentaries/hebrews/4-9.htm.

284. Hebrews 4:9. *Jamieson-Fausset-Brown Bible Commentary*, Biblehub.com. https://biblehub.com/commentaries/hebrews/4-9.htm.

285. Hebrews 4:10. *Pulpit Commentary*, Biblehub.com. https://biblehub.com/commentaries/hebrews/4-10.htm.

286. "How is Jesus our Sabbath Rest?" GotQuestions.org, accessed 3/22/23, 2023. https://www.gotquestions.org/Jesus-Sabbath.html.

287. Brown, Nathan, E. "An Exegetical Outline of Hebrews: "The Superiority of Christ and His Covenant," accessed 4/6/23: pp. 34–40, especially pp. 36–37, https://comeafterme.com/web_documents/English/Articles/Hebrews%20-%20The%20Superiority%20of%20Christ%20and%20His%20Covenant.pdf.

288. Greek. 2523. "kathizó," Biblehub.com. https://biblehub.com/greek/2523.htm. *NAS Exhaustive Concordance*: "To sit down, seated, appoint, rest, rested, settled."

289. The instances of imposing the death penalty for the willful violation of the Old Testament Sabbath Law are found in Exodus 31:14, Exodus 35:2, and Numbers 15.

It was, in part, those kinds of "laws," plus all the ones they simply made up, that the Pharisees continually tried to hang upon Yeshua so that, by them, they could kill Him.

Yet Yeshua's answer was to declare Himself Lord of the Sabbath! And for that answer, they accused Him of even more blasphemy, unaware that they were accusing the Creator of the Universe of claiming glory for Himself that He didn't "deserve." The Chaldean spirit is, indeed, a blinding demonic force.

290. Colossians 2. *Barclay's Daily Bible Study*, Studylight.org, https://www.studylight.org/commentaries/eng/dsb/colossians-2.html.

291. Colossians 2:16. *Coffman's Commentaries on the Bible*, Studylight.org, https://www.studylight.org/commentaries/eng/bcc/colossians.html. See also *Smith's Bible Commentary* (concerning Amos 8:9) https://www.studylight.org/commentary/amos/8-9.html.

"We do read of one day which was a feast day, the Feast of Passover, in which it turned dark at noon on a clear day. It could not have been an eclipse, because Passover takes place at full moon, and it's impossible to have an eclipse of the sun on a full moon. That was the day that Jesus was crucified. You remember how it declares that darkness covered the land from the ninth hour onward, sixth hour there was darkness over the land?"

292. Augustyn, Tim. "Bible Q&A: Is the Sabbath Day on Saturday or Sunday?" Open The Bible, 4/4/17, https://openthebible.org/article/bible-qa-is-the-sabbath-day-on-saturday-or-sunday.

"In Colossians 2:16–17, the Apostle Paul gives us three examples of things that Christians ought not judge one another over (and one of them is the celebration of the Sabbath). Keeping the Sabbath, by the way, is often the argument that is put forward for worshipping on Saturday rather than Sunday. "But Paul says that we are not to let anyone judge us over this matter. Think about what Paul is actually saying: We shouldn't let anyone judge us for keeping the Sabbath and we shouldn't let anyone judge us for not keeping the Sabbath. Why? Doesn't Paul know on which day the Sabbath should be kept? "He explains in the next verse. The reason we shouldn't let anyone judge us in regard to the Sabbath is that the Sabbath was a shadow of something to come. The substance, or the thing that the Sabbath was pointing to, is Jesus Christ.

"He is our rest. It doesn't matter whether you go to corporate worship on Saturday or on Sunday, because that's not what really matters. What really matters is that you find your rest in Christ! And you can (and should) do that every day of the week!"

293. Similarly, Romans 14:5 states: "One man considers one day more sacred than another; another man considers every day alike. Each one should be fully convinced in his own mind."

294. Early believers eventually began meeting on the first day of the week. A number of scholars attest that, at first, they continued their synagogue worship traditions on the designated Sabbath. However, they were soon expelled or castigated by Jewish people who were rejecting Yeshua as Messiah. While the early believers, including the Apostle Paul, would often still go up to the synagogues to worship with their friends and families—and to witness to them

about Yeshua—the Bible records that they also began to meet on Sundays, presumably in the evening hours, since that would have also been a work day. See examples in Acts 20:17, 1 Corinthians 16:1–2.

This appears to be the immediate context of Colossians 2:14–17 and Romans 14:5, as well as in other similar scriptural exhortations.

Following are the biblical facts that most likely led the early Christians to meet on Sunday for worship—the *first day of the week*, or *the Lord's Day*, according to John in Revelation 1.

1. The creation, especially of the earthly realm, was spoken into existence on the first day of the week. On that day, light was the first element to be called forth: "Let there be light." Yeshua is the Light of the World. He is the Light of Salvation. He is the Light of Life. He is the Creator of the universe! (See John 1, Colossians 1, Hebrews 1, and Revelation 4.) Therefore, the first day of the week would also become known as *the Lord's Day* (Genesis 1:3).

2. It was "early" on the *first day of the week* when the tomb was first discovered empty by His disciples (Matthew 28:1, Mark 16:1, Luke 24:1, John 20:1).

3. It was on the *first day of the week* when a number of the disciples first encountered the actual resurrected *person of Yeshua* (Matthew 28, Mark 16, John 20, Luke 24).

4. It was on the *first night* of the *first day of the week* when Yeshua first appeared to His disciples as a group, in the upper room where they were meeting (John 20, Luke 24).

5. It was one week later, again on the night of *the first day of the week*, when Yeshua appeared for a second time in that same upper room (John 20:26).

6. It was on the *first day of the week* (also known as the "Lord's Day") when John was caught up to the throne room of God and given the book of Revelation (Revelation 1). The Lord's Day was Sunday.

Pulpit Commentary: "On the Lord's day. The expression occurs here only in the New Testament, and beyond all reasonable doubt it means "on Sunday." This is, therefore, the earliest use of the phrase in this sense." https://biblehub.com/commentaries/revelation/1-10.htm.

Also see: *Expositor's Greek Testament, Ellicott's Commentary for English Readers, Meyers' New Testament Commentary, Cambridge Bible for Schools and Colleges,*

Bengel's Gnomen, etc., for the same conclusion concerning the Lord's Day. https://biblehub.com/commentaries/revelation/1-10.htm.

On the matter of Constantine's "declaration" of a "Sunday Sabbath," see Ayer, Joseph Cullen (1913). *A Source Book for Ancient Church History*. Vol. 2.1.1.59g. (New York: Scribner's) 284–285.

"Sunday was another work day in the Roman Empire. On March 7, 321, however, Roman Emperor Constantine I issued a civil decree making Sunday a day of rest [a Sabbath] from labor, stating:

'All judges and city people and the craftsmen shall rest [Sabbath] upon the venerable day of the sun [Sunday]. Country people, however, may freely attend to the cultivation of the fields, because it frequently happens that no other days are better adapted for planting the grain in the furrows or the vines in trenches. So that the advantage given by heavenly providence may not for the occasion of a short time perish.'"

295. Below are links to three helpful articles that demonstrate this truth.

1. Emily McFarlan Miller. "The Science of Sabbath: How People Are Rediscovering Rest—and Claiming Its Benefits," 1/31/19, https://www.ministrymatters.com/all/entry/9460/the-science-of-sabbath-how-people-are-rediscovering-rest-and-claiming-its-benefits.

2. Science Daily. "Dealing with digital distraction: Being ever-connected comes at a cost, studies find," Sciencedaily.com, 8/10/18, https://www.sciencedaily.com/releases/2018/08/180810161553.htm.

American Journal of Preventive Medicine. "Social Media Use and Perceived Social Isolation Among Young Adults in the U.S." Ajpmonline.org, 3/6/17, https://www.ajpmonline.org/article/S0749-3797(17)30016-8/fulltext.

296. Leavitt, Charles. *All Roads Lead to Rome: New acquisitions relating to the Eternal City*, College of Arts and Letters: Center for Italian Studies, 9/14/11, https://italianstudies.nd.edu/news-events/news/all-roads-lead-to-rome-new-acquisitions-relating-to-the-eternal-city.

"The proverb's origins may relate to the Roman monument known as the Milliarium Aureum, or golden milestone, erected by Emperor Caesar Augustus in the central forum of ancient Rome. All distances in the Roman Empire were measured from this point and it was regarded as the site from which all principle roads diverged. As such, artists such as Giacomo Lauro, often used it as a metaphor for the intensely cosmopolitan culture that has long been present in Rome."

297. Greek. 4633. "Skéné," Biblehub.com, https://biblehub.com/greek/4633.htm. Usage: a tent, booth, tabernacle, abode, dwelling.

298. John 7:2. *Pulpit Commentary*, "Feast of Tabernacles," Biblehub.com, https://biblehub.com/commentaries/john/7-2.htm.

"'Tabernacles' recalled in a festive form the time of Israel's wandering in the wilderness, when they dwelt in tabernacles. Joyfulness and astonishing ceremonial characterized the festival. The city of palaces broke out into booths of trees and leaves in every possible space, on walls and housetops in courtyards, and even in wagons and on the backs of camels.

"The people carried their palm branches and citrons in their hands, and great merriment, almost suggestive of heathen rites, prevailed. It probably gathered up about it, as some Christian festivals have done, other ancient or surrounding customs. The number of bullocks sacrificed during the seven days—one fewer on each day, beginning with thirteen—amounted in all to seventy (13 + 12 + 11 + 10 + 9 + 8 + 7 = 70). This the rabbis regarded as referring to the seventy nations of heathendom.

"Additional peculiarities were conspicuous in the immense number of priests who were required to take part in the sacrifices. The blasts of priests' trumpets which regulated the ceremonial, the great musical procession employed in brining water from the Pool of Siloam, then within the city wall, added another noticeable feature. The water was brought in a golden goblet, and poured into a silver funnel, which conveyed it by pipes to the Kedron, and was thus supposed to bless the thirsty land. This act was accompanied by singing the great Hallel, and the shouts and songs of Zion were heard far over hill and valley.

"At night time universal illumination prevailed, and huge candelabra in the temple court shed a radiance over the whole city. These peculiarities of the feast rendered it the most popular, if not the most sacred, of all the feasts....

299. *Cambridge Bible for Schools and Colleges*: "[The Jews' Feast of Tabernacles:] Again an indication that the Gospel was written outside Palestine: see on John 6:1; John 6:4. An author writing in Palestine would be less likely to specify it

as 'the feast of the Jews.' [It is most correctly called a "Feast of the Lord," or "the Lord's Feast"; see Leviticus 23:1ff]." https://biblehub.com/commentaries/john/7-2.htm.

300. "The One New Man – Spiritual Israel Theme of Revelation 21:12 Revelation 21:12." "Commentaries," Biblehub.com, https://biblehub.com/commentaries/revelation/21-12.htm.

Ellicott's Commentary for English Readers ("One new man"): "The representatives of all nations, and kindreds, and people, and tongues, are (Revelation 7:9) in the city of Christ; in Him there is neither barbarian, Scythian, bond nor free, but all are one. The diversities of human nationality and character, of age and race, and climate, are brought into one communion and fellowship."

301   *Pulpit Commentary* ("Spiritual Israel"): "Twelve; as signifying completeness (cf. Revelation 4:9; Revelation 7:4–8), and as being the number of the tribes of Israel, which are the type of the spiritual Israel of God."

Jamieson-Fausset-Brown Bible Commentary (Revelation 21): "The inscription of the names on the gates implies that none but the spiritual Israel, God's elect, shall enter the heavenly city.... The heavenly new Jerusalem is the consummation ... the elect Church of Jews and Gentiles being now gathered out: as the spiritual Israel."

Revelation 7:4. "Commentaries," Biblehub.com, https://biblehub.com/commentaries/revelation/7-4.htm.

Ellicott's Commentary for English Readers: "Thus the twelve tribes of Israel were the appointed witnesses of a pure theology and a pure morality in the days of idolatry and license; and later, the twelve Apostles became the inheritors of a similar, though higher, spiritual work in the world. The number twelve, then, stands for a world-witness of divine truth; and the fruits of this world-witness is a wide and sustained success: the twelve multiplied by the twelve a thousand-fold."

Meyer's New Testament Commentary: "[There is no] limitation of the one hundred and forty-four thousand to converted Israelites: 'Neither the Jews in contrast with the Gentiles, nor the Christian Jews in distinction from the Christian Gentiles, but Christians, the true Israelites, whether Jews or Gentiles [one new man of Ephesians 2]. The twelve tribes of the children of Israel are therefore identical with the people of God; only the latter are described in O. T. style, or typically, and as a living great organism… they are represented as the true Israel, as the numbered … one hundred and forty-four thousand.'"

302. Ephesians 2:6. "Commentaries," Biblehub.com, https://biblehub.com/commentaries/ephesians/2-6.htm.

Expositor's Greek Commentary: "Made us sharers with Him in dignity and dominion, so that even now, and in foretaste of our future exaltation, our life and thought are raised to the heavenlies where He reigns."

Cambridge Bible for Schools and Colleges: "Our great Representative is there, 'sitting at the right hand of God' (Colossians 3:1). We, as 'in Him,' vitally united to Him, are there also, in the sense of a supreme acceptance and welcome by the Eternal Father, and of the sure prospect of heavenly 'glorification together [with Christ]' (Romans 8:17).

303. *Bengel's Gnomen:* Ephesians 2:6. "Believers are already spiritually raised; they will be raised in the body; and to each of the two resurrections the sitting in heavenly places corresponds. They are not, indeed, present in heaven in the body, but they are so in point of right, and virtually in the spirit, and they have individually a seat expressly assigned to them, which is to be taken possession of at the proper time. They are for a while hidden in God; (Colossians 3:3) in the heavenlies."

Jamieson-Fausset-Brown Bible Commentary: "Believers are bodily in heaven in point of right, and virtually so in spirit, and have each their own place assigned there, which in due time they shall take possession of (Php 3:20, 21)."

"Jewish Population Rises to 15.3 Million Worldwide, with over 7 Million Residing in Israel," Jewish Agency For Israel, accessed 4/5/23, https://www.jewishagency.org/jewish-population-rises-to-15-3-million-worldwide-with-over-7-million-residing-in-israel.

304. Porat, Zev. *Unmasking the Chaldean Spirit*, (Crane, MO: Defender Publishing, 2022) Note: A great number of amazing examples of this truth are laid bare in this book. The two most prominent ones are what the Bible and modern archeology actually reveals concerning the genuine sites of the birth of Yeshua at Migdal Eder/Bethlehem, and the crucifixion/resurrection event of Yeshua on Golgotha—the place of "Goliath's head."